BEYOND THE GOPURAMS

Priti Aisola

BEYOND THE GOPURAMS

A Woman's Spiritual Journey Through South India

wisdom tree

First published 2014

Cover painting: Shuchi Chawla

ISBN 978-81-8328-365-6

Published by

Wisdom Tree
4779/23, Ansari Road
Darya Ganj, New Delhi-110 002
Ph.: 23247966/67/68
wisdomtreebooks@gmail.com

Printed in India

I dedicate this book to my parents,
my husband Ravi,
and our friend Chandrasekar,
an invaluable guide and companion
on many journeys.

Contents

Acknowledgements

My heartfelt thanks to the following people: Shyamala Sanketti for telling me about Wisdom Tree and persuading me to write to them; Chandrasekar Ramaswami for being a patient guide on our travels; Vidya and Venkat for their generous hospitality which facilitated our journeys from Chennai to the many temple towns in Tamil Nadu and made them a beautiful reality; my friend Mini Agarwal Dang for her sweet encouragement; Alex and Chitra for offering their home in Paris which made our trip to France a deeply cherished visit; Aparna, Sreedhar and their lovely twins for being there for us in Paris and India; Prof Subbarayudu for help with nagging grammar concerns; my parents, and family on both sides, for their love and unconditional support; my husband Ravi and my son Ananda for their heartwarming interest in my writing while pretending otherwise; my sister Shuchi Chawla for her painting (a labour of love), which is now the front cover image of this book; my publisher Shobit Arya for taking a keen personal interest in the shaping of this book; Papri Sri Raman for being a considerate and meticulous editor.

And to all the friends who haven't been named, all the guardian angels and invisible gracious guides and kindly spirits who can't be named, I offer my deepest gratitude.

I'll Renovate My Heart

Each day strips a beam from the roof
Each night loosens a brick, shifts a stone
Some mortar falls in the twilight hours
Do not collapse my house, my home
Outside the grass is seared brown, no bed
And there are no stars to gaze at
Grey-gripped the sky grimaces
Go where?
Home is where the heart is

I Am Home

Home is where the heart is
It's where we started
Where we belong

—McFly (British Pop Rock Band)

Home is where the heart is. Now, after a stay of close to six years in Hyderabad, the concrete form and delicate essence of this truism come to me with chiselled clarity. On the verge of our posting to Vancouver, I look back at our stay here with mixed feelings of pain, pleasure and gratitude—pain because of illness in the family and the loss of some dear ones and pleasure because of the exceptional opportunity it offered to reconnect with family and friends and forge new bonds with several others.

My husband, Ravi, is in the Indian Foreign Service. Apart from our visits to India during home leave, we had been away for nearly ten years. After a three-and-a-half-year stay in Paris, in August 2006 we came to Hyderabad, our home town. A home posting is rather unusual but we were lucky. The Ministry of External Affairs had opened a Branch Secretariat and a post to head it was vacant. Ravi requested for the post. My father-in-law was ill with a serious lung disease at that time. A Hyderabad posting would give us a chance to be with him and my parents who are settled here. Sadly, my father-in-law passed away a few weeks before we got here. This grievous loss cast a shadow on our homecoming.

I returned home with carefully garnered memories for company in backward-glancing moments. And the manuscript of a novel to keep me focussed in floundering moments. It was partly set in Paris, the attractive city that I had ventured to get to know a little—shyly at first and then with more ease and alacrity. Minutes before our arrival, as the aircraft began its descent into Hyderabad on 13 August, I am finally home, I told myself, yet I was apprehensive about the implications of this homecoming. I hoped it would be as simple as I tried to make it sound.

The monsoon was in full swing—very pleasant weather. It was certainly a great relief after Delhi's heat and unbearable humidity. I had spent the previous week in Delhi in a daze, shutting out all unpleasant sights and sounds, counting the minutes till I would be in Hyderabad in my parents' place in a green and agreeable colony. The only places where I felt at ease were my grandparents' home and Saravana Bhavan, where we would go for practically all our meals. I just felt vaguely threatened by something indefinable all the days that I was in Delhi. I have always feared Delhi. A city of savvy shopkeepers and astute politicians, its size, its belligerent commerce, its survival-of-the-pushiest code and one's own anonymity there, had made me shrink away from staying there beyond a few days. Coming from Paris, my eyes searched for beauty, craved for it.

A few days after we returned to Hyderabad, I had to go to the Shringeri Math, not far from our place, for my father-in-law's *masikam*, the monthly *shraadh* ceremony. I was unfamiliar with the nature of this ceremony. I felt comfortable and secure going to the Shringeri Math the first time because my sister-in-law and her husband were with me, while Ravi participated in the ceremony in the large rectangular room with four others, who were also performing it for one of their elders. After this, in the coming months, for the most part, I attended the *masikam* alone, with the exception of Ravi who was involved in this monthly ritual. On three occasions, my son Ananda was with me until he left for Montreal in December 2006. I used to be unsure of myself because, while I understand Telugu, I do not speak it fluently. This would make me vulnerable to the queries and looks of other people (the relatives of the deceased) who waited in the room with me while the ceremony was being performed. The whole thing would take around three hours, during which time I would sit along with the others in a different room before we were called for the ritual lunch.

To get to the Shringeri Math, one has to go through crowded bazaars and two railway crossings. Fortunately the Math is at the end of a quiet dead end street. A very functional place with no pretence to beauty, the Math's ordinariness is nevertheless redeemed by the trees, potted plants, flowering bushes and flowers within its walls.

I recall one particular day in October. The first flowers that greeted me were the mellow orange kanakambaram in a planter and the deep radiant-red and sunset-red ixora bushes. I took these colours with me inside when I sat for three long hours in the nondescript waiting room meant for relatives of the person participating in the *masikam*. We sat on patterned plastic floor mats, which have replaced the *chatai*s and *chapa*s of our childhood. It was my third visit here. Both Ananda and I were equipped with books. I hesitated to read for the first few minutes because I did not know what was appropriate in such a place and on such an occasion. I silently chanted the few shlokas of the Vinayaka stuti that I knew and repeated *Sri Rama Rama Rameti, Rame Rame Manorame...* several times. The others in the room were chatting in low voices about mundane and sticky domestic matters, health and family problems. The women had Telugu magazines that they flicked through desultorily. One older woman, who was very likely in her sagging sixties, yawned, rested her head on her elbow and stretched out on the floor mat. This was at eleven in the morning. The women stole glances at me and Ananda, trying to place us, figure us out. I was in a salwar kameez, which is not the norm in such a placc. Although the fabric was South cotton, Mangalgiri cotton to be precise, and I was wearing a big bindi and a mangalsutra, their curious, stolen glances told me that they were puzzled. My demeanour also did not encourage them to break the ice and venture into a conversation with me. Perhaps, I looked distant, reticent and inclined to remain silent. I looked around and took in my surroundings. The grey stone floor was oily, sticky, pitted, chipped and discoloured in places. A brownish-black uneven band ran across the centre of the floor. Two water drainage holes in the floor were blocked with cylindrical pieces of wood to prevent insects and rats from crawling in. The windows did not have wooden panes or frames because good quality teak is an expensive proposition. The translucent glass of the windowpanes was bordered by an iron frame, painted black. The window ledge had a spiderweb that moved in the breeze. The bluish-grey doors were speckled with dirty brown, dried water stains. The grey-blue wall of the room had become drab with time. It had darker bands and patches where the heads and backs of the people sitting on mats brushed it. The light and fan switches were grimy. The switchboard was greasy and dirty. The ceiling fan above us moved in a slow, desultory fashion. No amount of fiddling with the regulator could goad it to rotate faster.

I watched three ants explore the floor, each focussing on a separate stone slab as its demarcated domain. From the kitchen came different sounds: The stony roll of the wet grinder, the sprightly whistle of the pressure cooker, the clank of pots and pans and the banging of ladles against the sides of pots. In between was the erratic sound of someone slapping clothes against a stone or floor to wash them or beat the dirt out of them. A train rumbled closer and then clanged past, not far from the Math. All these sounds mingled with the sonorous chanting from the next room. The mixed aroma of incense, ghee and vadas drifted in and uplifted me. Everything was so familiar, yet it came as a surprising discovery after years of long absence from India. When we returned here irregularly, approximately once in a year and a half, I would re-experience the familiar sights and sounds, but more as a detached observer. Earlier, they had not penetrated my awareness as sharply as they did now. I guess it was because I was reacquainting myself with everything that I had left behind. After my return, some things jarred, others shocked, some things surprised and a few others came as a reassurance, tender, heartwarming or steadfast.

The grey-white boundary wall of the house was suffocatingly close to the window. The dhatura plant raised its noxious head above the wall. Not far behind was a tall, prosperous mango tree with dense abundant leaves. It seemed to dwarf the other trees in front of it. Small portions of the sky were visible like uneven paper cut-outs, shaped by a child's fanciful hand.

I started reading and making notes. I could feel the occasional glance of a slender, balding middle-aged man on me. He had been narrating the history of his afflictions and I caught scraps of that narrative. I looked up from the book and met his eye. He addressed me abruptly in English, which sounded so much like Telugu because of the accent and the way he intoned his sentences. 'Excuse me to disturb you. You read. You make notes. Are you a teacher?' 'No,' I replied softly. 'You research?' 'No. I am reading for pleasure.' I waited. 'Are you Telugu?' I shook my head slowly. He waited. 'I am from the north,' I explained reluctantly, with some measure of defiance and a hint of displeasure in my voice. I did not explain any further. He was decidedly curious. The others in the room were all ears. 'Are you a Gujarati?' he wished to know. 'I am not,' I replied brusquely. He wouldn't give up. 'Are you from UP or Punjab?' 'I am from both, but more so from Hyderabad. My parents have lived here since 1976. This is home,' I explained. I did not wish to satisfy his curiosity any further and turned away to read when he said, 'North or south...you are a human being.' I was aghast at his flimsy charity camouflaged as a Eureka moment, but soon realised that he meant no offence. It was an involuntary and harmless statement, though thoughtless, which posed as tolerance in his mind.

After coming back to India, I was increasingly becoming aware of how much the specifics of one's origins mattered here. This was unlike life abroad, where one was part of the disparate and amorphous corps diplomatique, or the NRIs, who are a curious blend of financial success with its assertion of a new identity, nostalgia, a harking back to roots and the need to project a unified face of India, which reflects both its diversity and divisiveness. Living in India, outside of the cosmopolitan veneer of the big city élite, was to become acutely aware of, and be reminded of, the precise details of one's identity—region, religion, language and caste. This presented the challenge of learning to locate oneself in, and assimilate into, a particular community. Once again, I had to come to terms with this reality.

The life of Ramana Maharishi kept me company that day and contained my irritation.

Each *masikam*, I would take my reading and my cross-stitch embroidery to the Math. The embroidery and the pattern book—titled in French—would awaken the curiosity of the women sitting in the room with me and they would ask me to show the book and what I was doing. My hesitant and uncertain Telugu invariably gave me away. They would wonder where I was from and ask questions about my marriage to Ravi. I did not flinch. I learnt to accept their curiosity, take it in my stride and respond with quiet dignity. On one occasion, one of them conceded generously, 'It doesn't matter where you are from. You are an Indian.' There was no hidden barb there. They did not know how to tread carefully in personal areas and I smiled and continued to read.

Each *masikam* and *shraadh* that I attended at the Shringeri Math, the ritual *prasadam* lunch would be served around one. The first two or three *masikams*, when I sat down with the others to eat, I was self-conscious and shy. A slow eater, I would struggle with *pappu annam* (dal and rice) while others would've adeptly moved on to second and third servings or *charu annam* (rasam and rice). We would sit on long mats on the floor and eat out of large, flimsy paper plates covered with a thin sheet of aluminium. Invariably, this was the *shraadh* menu—a fiery-sweet ginger chutney, searingly spicy roasted sesame powder, boiled, skinned green gram dal, a sweet-sour, spicy bitter gourd or yam or raw banana preparation, a tongue-chafing bendakaya (okra) or dondakaya (gherkins) preparation with cumin and red chilli powder, an under-sweet watery *payasam*, crisp, oily vadas, a rasam that I never tasted and sour buttermilk. And, of course, a mound of rice with two drops of ghee that I always wished I could give away to a hungry mouth. The meal would conclude with a loud satisfied belch from the priest, who was always, for some reason, indulgent and gentle towards me and sterner towards the others. And each time as we would step into the backyard and await our turn to wash our hands at the long rectangular trough-like cement sink, I would gaze longingly at the bilva tree with its hard woody fruit and dark trifoliate leaves and wonder if I could get at least one fruit to take home. I never asked because something told me that the leaves and the fruit would only be used for pujas and religious ceremonies. I had last tasted the fruit as a child, had enjoyed the sherbet made from the pale-peach, fibrous flesh of the fruit and knew of the medicinal value of the bilva root, leaves and fruit.

I went to the Shringeri Math once a month for the first year of our stay in Hyderabad and three or four times a year during the next five years. With the passage of time, I was less bothered by the people's unabashed curiosity and interest in me as an outsider. I learnt to relax and accept all my experiences there as an integral and inevitable part of my homecoming. 'I am home' gradually began to mean something positive and promising for me. It gave me a chance to travel in my country, primarily to the different temple towns in Andhra Pradesh, Karnataka and Tamil Nadu. As I experienced each of these places, my homecoming resonated with meanings I had never dreamt of discovering. It enriched my stay in India in ways I had never even remotely contemplated. What follows is a narration of those journeys, without and within.

Monkey Business and Mahabalipuram

Chennai is home for Ravi, an indelible part of his memories—his years of childhood and youth with their turmoil and joys, his childhood friends, his college mates; Mylapore and Triplicane, the beach, the Kapaleeshwar temple, the British era structures, some still surviving doggedly, some razed to the ground; Carnatic music and the various *sabhas*. A nostalgic connection with all its dicey pitfalls and its cosy reassurances. And after so many years of marriage I was going to discover the many dimensions of his home. I was in Chennai with Ravi for the music season, full of anticipation and some trepidation because I would be attending the music festival at the august Music Academy for the first time.

A pleasurable and heartwarming aspect of this visit to Chennai was an opportunity to reconnect with Chitra and Alex, our friends from Paris. Chitra was visiting her parents in Chennai. It was a trying time for her as her father was ailing. Keen on giving her parents an outing as the year drew to a worrisome close for her, all of us decided to go to Mahabalipuram.

After seeing the shore temple, we were going to see the old lighthouse which is around a thousand years old. Chitra's parents decided to sit on a stone bench in the open, tree-filled, shady area at the base of the cave temple as her father would find it very strenuous to make the climb. The afternoon sun added to his fatigue and unease. We walked up the sloping path that led to the Mahishasuramardini Mandapam, which is a temple created out of a huge rock. It is supported by cylindrical pillars that have no carvings on them. At this rock-cut temple we saw Mahishasuramardini in bas-relief on the wall to our right. The goddess Durga here is full of divine fury and fiery energy as she kills Mahishasura, the buffalo-headed demon. In stark contrast, on the long panel opposite, is Lord Vishnu as Anantshayana. He is reclining peacefully on Adisesha. He is in an impressive state of repose on the massive coils of his serpent bed. As we face Lord Vishnu, to his right, very near his feet, is a standing figure in a belligerent posture. He has a weapon in his lowered right hand which is positioned across the body and touches his upper left thigh. His look is full of defiance and arrogant power. He is looking sideways and his chin is parallel to his right shoulder. He looks ready to assault someone or protect Lord Vishnu. Another figure behind him, who is looking over his shoulder, places a restraining hand on his arm (at least that's how it seemed to me). Both these men have tall, elaborate headdresses. I would have loved to know the story of this tableau—roused energy and restful sleep were juxtaposed here.

We walked up the steps to the old lighthouse which itself is a temple called the Ishvara Temple. There were a few monkeys around and Ravi had warned me to be careful and not do anything to attract their attention. The old lighthouse has a metal railing running around it for the safety of visitors. We had just turned the corner and were near the virile lion figure at one of the corner pillars when I noticed a monkey on the rock below. While seated it was bending forward to lick a small patch of wetness there. I thought to myself, 'Poor thing, it is thirsty.' I had barely turned away from it when there was a sudden movement near us and in one swift, deft and unaggressive move the monkey took the water bottle that was in Ravi's left hand. We watched the monkey now, curious as to what it would do with it. It sat down on the rock below and then effortlessly and quickly unscrewed the lid of the bottle, as if it had been doing this all its life. I thought it would raise the bottle to its mouth and drink water just as we do, because it had looked so human earlier. Instead, it spilt the water on the rock surface, flung the bottle away and bent forward to lap up the water quickly to slake its thirst.

I said to Ravi, 'Poor thing, it must have been very thirsty. Did it scratch or hurt you when it took the bottle?'

'No, I just felt a mild tug. Basically I was taken unawares.' Ravi became extra cautious afterwards and began worrying about his expensive sunglasses. The monkey might just show evidence of another form of human behaviour – take the sunglasses to shield its eyes from the sun, was his argument.

I laughed, 'How will a leaping monkey keep the sunglasses on?'

'That's not my problem. I just don't want it being attracted by my sunglasses.'

'Very far-fetched!' I said, amused.

This monkey episode reminded me of my childhood visits to the town of Dibai in Uttar Pradesh. It happens to be my birthplace. It used to be a village then – a village filled with monkeys (raided by monkeys, I would say). It had far too many of them for my comfort. I must have been very young, a little over two, I think. I am not very sure how old I was then. On a winter afternoon, I was sitting on a charpoy in the courtyard of my dadiji's home. My mother and dadiji were with me. The kitchen was set apart from the rest of the house and was at the other end of the open-to-sky aangan or central courtyard, right across from the rooms. Fearfully, I had been watching a monkey sitting on the boundary wall that we shared with the neighbour's house. I pestered my mother to go inside the house with me. I had a positive horror of monkeys and she felt, I understand now, that if I got used to seeing them around me, I would overcome my fear of them. She asked me to sit closer to her and dadiji said, 'Why are you afraid when I am here with you?' My mother told me years later that I replied, 'Because you can't jump like the monkeys.' Within minutes, the monkey that had been biding its time on the wall jumped down, picked up one of my mother's Bata rubber slippers. I shrieked and hid my face against my mother. The detestable creature climbed the wall, sat there chewing the slipper and then hurled the disfigured thing onto the ground. I can still recall my fear and disgust at the sight of the unsightly slipper.

The toilets were not in the house but across the street in a row. I used to be so terrified of the monkeys that I had to go through a major brainwashing by my mother and a lot of coaxing before I felt comfortable stepping out. I had to be reassured a million times that there was no monkey prowling about and my mother had to stand guard at the door and keep calming my fears.

Strangely enough, I am not afraid of them at all now. And I was not afraid of the monkeys of Mahabalipuram.

Chidambaram

As part of this trip to Chennai, Ravi had planned a visit to a few temples in the Thanjavur region and around. The first of our journeys began with the start of the new year—January 2007.

From our guest house at Ashok Nagar in Chennai, we drove to our friend Chandra's house. We had known him since our posting in Damascus, where we'd first met him. He was going to go with us on our visits to temples. In fact Chandra became our unproclaimed, steadfast guide and narrator of stories and anecdotes on this trip. I was ignorant of the significance of the temples we were going to visit and the *sthalapuranas* associated with each of them, and he was an inexhaustible library of information. Above all, he was patient, very patient with me. I troubled him with endless questions, sometimes about the most obvious and simplest of things and he replied very calmly and conscientiously as if he were explaining something to a curious child. I was amused at times because I did already know the meaning of some of the Sanskrit terms he used, but I guess my persistent questions gave him the impression that I was totally unaware of most things to do with temples, their history and significance. However, it was also true that what was common knowledge for someone who belonged to this region and was raised on stories and legends associated with the temples, was a discovery, a beautiful revelation for me.

We drove from Chennai to Chidambaram in Chandra's friend's car. On the outskirts of Chidambaram, we crossed a canal filled with water hyacinth—neelambala. A bund with thorny bushes skirted one side of the canal and wild plants and weeds with long, tangled arms barged into the water insidiously, choking the canal. Quite a disagreeable sight! As we neared the main street, the pleasurable smell of ghee and *sambhrani* filled the air and greeted us with an auspicious welcome. We got off the car and saw the main temple chariot and learnt that the temple chariot procession had been delayed by more than a couple of hours. We were grateful for this delay because we would now see the *ratham* being pulled. There were people and people everywhere. The whole atmosphere was festive, colourful and charged with devotion. Most of the women looked fresh and lovely in their richly coloured Kanjeevarams or bold floral synthetic saris. They had taken great care to adorn their hair with jasmine and kanakambaram or jasmine and pink arali flowers. The more traditional Brahmin women were in their madisars. Women, young boys and girls vied with each other in decorating the road with *kolam*. With small plastic bags in their hands, they bent down to draw simple or elaborate and exquisite *kolam* designs on the road. They were oblivious of everything but their own desire to adorn the path where the lord's chariot would pass. I think the street must have been sprinkled with water beforehand to allow the *kolam* patterns to adhere. It was a brisk, smiling business day for the vendors. A young boy was selling flutes and an old man staggered forward with his multicoloured burden of paper windmills. Balloons of different shapes and sizes bobbed up and down in the hands of a seller. Another vendor was enticing children with soap bubbles. A makeshift contraption, which was an elongated handcart with wheels and a cycle attached in front, passed before us. A man sitting on the cart announced something on a loudspeaker at regular intervals. A boy sat beside him with a regal posture which said, 'I am the king of all I survey'. A man sang from the *thevarams,* hymns of the Shaivite saints—totally absorbed in his singing as he clanged the small cymbals against each other. Men walked past, carrying lighted torches with dark smoke trails—kerosene-soaked cloth, each tied to the top of a long stick. Others carried long-stemmed *sambhrani* pots.

I turned to my right and saw the *ratham* sway ponderously and then lurch forward. It was being pulled by two rows of devotees gripping the two thick ropes with such tenacity and faith as if their entire life and future depended on it. The *ratham* was a several-tiered deep brown wooden vehicle replete with ornate carvings and figures. It had a multicoloured conical canopy fringed with torans. From the wide edges of the canopy were suspended long lanterns made of colourful fabric. On the widest tier sat the young sons of the *dikshitar*s, the temple priests. In their white veshtis and well-oiled dark hair tied in a side knot, they looked precocious and privileged. The *ratham* was garlanded with flowers so that Lord Nataraja, Lord of the Cosmic Dance, and his consort, Sivakamasundari, would have a fragrant ride.

For the people thronging there, it was a sacred duty, a blessing to be able to pull the chariot of Lord Nataraja and Goddess Sivakamasundari. Ravi asked me, 'Would you also like to do it? But you must be careful when they suddenly stop pulling as they fall forward and then backward. You will get crushed if you are not careful or your foot will get squashed.'

'But I can't see even a centimetre of free rope where I can place a single finger or the tip of one.'

'Are you crazy? A single finger won't do. That finger will snap. One has to get a good grip,' said Ravi irked. 'Follow me. We just have to push our way in.' He charged ahead confidently.

I was in awe of the divine frenzy of the devotees. With so many hands gripping the stout, coarse rope, with so many bodies tugging, pulling, straining at the rope and so eager not to be left behind in this privileged service to Lord Nataraja, where did I, a novice in devotion and hesitant in service, stand a chance?

'Come on, follow me. Don't stand there wondering. Hurry,' said Ravi, with some impatience.

'What about my slippers? Everyone else is barefoot.'

'Well, can't be helped. Why didn't you leave your slippers in the car when the three of us did?'

'I didn't anticipate the fact that I might want to pull the chariot. Hopefully no one will look at my feet and disapprove.'

'That's not the point. This is a divine chariot. Let's not debate this any further. Just follow me.'

Ravi plunged into the thick mass of people and I followed, slightly dazed by the charged ardour of the people around me. He got a grip on the rope and then created space for three of my fingers which felt the rough stout rope but had no grip around it. I realised too late that I was the only woman for that stretch of the rope. My arm was wedged between two bodies and one part of it rested against the sticky, sweaty, red T-shirt of a young man who was quite oblivious to me and my sense of discomfort. Then I felt the rope being yanked, hauled forward and I felt the pressure and heave of several bodies around me. I released the rope, stumbled. Someone's foot crushed mine. I felt Ravi grip my arm, steady me and pull me out of the dense mass of people. 'Are you okay?' he asked.

'Just hot, and my foot is covered with dirt.'

'That's nothing as long as you are not hurt. Don't be so finicky.

Look at the white woman there. I have been watching her. She just hasn't let go of the rope. I am pretty sure she has been pulling the rope from the time the procession started. Her face is gleaming with sweat. Her hair is all over her face but she is unfazed.'

I looked at the white woman with lank shoulder-length hair, her sweaty forehead plastered with stray strands of hair. In her late forties or early fifties perhaps, she looked quite attractive in spite of her state of disarray.

I wonder who she is and why she wants to be a part of this, I thought to myself. Then I looked at the different faces of devotion, of *atmasamarpanam*—the need for submission to something larger and higher than oneself.

We had turned right onto another street where a temporary platform had been erected against an open *mandapam*. Here, the deities would be transferred and received from the temple chariot at the end of the procession so that they could be taken for the *abhishekam* which would happen in the very early hours of the next day. The bamboo scaffolding looked very makeshift and shaky. Also, the horizontal wooden planks seemed too clumsily and inexpertly placed to bear the weight of the priests and the bronze idols. I looked at the whole arrangement rather sceptically.

It was dusk and the *ratham* was very close to the temporary platform. Now the challenge was to have the latter aligned perfectly with the *ratham* so that transferring the idols wouldn't be a problem. At this time I learnt that in Chidambaram the *moola murti* is also the *utsava murti*. The fervent need of the people to pull the chariot, to embellish its path, to touch the chariot and the elephant drawing it, made even greater and more heightened sense to me now. More and more people had congregated on the street. Among them were weak old men, women, children led by the hand, children mounted on hips and children riding on shoulders. Five or six young women constables were trying to manage the crowd along with other policemen. They were better at chatting with each other and giggling over their helplessness and timidity in the face of this crowd than at directing and controlling it.

We stood against a new *ratham*, worth thirty lakh rupees, donated by somebody, and waited with focussed patience for Lord Nataraja's *ratham* to be perfectly aligned with the temporary platform. The *ratham* was being pulled in small jerky and uneven jolting movements and we were concerned. The new *ratham* was very close to the wall of some houses and in between this chariot and the wall was another scaffolding of metal bars. This created two disastrously narrow passages between the new *ratham* and the wall. We stood against the corner of the *ratham* at the edge of one of these narrow passages thinking that we were safely out of the path of the *ratham* pullers. Soon several agitated shouts and cries of panic rose in the air. With rude sweeps and shoves of the hand, all of us were told to clear the passage as the rope pullers were about to move into the narrow passage close to the new *ratham*. People pushed, shoved, shouted, squeezed past, flung their arms around in helpless confusion and jammed their elbows into each other to move away. An old woman was quickly helped away from this dense mass of agitated people. Two children started crying. A woman screamed angrily. The rope pullers at the left front end of the rope thrust themselves into the constricted passage heedless of its suffocating closeness. Rather, they were thrust into it by a momentum, powerful and dangerous—the collective strength of all the rope pullers who were oblivious to the risk to their life and clueless about the combined, uncharted strength of a people impelled by blind faith. I marvelled at them and also blamed the *dikshitars*, the security officials and the police force for not paying enough attention to the safety of the devotees. There was a stampede waiting to happen. The invitation was loud and clear. We were all afraid. Ravi was apprehensive. The petite women constables panicked. Trying to shield themselves, they took cover behind Ravi's ample back and giggled nervously. He looked at their fear and his own fear and decided that the whole business was too much for him. 'In a few moments, there will be a stampede. I am getting out. Let's go.'

'I am staying.'

'Are you out of your mind? Come,' he said imperiously.

'I am staying. Your friends are here. Nothing will happen.'

'Don't be an idiot.' He clutched my arm and pulled me towards him.

'Go, Ravi. I am staying.'

He turned away from me. Using his bag as a weapon, he carved a way out for himself. Within seconds there was another massive tug by the rope pullers and people jammed into me. I struggled to steady myself. Something scorched my entire arm. I screamed. I saw the smoldering *sambhrani* ashes fall and then slither off my entire left arm, which was partly covered by my navy blue chiffon dupatta. My arm was slightly red and that was about it. I had been saved but the *sambhrani* had burnt holes into my brand new dupatta. A man with a *sambhrani* pot propped on a long stick had been standing behind me, against the *ratham*. He had lost control and the *sambhrani* pot had toppled over. Concerned, our friend Chandra asked me, 'Are you okay?'

'Yes. It's nothing much.'

'Are you sure?' Then he laughed. 'Consider this as the Lord's *prasadam*.'

'Do I have a choice? Is there any other way of looking at it?'

Soon the crowd became calmer and the agitation simmered

down as the *ratham* had come to a complete stop. All of us waited eagerly for *darshanam* of Lord Nataraja and Sivakamasunadari but the *dikshitar*s had focussed the spotlight on the crowd so that we wouldn't be able to see the deities when their ornaments were being removed before the transfer across the temporary platform. Blinded by the light we felt cheated. Disappointed, we left for dinner. After dinner as we drove towards the PWD guest house we noticed, to our left, the tall illuminated outline of a well-known structure framing an arched passage for vehicles. Both of us exclaimed in surprise, 'The Eiffel Tower!' It was part of the decorations for the All India Science Congress being held in Chidambaram that year.

Paris had been with me and followed me during my stay in Chennai as I attended the *kutcheri*s at the Music Academy and it had decided to inaugurate this journey to the temples too. I had met at least seven people who were either from Paris or associated with Paris in some way. Amazing how some things never really leave you! I guess one's continued search for them, whether expressed or unvoiced, keeps them in close proximity. I have also heard people say that you do find what you actively or sincerely seek.

The PWD guest house was a very functional place. We were welcomed by a host of people (all idlers, all hangers on, most of them decrepit looking) as they had been told that a senior IFS officer was going to be staying there. We had decided to stay only in government guest houses because we were travelling on a tight budget. Also, because of the Science Congress, the better-maintained government guest house was unavailable. One look at the room and I knew that I would have to ignore the dusty chairs, the threadbare white bedsheet, the dressing table squatting on its chipped haunches, the mirror layered with dust, the dead air conditioner, the stained plastic bucket in the bathroom and a non-functioning geyser. I would have to pretend not to notice the dead insects spattered around and crumbling leaves sprinkled in the small enclosed rectangular space with a broken armchair and a large grille window overlooking the backyard.

We got barely three hours of sleep and were up at one so that we could bathe and then go to the temple for the special *abhishekam*. The hot water had to be fetched from the neighbouring bathroom. In no mood to get into a sari at that hour of the night, I had asked Chandra whether I could go in a salwar kameez. While I wanted to be comfortable, I didn't want to be frowned upon by the orthodox devotees and the priests.

It was slightly cold at that hour of the night. We left our slippers in the car and entered the temple from the west *gopuram*. The courtyard of the outermost *prakaram* was full of people sleeping on the floor. Covered with shawls, blankets, thin sheets, exhausted by travel and lack of proper resting places, people were sleeping in various states of stupor. The place was littered with paper plates, small plastic cups, plastic bags, banana peels, stained flyers and soggy newspapers. Someone blew his nose loudly, sullied the temple courtyard floor, and I squirmed. I was disappointed at the state of the temple, but with so many people gathered, this mess was a given. I wished that some garbage bins had been provided and the people sufficiently warned by the *dikshitar*s or the cops not to litter the place. People needed to be educated on keeping the temple premises clean but apparently those who ran the affairs of the temple were doing nothing about it. In several places, the stone floor felt sticky and soiled under our feet. For me, the litter and the unclean floor took away something from my sense of the sacred. At the same time, I was in awe of the bhakti of the people who had come from far and near and put up with travel fatigue and a lack of board and lodging in order to witness Lord Nataraja and the *ananda tandava*.

We skipped over sleeping bodies, gingerly stepped past reclining forms and slowly found our way to the thousand-pillar hall. Here the central aisle was free so that the water in brass pots for the *abhishekam* could be passed from the hand of one *dikshitar* to another with ease and efficiency, till each could be emptied into a massive copper container placed at the outer edge of the raised platform of the *Raja Sabha*. At this time Chandra told me that Shiva is *abhishekapriya* whereas Vishnu is *alankarapriya*. It was around three in the morning and the excited anticipation in the air was palpable. A rope connected the pillars on either side of the hall. It was adorned with auspicious mango leaves and tender coconut leaves knotted and shaped into a three-petal decorative motif. There was the combined smell of sleep, unwashed travel-fatigued bodies and camphor in the air. Some people who had no place to stretch themselves were sleeping on folded arms. Most of the *dikshitars* had their hair tied in a left topknot. One of them was dressed very brightly in a magenta angavastram with gold thread embroidery. Two foreigners sat on the steps leading to the *mandapam* of the *Raja Sabha*. One of them was dressed in saffron robes and the other was wearing a yellow angavastram with something written on it in Hindi. I could not read it from a distance but I was sure it either had some common religious chant or *Hare Rama, Hare Krishna*. The moon was beautiful with the white clouds sailing before it, revealing and concealing it from moment to moment. The next day would be full moon day.

Soon the chanting began behind the blue and white curtain that concealed Lord Nataraja and the Goddess Sivakami. Around half-past-three, all the *dikshitars* who had been sitting on the steps went inside the enclosure which had the deities and the grille aluminium collapsing gate was pushed back further. In the open courtyard to our left, someone started playing the cymbals. The moment of *darshanam* was drawing closer and the people waited with impatient fervour and prayerful anticipation.

The curtain was drawn aside and shouts of joy and tear-filled gratitude rose in the air. I struggled to get a good view of the *vigrahams* of Lord Nataraja and Goddess Sivakami. I had to look past and above the excited heads piled up ahead of me. The Nataraja was resplendent. Of a reddish copper hue with an underlying touch of silver, it was much smaller than the idol I had visualised. I couldn't see the idol in its entirety. I could see the face, the *abhaya hasta* and the hand pointing to the raised foot that offers release. Radiant, the face exuded light and glory. I had never seen a more beautiful and captivating deity. I had come across the significance of the dance of Shiva for the first time in Ananda Coomaraswamy's book by the same name and had marvelled at its rich metaphysical meanings.

The first *abhishekam* was with *vibhuti*. Like a grey veil, it concealed the radiance of the idol but enhanced the divine mystery. It was followed by *abhishekams* with milk, curd, sandalwood paste, honey, turmeric and coarsely blended fruit that looked like mashed bananas, crushed grapes and apple to me. After each *abhishekam* the *vigrahams* of Lord Nataraja and Goddess Sivakami were washed liberally with water. Each *abhishekam* was an experience worth remembering, intensifying and heightening one's sense of the sacred. Each of the ingredients used, contributed to the splendour of the idols and seemed to bring forth their rich beauty and essential glory. Golden, warm brown, antique bronze, reddish copper hue, milky or creamy white, silver tinged, rich ochre—these were the colours that one could see in the idols. Each *abhishekam* transformed them and made them radiate a beautiful energy and blessings to all present. If the divine has form (*swarupa*), qualities and attributes (*suguna*), and if this sublime form has the ability to move, elevate and even momentarily transform the consciousness, it had all of these that morning. I was amazed and touched by the devotion of the people who sat with folded hands or lifted their hands in prayer, ardent appeal and submission before the God that stood in their midst and exuded the most beautiful sacred energy. From where I was seated, I could see Lord Shiva's second left hand pointing downward to the lifted left foot that offers deliverance. The right hands were not clearly visible from where I was sitting—one of them holds the drum—*damaru* or *udukkai*—and the other is raised in the *abhaya mudra* (do not fear). I could see part of the *tiruvasi*, the encircling arch of glory, touched with flame along its circumference, but my focus was on the raised left foot that ceaselessly offers release or the promise of one. For most people gathered there, the religious or metaphysical significance of the dance was not a prime concern or the moving force behind their presence—they may not even know about it. It was enough to know that here in Tillai (the whole area was originally a forest of tillai trees and shrubs) or Chidambaram, Patanjali and Vygrahapada had witnessed the divine dance. It was more than enough to believe that at the time of *Arudra darshan*, which was a few hours away, Lord Shiva would re-enact the Cosmic dance, which would re-energise them and the entire world. In fact, it was a source of great joy and liberation to believe this. It would add nothing significant to their joy and devotion to know that Lord Shiva's dance represents five activities (*Panchakritya*), which are—creation, preservation, destruction or dissolution, veiling as also giving rest and, finally, grace or salvation. For them Lord Shiva was right before them and they would witness his dance of bliss. Uncluttered by knowledge or awareness available to scholars, there was something cheering, fresh and touching about this spontaneous form of devotion that I saw in the mass of common humanity here.

We left the temple around six in the morning and Ravi was exhilarated because it was his birthday and the day had begun very ceremoniously and auspiciously. I was happy to see him so serenely happy. As we walked out of the gateway from where we had entered, we saw quite a few people sleeping on either side of the pathway. We decided to have our morning tea or coffee before going to the guest house. The road and the roadsides were choked with trash—paper plates, plastic cups, flyers, soiled leaves which had been used to eat tiffin or some dish like tamarind rice. I was aghast. On any other day and at any other time, I would have protested about having to walk barefoot and negotiate my way through this unsightly trash but that morning I decided to ignore it and treat it like a minor inconvenience. The coffee or tea-*kadai* was open and, at two or three tables, some people had already ordered their idlis and vadas for breakfast. The coffee was superb as expected but the tea was a strong bitter decoction as we had asked for milk and black tea to be given separately. It was a strange and novel request for them. They were confused and disgruntled at having to deal with something so out of the way, early in the morning. Also, they must have been catering to a barrage of customers over the past few days. It was a cool morning and the hot coffee felt good although it was too sweet to be perfect. I had forgotten to tell the waiter, 'Sakkarai or sugar *kammi*'. The last word is similar to the Hindi word *kam*, which means less.

The guest house smacked of pitiable neglect, looked derelict, smelt of sleep-sluggish bodies, but that was the only place for rest and a bath before we went back to the temple for the

Arudra darshan. I was looking forward to seeing the *Chit Sabha, Kanaka Sabha* and *Nritya Sabha*. This would help me ignore my physical surroundings.

The same evening we visited the temple at Sirkazhi. This was the beginning of my experience of Shiva in his different forms, a journey that became richer with meaning as the stories around each form unfolded in various temples that we visited. However, a clear knowledge of the mythic stories did not dim the sublime mystery that emanated from each form.

At sundown we reached Sirkazhi, which is not far from Chidambaram and the Vaitheeswarn Koil. Sirkazhi is a centre of worship of Bhairava, Shiva's 'dreadful' form, which he assumed when he decapitated Brahma, his father. Tormented by this grievous sin, Shiva wandered the earth, restive and impoverished. I had never seen either a sculpture or an idol of Bhairava. I expressed my apprehensions about seeing a Bhairava shrine. Chandra calmed me by giving a metaphysical explanation for Shiva's fearsome aspect: 'While he is fear-inspiring, he also protects the Universe. There are eight forms of Bhairava. As Kala-Bhairava, he makes *Kala*, Time, or God of Death submit to him. He is also known as Papa-bhakshana as he devours the sins of his devotees.'

I was still a little fearful, 'That's not an agreeable description. Why not the Papa-Vimochana murti, one who grants freedom from sins?'

Chandra was amused, 'You want a benign description? That follows logically, doesn't it? The benevolent and the fearful make a complete picture. Anyway, understand the Bhairava iconography and the history of Bhairava worship in India and elsewhere. After that you can decide what form of Shiva you are comfortable with.'

'I already know—Nataraja.'

Chandra chose not to respond to my childish spontaneity.

Brahma teertham, the temple tank, was the first thing we noticed when we entered the temple premises. A kid was scrubbing himself vigorously on the tank steps. Chandra asked us to sprinkle the sacred water on our heads. While Ravi did it with great gusto, I did it gingerly. Standing on the steps Chandra briefly narrated the story of Sambandar, who is associated with Sirkazhi: On the banks of the temple tank, as a very small child, Sambandar was left alone by his father who had gone to bathe. Hungry, the child began to cry. Shiva and Parvati were passing by. Moved by the child's crying, Shiva asked Parvati to feed him. She nursed him with the milk of knowledge and the child, who grew up to be a venerated Shaivite saint, came to be known as Thirugnana Sambandar.

In Sirkazhi Shiva is enshrined in three different forms—Brahmapureeswarar at the ground level, Thoniappar at the middle level and as Sattanathar (Bhairava) at the top level. Four things stand out in my memory of Sirkazhi—its connection with Thirugnana Sambandar, the *Sattanathar sannidhi*, the Ashtabhairava Mandapam with its heavy silence resonating with the palpable presence of eight Bhairavas and the temple's singular form in the gathering dark. The temple seemed to have unseated itself from real time and space and drifted into the realm of the impalpable and the mysterious.

From the *Sattanathar sannidhi* one can get a view of the temple towers, *mandapams*, *prakarams* and the surrounding areas. The moon was out. In the hushed moon-painted dusk, the dark green form of the palm trees silhouetted against the darkening sky looked like entranced sentinels in a dream-daze. Those moments were magical. I was awestruck by the silent potent presence of Sattanathar and his speaking eyes that had none of the frantic terror I had imagined. At that time Chandra suggested that we should see Vaitheeswaran Koil also on the same evening. But I was in no mood to rudely puncture the experience of Sirkazhi and make a transition to a different experience. And I had a premonition that Vaitheeswaran Koil couldn't be done in a hurry. My decision changed the course of our journey in a dramatic way.

Vaitheeswaran Koil

Ravi's long-standing desire to visit the Vaitheeswaran Temple (Koil/Kovil) was fulfilled the next morning, a visit that changed something in both of us and reawakened in me the need for a new perspective on life. Eager to be in time for the *darshanam*, we drove out of Chidambaram without breakfast. We could have an early lunch after seeing the temple. It was only after we were on our way that I realised that I was going to see the shrines of Lord Vaidyanatha and Lord Dhanvantari. The latter, the God of Ayurvedic Medicine, is an avatar of Lord Vishnu and the deity to whom my Tuesday fasts had been dedicated for over four years. I had kept the Tuesday fast without following any rigorous ritualistic discipline or any form of formal prayer to this deity except for chanting the Dhanvantari Gayatri Mantram that goes like this:

Om tatpurushāya vidmahe
Amrit kalasha hastāya dheemahi
Tanno Dhanvantari prachodayāt

In Vaitheeswaran Koil, Lord Vaidyanatha or Shiva as the Divine Healer, cured Angaraka or Mars who was suffering from leprosy. Hence it is believed that a dip in the holy tank of Siddhamritam will cure sincere seekers of all ailments.

It was late morning by the time we reached. There weren't too many people at the temple. As soon as we entered, we were pestered by a man to buy the *archana samagri* from him. The shops had virtually no customers. Flowers, puja materials, brass lamps and small brass idols, clay lamps and Vinayakas, glass bangles, cheap bright jewellery, everyday steel utensils, brass pots—the shops were full of these things. The temple tank, known as the *Siddhamrita teertham,* is to the south of the temple of the goddess Thaiyal Nayaki. Before we went there we bought rock salt and jaggery from two men who had packed salt, pepper and jaggery separately in small plastic packets and laid it out on two long tables. As we walked to the *teertham,* Chandra told us a story about it. He said, 'It is strange and interesting that there are no frogs and snakes in and around this tank.'

'What is the reason for this?'

'The story goes that when sage Sadananda was meditating on the banks of this tank, a frog which was being chased by a snake leapt on him. Disturbed in his meditation, he pronounced that no frogs or snakes would be found in the tank or close to it.'

'How do you know all these stories?' I asked, surprised.

'We grew up on such stories and I am interested in the *sthalapuranam* of each temple I visit.'

'I think I have had a very deprived childhood since I don't know any of this,' I said with a laugh. Then I added, 'I was raised on the Ramayana and Krishna Leela; that explains my ignorance.'

'You can read up about these temples, their history and the myths and legends associated with them now.'

'I suppose so.' What about my son Ananda? I haven't done enough for him in terms of such stories, I thought to myself.

We went to the *teertham,* tore open the salt packet and put the contents in the water. Fortunately, there were garbage bins for the empty plastic packets. After opening the jaggery packets we took it in our right hand, lowered this hand into the water and allowed the jaggery to dissolve in it as much as it could. We were asked not to throw it into the temple tank but offer it in this fashion. I have no idea what the significance of this gesture or ritual offering was and what the salt and jaggery stood for. I forgot to ask Chandra what it meant as I am pretty sure he would have known the significance of our offering. Why did it have to be salt and jaggery and not something else? We also chanted a small mantra for health and well-being.

After this we went back to the two men who had given us the salt and jaggery. They now gave each of us a packet of salt and pepper, which we were supposed to circle around our heads thrice while chanting a short shloka which meant, 'Free me of the consequences of the sins of previous births. Free me of the pernicious effects of drishti or the evil eye. Take away all my afflictions and health problems.' Then the contents of the packets were emptied into the metal containers standing on the edge of the table and a tiny piece of the rock salt and a few pepper grains were given as *prasadam.* They were sharp and spicy on my tongue but I enjoyed the mildly hot sensation.

After we performed the *archana* before Lord Vaidyanatha, as we were doing the *pradakshina* around his shrine, we saw magnificent bronzes in an enclosed rectangular raised gallery adjacent to the innermost *prakaram.* One of them caught my attention. Shiva and some goddess stood at an angle and Shiva had his right hand under her arm. The two forms were beautiful, more like dancers, graceful and expressive.

I asked Chandra, 'Do you know what form of Shiva this is?'

'I don't know the name. It appears as if Parvati is upset with Shiva and as she turns away from him, he is trying to placate her.'

'Are you sure? Sounds charming but I am not convinced. Let's ask the priest.'

We asked one of the priests who was at the other end of the *prakaram* and he said that the *panchloha* representation was that of Shiva as Gangadhara. I couldn't comprehend how it stood for Gangadhara but I was not there to question the priest's knowledge. If I knew Tamil, I might have probed further and asked him to give a detailed description of these two statuettes standing in such attractive proximity to each other. I had seen colourful calendar pictures of Shiva as Gangadhara, where the tamed and contained river flows from his locks as a regulated thin arc-like jet of water and then goes to the Earth. Thus released in this controlled manner, the Ganga is prevented from destroying the Earth with her might.

After praying before the shrine of Thaiyal Nayaki, who holds the *sanjeevani thailam,* the medicinal oil for all ailments, we walked back to the entrance of the temple. I don't recall seeing the shrine of Murugan, who is known as Selvamuttukumaraswami here. As our son's middle name is Coomaraswamy, which is among one of the many names of Lord Murugan, I don't like to miss seeing him. Strange, how I didn't have any recollection of either being told of his presence there or of visiting him! At the entrance, we were besieged by beggars. I gave three of them some money and all the coconuts and bananas we had with us as *prasadam,* but they still came after us with pleas of *'pasi, pasi'*—hunger, hunger. I would have given them more but I had an unpleasant sensation of being harassed and I let my annoyance curb my generosity.

Also, the three women were young, looked reasonably presentable and healthy. Later, Chandra told me, 'Since this temple attracts a lot of devotees, the beggars here have good earnings and some of them have become regular moneylenders to those not as fortunate as themselves to make a decent living by begging.' This appeased my sense of guilt at not having given them more.

On our way to lunch I spotted the Sivanadi Jyotisham place. I was startled because I had forgotten that this temple town was known for its *nadi jyotisham*—something that Ravi had been talking about for several years. Ravi was busy chatting with his friend, so I didn't get a chance to tell him about my discovery. We had lunch at a place called Sadabhishekam—it had nice cottages, rooms to let, small neat patches of lawn and potted plants and flowers. The golden-yellow and pink arali were in abundance. It was a pleasure to see so much colour and soothing green. It was laundry day at that place because they had hung out the sheets and spread them to dry on the grass and the sandy patches. The restaurant was deserted except for two foreigners. We were concerned that the food would not be fresh as they didn't seem to have any customers. The food was tolerable and reasonably fresh but had a liberal quantity of onion and garlic, which I dislike in any afternoon South Indian meal. The *vata kozhambu* was oily and spicy.

During the conversation at lunch, *nadi jyotisham* was mentioned and Ravi said that he was debating whether he should consult them. Then, within minutes, he made up his mind that he was going to do so. I was apprehensive and uneasy because I didn't want us to know our future. Ravi said that he would consult them about his health and ask them for various *pariharams*. That's all. I didn't contradict him or try to dissuade him because he believed that any present suffering and physical pain is partly a result of karma. Also, he had been talking about *nadi jyotisham* for years.

We entered the Sivanadi Jyotisham place. The street was quiet whereas my heart was pounding. I was afraid. I didn't know exactly what we were getting into and what we were in for. The people at the reception desk were very courteous, pleasant and casual. They called a *nadi* reader to explain the process to us and also to ascertain our specific requirements. It all seemed as matter-of-fact and relaxed as finalising a travel itinerary. Here we were tremulously eager to see our future and fearfully curious to catch glimpses of our past lives. It was a major, momentous and life-changing decision and it was all being treated very nonchalantly. I guess it was an everyday affair for them and perhaps a matter of running a sound business. Even if one totally ignored the moneymaking angle of this set-up, still there was every reason for an unemotional approach because the *nadi* readers involved in this entire enterprise had to be detached people; otherwise their lives would be affected by the recounting of the history of the great many lives they looked into. Charting the course of someone's life is a very demanding task. It can be a very dangerous, damaging and potentially enervating experience—putting together and interpreting the course of other lives—if one has not prepared for it through meditation, prayer and rigorous self-discipline. I hoped that the *nadi* readers were spiritually and mentally equipped for their task. The people at the front desk seemed like ordinary clerical employees.

We gave our thumb impressions and then waited. After figuring out and defining the classification or category each thumb impression came under, the *nadi* reader would be able to locate the four or five bundles of palm leaves that matched it. Each bundle had a set of leaves which are punched with two holes and tied and held together between two wooden frames. As we waited with restive curiosity and anxiety, I looked around to calm myself. I told myself, 'It's such a peaceful day and it's so calm in here. There's no reason for you to work yourself up into a panic.' It is difficult for me to explain, but at that moment the thought did not even cross my mind that I could arrest the process that I had set in motion. It was almost as if it was destined to be so and I was destined to completely forget that I still had a choice in the matter.

Ravi, Chandra and I sat on the long seat covered with deep blue fabric. The front room was also blue. On the front desk was a clay model of Shirdi Sai Baba. I was looking at the pictures of the Puttaparthi Sathya Sai Baba and Ma Amritanandmayi when a mendicant called out and someone stepped out to give him food in a banana leaf packet placed inside a plastic bag. He asked in Tamil, 'What are you giving me today? (I had begun to understand simple sentences in Tamil.) 'Idli, or pongal?' 'Pongal,' came the half-amused answer but the voice was gentle...indulgent. Yes, that's right, be gentle, I told myself, for a mendicant is entitled to preferences too. Then I turned around to look at the other pictures—Vishnu as Anantshayana, the *utsava murti* of Lord Venkateshwara, Bhudevi and Sridevi, a mature and serious-looking Vinayaka (I have a preference for a childlike Vinayaka) and Lakshmi. On the triangular wall right behind the reception desk were other pictures—a black and white picture of Krishna as a baby, a mosque, Vinayaka and Jesus in one picture, Tirumala Venkateshwara in a gold flower and leaf frame and a framed picture with four yantras engraved on a gold plate. In front of us was a staircase leading to the rooms on the first floor and to our right was a U-shaped doorway with a mirror above it. Right next to the staircase were U-shaped windows with blue frames and white decorative grilles, festooned with colourful ribbons to herald the new year and more future-craving, future-hungry clients, I suppose. There was a clock above the window and next to it was a plaque announcing two aphoristic sayings: All deeds are yours. Many receive advice. Only the wise profit by it.

The doorway led to a passage with a long armchair and a large plastic water container with a tap. There were several rooms to the left of the passage as in a train. Cutting across the doorway at the end of the passage were two branches of a banana tree. I could see a stagnant water pond with low rambling shrubs, wild plants on the bank closer to us and tall wild grass at the other end. A white house with a tiled sloping roof stood just beyond the pond. Sitting in this place, nothing looked ordinary or commonplace. The pond, the plants and the house—everything seemed to have other meanings and they were all invested with an atmosphere that did not belong to the quotidian world of humdrum activities. To me the passage seemed to offer exit, escape—I couldn't exit from the doorway of entry, I felt.

Across the street from the entrance to this *nadi jyotisham* place was another nadi nilayam. There was a pungai or the pongamia tree in the front yard. This tree has medicinal value and is used in the treatment of asthma and tuberculosis. It was a lovely large-spreading tree with low branches partly covering the façade of the house next to the nadi nilayam. Everything was in its place, except for my wayward desire to know a part of my future—what profession or career could I hope to follow? At this middle stage of my life, after having led a wandering life, I craved to know what kind of work would offer me something more than the regular sort of satisfaction. I suppose I could have answered this question myself, but I was curious about the predilections and innate tendencies that my horoscope would reveal. Call it laziness to think for oneself and work hard towards a goal. Call it stupidity or by any other more penetratingly accurate name. Basically, I was conflicted and I wanted a way out and I was banking on this place to give me some direction or the glimmerings of an insight. I did not want to take up just about any teaching job that came my way and I had no confidence in my ability to focus on writing as a career. When so many are writing, what special promise does it hold for me, I would ask myself. Would I be content to write for myself alone and not hope that I would be read by others? I wasn't sure that I could be so detached here. Also, while I did wish to write, I recognised the need in actual life to be very careful and frugal with words because I had experienced how much disquiet, misunderstanding and heartache words could cause, if they are not used with restraint and concern for the other. Words must be used sparingly and in accordance with the imperative need of the moment, I often reminded myself.

There was a narrow passage in between this house and the neighbouring one and from there came an appetising smell of curry leaves being roasted in ghee. As the aroma drifted in, I was filled with a sudden desire for coconut rice, just a taste of it. I don't know where this wayward association of curry leaves being roasted in ghee and coconut rice came from but it was there like a clear mental image. We had already eaten, so there was no question of hunger. I could lucidly visualise the coconut rice—grated coconut seasoned with mustard, cumin, Bengal gram, washed black gram, groundnuts, green chillies and curry leaves. The different colours there—white, black, green, golden-yellow and a warm brown—made the craving stronger. Then there was an overpowering smell of sambhar powder and my desire evaporated.

Soon the *nadi* readers appeared and they led Ravi and me to separate rooms. My *nadi* reader asked me if he could speak in Telugu. I said yes, as long as it was everyday Telugu and not the literary kind. We sat facing each other across a large, sturdy writing desk. The room was small, cosy and very quiet but my heart and mind were full of apprehension and disquiet. At the same time, there was some excitement about the procedure and the course this whole *nadi* reading would take. The astrologer had a bundle of palm leaves before him, tied together with a thick cord. He told me that he would read out statements from each leaf and I would have to respond with a yes or a no, till he finally discovered the palm leaf that would have all my coordinates—name, date of birth, parents' names, number of siblings, marital status, children, education, husband's profession and so on. I would have to listen very carefully and respond very truthfully, otherwise the whole process would be a futile exercise or a very long-drawn-out one or I might end up with someone else's palm leaf if I did not pay very close and meticulous attention to each and every statement that was made. I was now afraid of slipping up or giving a wrong response in my nervousness. Really speaking, I wasn't all that nervous—just anxious and perplexed by this entire *nadi* reading business. I felt that I had left the world of everyday normal life behind me and was afraid that I might never be able to return to it as before—that something in me would change radically because of this experience and I would look at my life and my place in the world differently. Or, I would carry something of this experience within me all the time—it wasn't a very reassuring thought. Even if nothing unsettling or unpleasant was revealed, it would stay with me, I knew, and affect my way of going through life and my interactions with people. Whether this was desirable or not so desirable, I had no ability to judge then or think clearly of the impact it would have.

The *nadi* reader opened the bundle and after chanting something, he began to read out each palm leaf in a manner that was somewhere between chanting and singing. It was in Tamil. He translated each statement into Telugu and I had to respond with a yes or a no. For example, your name begins with 'Ga Gi Gu'—No. You were born in January—No. You have two sisters—Yes. He must have made over fifty statements to which I responded. In the first bundle, if on a particular palm leaf some of the personal information matched, the rest did not. After ten to fifteen minutes of search, he came back with another bundle and said that if he didn't find my palm leaf in this one, then we would have to go through a third one. It was also possible that my palm leaf wouldn't be found there and I would then have to look elsewhere, in some other Nadi Jyotisham centre. We had been warned when we entered that we must be cautious because there were some impostors and frauds floating around. In the second bundle, he found my palm leaf or *nadi*. I was amazed. He started reading out the entire basic personal information, like one's biodata—date of birth, parents' names, number of siblings, husband's name and so on. I wondered if he had had the time to collate all the information and present it, based on all my positive responses. While it was quite possible, I didn't think it was the case here, because he had made no written notes based on my responses and he would have to be very bright to recall and put together all the relevant information that emerged from my affirmative answers. His power of concentration would have to be remarkable and his memory sharp and clear. I was impressed. Then he told me that he needed some time to make my horoscope and work on the various general predictions, the past life information and the specific career or profession-related question I had asked. The first step of discovering the correct *nadi* was behind me. Relieved, I did not want to think of what lay ahead. Ravi's *nadi* was found in the third bundle.

Ravi and I went to the front room and waited for our horoscopes to be made, interpreted and a detailed analysis and prediction written down in notebooks. It would take more than a couple of hours, we were told. Ravi and I hesitated to exchange notes there about our respective experiences.

While waiting there, before Ravi joined me, a man had walked in and asked if I was interested in special tea. He spoke Tamil but I could get the question as he said 'special tea'. I replied, '*Venda,* thanks.' As I looked out of the door, I saw a large cylindrical drum-like steel container with a tap strapped to his bicycle. A small stack of tiny plastic cups peeped out of a polythene bag looped over the handle bars. I would have said 'yes' if my stomach wasn't churning and if the tea was offered in something other than plastic. Any hot drink in plastic cups is distasteful. He asked me again in a persuasive tone, 'Special tea?' I guess he saw me eyeing the steel container. I wondered what special tea meant in Tamil Nadu. More than the usual amount of milk, I suppose—just as *payasam* was not plain *payasam* but pal *payasam* if the milk there had to be highlighted. I don't think he meant masala tea or cardamom tea.

I was getting increasingly anxious, waiting for our horoscopes to be made. After Ravi came out of the room where he had met with the astrologer, I suggested to him that we should walk around a bit. We went to the car and woke up Chandra who was sleeping on the back seat. The road was peaceful and there were very few people out on the street at that hour. It must have been around three in the afternoon. The quiet somnolent road seemed to ridicule the turbulence that rose and fell in the pit of my stomach. Why had I allowed myself to be tempted by this *nadi jyotisham*?

Such curiosity, if not perverse, was in rotten taste and very foolish. All the words of consolation that I repeated to myself (I am a very fortunate human being and have a very bright future) began to sound false and slightly hysterical. So I decide to chant *Aum Namah Shivaye,* but even that was said with such desperate quickness that very little of it actually penetrated my inner self.

A tea-*kadai* was open. We climbed the three or four steps which led to a small rectangular raised platform or veranda. We asked for tea that was not strong. I do not think the request made any sense to the tea-*kadai* owner. When Ravi noticed the look of incomprehension on his face, he asked him to give the two of us the decoction and milk separately. We were complicating things for him considerably. Ravi asked me to supervise the preparation while he and his friend sat down on a low, long backless bench and chatted. I noticed a very innovative and interesting contraption for making tea. When I commented on it, Chandra told me that it was fairly common in Tamil Nadu. Common or not, I was impressed by the resourcefulness of the people and the ingenious device. On a kerosene stove, the tea shop owner had placed a large brass pot, which is generally used to fill and store water. It had a brass tap to get hot water. On its right was a hole from which hung a long-handled narrow cylindrical steel jug and a narrow sack-like tea-stained sagging cloth strainer. A steel utensil with milk in it was placed at the mouth of the brass pot. It was a clever contraption—a novel tea-making experience for me. We were given the tea decoction and the milk separately. The decoction was strong, thick and potent. Ravi diluted it with hot water and it was still strong and bitter. He asked for some more sugar and added just the barest trace of milk, but it failed to make an ameliorative difference. He gave up and left it after just touching it to his lips, afraid that it would keep him awake the whole night. Glad for something warm, I had mine. It had already turned tepid after being poured from one little vessel to another to mix the sugar. For someone used to a large mug of tea, this was a thimbleful in quantity, but potent.

The tea shop owner gave me a metal chair to sit on as he realised that we were in no hurry to have our tea and move. A little away from the stove, there was a long sun-paled wooden box with two doors, perhaps to store tea and sugar. On top of it were large plastic jars with biscuits, muruku, samosas and some brown and yellow sweet that looked like a shabby imitation of Mysore paak. We had our tea and chatted to the intermittent sound of a middle-aged woman sandpapering the door behind me with slow, lethargic movements.

We talked about various things, about *pariharams* and their efficacy, about the absolute necessity for faith while doing these, about people with marital problems and serious health problems who consulted astrologers, about politicians and people in serious legal tangles who sought the help of astrologers to find out when their favourable time would come. All these discussions did me no good and I regretted my curiosity. How was I to ensure that the astrologer would restrict himself only to one specific area – my concern about the future of my writing and whether I should pursue it or not. We had told them that we were not keen on any detailed predictions about the future but would they remember and avoid all unpleasant areas? I was glad that Chandra had not given in to curiosity and remained steadfast in his refusal to consult the *sivanadi*.

What followed at the Sivanadi place, the interpretation of our horoscopes and the foretelling of our futures, I have chosen to keep to myself and over a period of six years have gradually allowed the distinct memory of each to smudge and pale away gradually. I have never gone back to listen to the audio recording of the predictions. And I never will.

Our Guide at Darasuram

The interpretation of our horoscopes by the *sivanadi* astrologers initiated the need for a series of *pariharams* at different temples—Tirukkadiyur, Suryanarkoil, Tirunallar, Uppiliappan and two or three others. Performing pujas, saying special prayers, getting together ingredients for specific ritual offerings preoccupied me so much and filled me with so much trepidation that I couldn't look around and enjoy those temples and make mental or actual notes about any of them. Hence they figure only as mere names here. When we reached Thanjavur on 7 January, I was more relaxed.

The Circuit House in Thanjavur, where we had booked rooms for our stay, had poorly-maintained spacious grounds. These could've been made to look more agreeable and cheerful. Time's benevolent neglect was evident. Our room was large, sparsely furnished and dusty. The bedcovers had so much dust in them that it triggered Ravi's nasal allergy within a few minutes of our retiring to bed for the night. Bouts of sneezing, a runny and itchy nose ruined Ravi's sleep and he woke up feeling miserable, unwilling for an early start to our day.

After lunch in Thanjavur at the Meenakshi restaurant, we left for the Airavateshwara Temple in Darasuram, which is thirty-four kilometres from there. Built in the twelfth century by the Chola king Raja Raja II, it is a UNESCO World Heritage site. The constable who was with us had noticed my keenness to have a guide explain some of the salient features of the temples we visited, so he had arranged for one for that temple. He was not really a guide but someone who had voluntarily renounced the life of a grihastha in order to follow the spiritual path. Our car stopped in front of a shop and he got in. He was short and stocky—a big-boned man. While he was not handsome, there was something striking about his personality. Wavy coal-black shoulder-length hair, an ample forehead, large dark eyes, a prominent nose, a wide mouth with full lips and large hands—this was our guide. He claimed to know some English. While he could understand perfectly what was said in English, he could not respond with ease or fluency. Therefore he spoke only in Tamil. I was both angry and sorely disappointed because I would understand very little of what he would explain about the temple. I knew that Ravi would find it tedious to translate and it would take a lot away from his enjoyment of the temple. Chandra would oblige, but it would not be fair to pester him with insistent questions about the description and narration in Tamil.

It was a very short drive to the temple from our guide's shop (I am going to call him by this name for the sake of convenience). The temple had a lot of empty space around it and the surrounding area was green and pleasant. A tourist bus, which had brought foreigners, was parked in the car park. Some of them had gathered in a group around the Nandi pavilion and others were seated on the parapet wall, which enclosed the Nandi and the Sapt Swaras steps. At that time, I had a distinct feeling that I was not going to see a thriving temple, aromatic with sacred energy, but an interesting historical monument. The guide took off in Tamil and after listening to him keenly for a few minutes, I guessed that he was talking less about the temple, its history and architecture, and more about himself and how he became a seeker. I got weary of trying to put together the bits and scraps of Tamil I understood to give me a coherent picture of the subject being discussed and moved away. Ravi and Chandra were very engrossed in their conversation with the guide. Two tourists were about to leave the *prakaram* and exit by the gateway under the inner *gopuram*. I noticed that the woman was smoking and I asked Ravi, 'Is she allowed to smoke in here?' Before Ravi could respond, the guide turned to the woman with a smile and said, 'Don't smoking. This is temple.' She was apologetic and looked sheepish. The guide then continued with his discourse in a very involved and impassioned manner. I caught a frequent mention of the word siddha. I was interested in knowing about the niche statues on the eastern side of the Maha Mandapam but the guide was on his own trip and either disinclined to share information or was himself unclear about the specific aspects of the temple.

I moved away from the three of them, went up the east side steps of the Maha Mandapam or the chariot *mandapam* and sat down on the topmost step. The sun was beating down on my right shoulder. Looking down over the banister of the stone steps, I could see the horse, the chariot wheel and the battlefield elephant with its curved trunk. I marvelled at the artistry and the unique inclusive perspective of the sculptors of the Chola times. On the pillars of the *mandapam*, I could spot the figure of Yali, the mythological animal. I was wondering whether I should wander away and explore on my own when I heard a woman tourist call out to her husband in French. He was standing a few steps behind me, next to one of the outer pillars. At the sound of French, my ears perked up. Standing at the foot of the steps, she was taking his picture and he was positioning himself in the right spot. He asked, '*Est-ce que c'est bon?*'

She called out, '*Presque bon.*'

I felt nostalgic about Paris. *Paris tu me manque,* I whispered to myself. Soon after, the three of them joined me and I could not indulge my nostalgia any more. The stones inside the *ratham* felt cool, very cool under my feet.

Having read up a little bit about the temple, Chandra showed us some of the miniature sculptures on the pillars—there was a Vinayaka with a sacred thread and a Nartana Vinayaka. We saw the Shiva-Parvati *kalyanam,* a very small Somaskandamurti, Ardhanareeshwara and Airavat. Next to the lingam in the main sanctum was an elephant in metal painted white—Airavat. The *avudaiyar* of the lingam had a lotus petal pattern. As the water level is generally high in the temple well, the *avudaiyar* conveys the impression of a lotus floating in water. As we faced the sanctum, to the left of the entrance was Krishna dancing on Kaliya.

The more I saw of the temple, the less satisfied I was with the casual cursory way in which we were seeing it. In addition, I felt more like a tourist here than a devotee. The guide, who had read quite a few of the religious texts, was engaged in rapid uninterrupted discourse with Ravi and Chandra. I wish he had given them some respite from his ceaseless exposition on one thing or another. As we started walking along the outer *prakaram,* Chandra pointed out the sculpture of Shiva as Dakshinamurthy on the south side of the *vimanam.* Dakshinamurthy in *chin mudra* is surrounded by four rishis. Austere, simple, in a yellow veshti, without *vibhuti* or sandalwood paste and *alankaram*—I liked the deity this way. Chandra also pointed out the Sharabeshwara shrine and the window near it made of stone. If he hadn't told me, I would have assumed that it was made of wood. The impression of wood was very convincing. Shiva as Sharabeshwara is an eight-legged creature, part lion and part eagle. This incarnation looks as fierce and invincible as that of Vishnu as Narasimha. In fact, Shiva took this form to quell Narasimha's untrammelled fury. I wondered if the origin of this form of Shiva had anything to do with the Iyer-Iyengar rivalry and each one's claim to supremacy.

I had now begun to recognise the various forms of Lord Shiva and I had noticed that Shiva as Lingodbhava always faced west and was located in the rear niche, behind the Shivalingam in the main sanctum. I hadn't yet asked Chandra to tell me the story of the Lingodbhava murti since the guide was expounding non-stop in a theatrical manner. Disinclined to look at the niche sculpture vacuously and walk away, I interrupted them. Chandra told me the story patiently:

> The story goes that one day Vishnu and Brahma began to argue about each one's superiority. While they were engaged in this strident conflict, a huge lingam of fire appeared before them. Desirous and curious to discover the origin of this massive column of fire, Brahma assumed the form of a swan and flew upwards while Vishnu assumed the form of a boar and dug into the earth. They searched for several days without any luck. Tired of this futile quest, the two of them surrendered to the column of fire with prayers. Shiva appeared out of this column of fire. His form was magnificent and awe-inspiring, with a thousand arms and with the sun, moon and fire as his three eyes. He had a pinaka bow, a trishul and wore the hide of an elephant. Addressing Vishnu and Brahma in a powerful voice, he explained that the two were born out of him initially. Later, they separated into the three different aspects of divinity.

Chandra added, 'Really speaking, the three were part of the Supreme *Brahman*. Look, you can see Brahma and Vishnu in the niches on either side.'

Lingodbhava murti would now speak to me. Each time I looked at it, it would have a unique voice and a story to tell.

While walking along the outer *prakaram,* I noticed that the temple was replete with small sculptures depicting the socio-cultural life of those times. The few small panels I noticed were – a standing pregnant woman supported by two women on either side, a human wheel, women training with weapons, men wrestling and men engaged in sword-fighting. A curious one showed a monkey removing lice. On the north façade of the temple, I noticed a small mount Kailash being lifted by Ravana, and smaller panels showing the life of the Nayanmars. At this point, when I was writing something in my notebook, a pretty young girl walked up to me, peeped over my shoulder and said, 'Handwriting super.' I was in fact scribbling something hastily as the three men seemed to be in a hurry to leave. I turned around surprised and said, 'For me, not super.' She smiled brightly and asked, 'Rupees, please.' She was well dressed and had flowers in her neatly braided hair. This annoyed me because I saw no reason for her to beg and it sounded more like a demand and a gamble than like a real need. I also wondered if her praise of my handwriting had been a clever strategy to soften me. I told her firmly, 'I am not a tourist.' She walked away jauntily, unperturbed by my refusal.

We were going away without seeing the next-door temple of Deva Nayaki when the guide persuaded us not to do this. I was glad we saw her shrine because she was very beautiful and serene. The temple was also very peaceful and peace-giving, very calming. The only unfortunate feature of this temple was that it was full of stagnant water in places and the various establishments responsible for its maintenance were quarrelling over who would take care of certain aspects of its upkeep. The stagnant water prevented us from doing a full *pradakshina.*

When we dropped the guide off at his shop, he insisted that we step inside and sit with him for a few moments. While waiting for tea from a tea shop nearby he spoke continuously and eloquently in Tamil about his reading and life experiences. The wall behind him and the one to his left, had pictures of deities, spiritual masters, religious leaders, sages, a couple of siddhas, thinkers and remarkable people like Mother Teresa. What was curious and interesting was a large picture of him, with compelling smiling eyes. I am generally wary of people who advertise themselves in this way. He had a captive audience and he made the most of it. Later, Chandra gave me a gist of what he had said:

> Right from his early days, he had been exposed to siddha literature and practices. His grandfather was a well-known siddha and his father, who had followed the spiritual path, had acquired certain siddhis. Our guide's main source of inspiration or guru was one of the Shankaracharyas of Joshimath (Badrinath) who later moved to Tirukovilur near Tiruvannamalai. Many years back, the guide had travelled with some of his friends to have a *darshan* of the acharya. He was unwell on that occasion. In some mysterious way, he was helped by the acharya to complete his journey. His entire experience during that journey was a revelation about some essential truths about human life and this strongly impelled him towards the spiritual path. He renounced family life. He left his wife after six months of marriage. She was pregnant at that time.

Poor woman, I thought to myself.

Chandra told us that our guide had a son who was twenty-two. As an integral part of his sadhana, he cooked his own food which was *satvic*—fresh, bland and prepared after a ritual bath and prayers. He ate just one meal around noon. He claimed to have reached a stage where he could manipulate his kundalini for his energy needs and thereby manage with just one meal a day.

Quoting a few instances from Siddha philosophy, Tamil religious literature, and his observations of people, he spoke about sex and how potent a force it is in human life. One of them was rather graphic and unabashed in its details. It is not for any of us to judge the state of a man's soul or the progress he has made on the spiritual path, but I did wonder about his noticeable preoccupation with sex. At best, he could be described as a seeker.

Our guide had a small garden with a little patch of grass, two rose plants with large vivacious pink roses and a kitchen garden. He insisted on showing us his meditation room, which was on the second floor. For some inexplicable reason, I wasn't keen on entering it. The room was at one extreme corner of the landing on the second floor; it had a low roof and a window, which he claimed remained closed most of the time. He did not want sounds from the outside world to penetrate. The curtain drawn across it was dense and dark. Bronze statuettes of gods, brass lamps, two brass female figures with lamps, incense sticks, camphor, rounded polished stones and a small mandiram—this was the room. The ceiling was painted with constellations, which were visible only in partial darkness, after the electric light was switched off. The décor was a curious mix of the traditional and the unconventional puja-cum-meditation room. I thought he would let us take a brief look at this room and then show us the way down, but when he suggested that we enter the room, close the door behind us and sit there for a few minutes, I was a little uneasy. I didn't want our energies to be a part of that very personal space of his and I was also apprehensive about the kind of vibrations his energy would emit in that airless closed room—my fears were unfounded. The coarse blanket on which I sat felt uncomfortably warm under me and I wondered whether he used that in summer too. He just asked us to meditate for a brief while and after we made a concerted attempt to be still, he was ready to let us leave the room. I was glad to be released. On my way down the staircase, I noticed that a tall coconut tree penetrated the terrace and raised its proud head higher than the roof of the house. The tree had not been felled at the time of the construction of the house—an act of charity and respect for life, I thought.

We said goodbye to our guide. He folded his hands and said to me, 'Goodbye, sister', with unusual emphasis on the last word.

Sweta Vinayakar and Tiruvaiyaru

Apart from the temples that we visited to do our *pariharams*, we visited other shrines based on Chandra's suggestions. One such temple was the Dhenupureeswarar (Shiva) Temple at Patteeswaram. I had never heard of it, I admitted to Chandra, somewhat ashamed of my ignorance.

As we neared the temple town, Chandra explained: 'Patteeswaram got its name from Patti, Kamadhenu's calf, who is worshipped here. Patteeswaram is very special to me, as goddess Durga, in that temple, reminds me of my mother. As Jagan Mata, she is indeed the mother of all beings. But my fond thoughts of her are mainly from her image in that temple. In almost all Shiva temples, we see Durga as a small niche figure dressed up in a long skirt. But in the Patteeswaram temple, she has a separate shrine with a life-size image wearing the traditional madisar of Tamil Iyers. Also, her posture and facial expression project motherly care and maternal solicitude, while anger is the typical expression of Durga in most temples. From Patteeswaram she seems to be keeping an eye on her two children playing near the river—Sweta Vinayaka at Thiruvalamchuzhi and Swaminatha at Swamimalai. Incidentally, Patteeswaram is the Durga kshetram as per a Thiruvidaimarudur-centric layout. You may recollect that Sirkazhi is the Bhairava kshetram.'

Chandra looked visibly moved as he thought of his mother and the Universal Mother, Durga. As they fused in his emotions and memory, he took a few moments to continue his narration, 'The temple is also closely associated with Rama, who was afflicted with three *doshams* or sins for killing Ravana, a Brahmin, an able warrior, and a great patron and exponent of the fine arts. Killing Ravana brought upon Rama the third *dosham*, the *chaya hatti dosham*. Rama performed penance for this sin when he installed a Shiva lingam at Patteeswaram.'

He paused and asked, 'Do you know why the Nandi is not directly opposite the lingam, why it seems to have moved a bit from its original position?'

I shook my head sheepishly. 'No guesses.'

Chandra smiled and said, 'In the intense summer heat, Tirugnana Sambandar, a child poet, was on his way to worship Shiva or Dhenupureeswarar. Concerned about his devotee, Shiva had a canopy of pearls erected all along the way to shield him from the sun. Very eager to see Sambandar, he also asked Nandi to move a little bit so that he could see his bhakta as soon as he entered the temple. Nandi obliged. An annual festival in the Tamil month of Ani commemorates this incident.'

With the deeply uplifting story of Shiva's compassion for his devotee for reassuring company, we headed for the Sweta Vinayaka Temple in the Sivan Tirukkovil. It has the sweta or white Vinayaka, created by Indra out of sea foam. It was dusk by the time we got there. With only a handful of people around, we got an uninterrupted *darshanam*. In spite of this, I could not see the image very clearly, no matter how much I bent forward or how intently I peered into the sanctum. At that time, I did not realise that my long distance eyesight had weakened. I was disappointed that I could not see this singular image of Vinayaka.

Ganesha or Vinayaka is a much-loved god who inspires the modern craftsman or artist in a unique way and lends himself very easily to depictions in interesting, sometimes unconventional, forms. My first experience of the contemporariness of the Ganesha figure was in Mahabalipuram. In some of the smaller statuettes, he was shown with a keyboard before him. Since he is a scribe and a scholar, this comes as no surprise. It is his location in the present day scenarios and settings, and thereby his greater accessibility, that makes one smile. Two months later in Mangalore, when we walked into an arts and handicrafts emporium, I saw a curiously depicted bronze Ganesha. Like the hand-rickshaw pullers of Calcutta, a strapping Ganesha was pulling a handcart in which his *vahanam,* the rat, sat very comfortably and regally. As we know, Ganesha was created by Parvati using the turmeric paste with which she had anointed herself. I remember reading in some book by Devdutt Pattanaik that when Ganesha receives the elephant head from Shiva, he becomes the means by which Shiva the ascetic, the inward-looking hermit, enters samsara and participates in it as a householder. With his lower part created by Parvati or Shakti and the upper part created by Shiva, this endearing deity brings together in his form the contrary forces and worlds that Shakti and Shiva represent.

While reading WJ Wilkins' book on Hindu mythology, I later learnt that the Puranas give different accounts of Ganesha's origin. One of them quoted by Wilkins is from the *Varaha Purana.* According to this Purana, Ganesha is said to have been created by Shiva alone, on the appeal of the gods and the sages who prayed to him that he alone could create a 'being capable of opposing obstacles to the commission of improper acts'. After hearing this prayer of the immortals, Shiva looked at Parvati and when he was contemplating how he could fulfil the wishes of the gods, a youth of extraordinary beauty came into existence from the radiance of Shiva's own countenance. On seeing his beauty, Parvati was jealous and in a moment of anger pronounced a curse on the captivating youth. She said that his beauty would be soon gone and he would have an elephant's head and a large belly. Shiva then called the youth his son and named him Ganesha, the chief of the Vinayakas and Ganas.

Ganesha is a very accessible god, easy to please and venerate. I remember when I was doing the Art of Living course a few years ago, on one occasion, after the *Sudarshan kriya,* when we were asked to meditate, the image that leapt before my inner eye and stayed there, was that of Ganesha. A young and playful Ganesha kicks a ball all over a meadow. He does it with grace and style and the delight on his face is writ large. That evening his pleasure was so palpable to me that I smiled openly. Each time after that, when I tried to meditate, this image followed me or, perhaps, I was reluctant to let go of something so delectably amusing.

Since childhood I have known the Hindi expression '*Sree Ganesh karna*'—to start something new auspiciously with the appropriate puja and prayers. However, I had never seen Vinayaka sthapana or the installation of the Vinayaka image in a home before any ceremonious event like a wedding or an *upanayanam,* the sacred thread ceremony. I finally got to see Vinayaka sthapana being done in the month of May, in the house of my sister-in-law Subhadra, several weeks before her daughter's wedding. It was essentially a women's event and a minimum of five married women were required to participate in it. All of us rose very early as the *muhurtham* was at 6:53 am Subhadra did her usual daily puja and then chanted the 108 names of Vinayaka.

Some preparation preceded the Vinayaka sthapana. We placed a small stone grinder, that is, a grain mill, on a clean piece of cloth. The grinder was adorned with kumkum and turmeric. Nine threads coated with turmeric paste were tied around the stationary bottom grinding wheel. 'Why nine?' I asked. No one had a clear answer. Then someone said it might have something to do with the navagrahas. Whole black *chana* was placed in a large steel *thali* or *kancham* next to the grinder. A mortar and pestle with whole turmeric was also placed next to the grinder. On a soft new handloom towel, a kilo of rice, whole turmeric with sprinklings of kumkum and a few coins were placed. At the time of the *muhurtham,* all of us took turns to grind the black *chana* which had to be put in the circular channel in the centre three times. The grain mill did not have a wooden stem that we could hold to turn the upper stone, hence we used our hands to rotate it. Two women had to do it together. We enjoyed ourselves immensely as it was more like playtime for us. Our mini exercise brought back memories of earlier times when there were no mechanised grain mills. The *chana* that had split into uneven halves was then gathered and tied along with the rice into a neat bundle. These would be used sometime before the wedding to make *undralu* or rice *rava* (semolina) and Bengal gram balls. Eaten with hot ghee and maangai, sliced mango pickle, these are divine.

After this procedure, one of the women made a Vinayaka from rice flour and thick turmeric paste. This little idol was placed on betel leaves and delicately adorned with kumkum. Although clumsily shaped and too tiny to have any distinguishing features of Vinayaka, devotion and love for this deity made all the women believe that they had created Vinayaka and ceremoniously given him a place in that home. After this, the idol was placed on a clean plastic sheet and around him were placed little mounds of *vadiyalu* made from washed black gram dal batter, spiced with cumin, asafoetida and red chili powder.

The preparations for the wedding could now be initiated. This ceremony was a miniature version of all the preparations for the festive cooking that would take place around the time of the wedding and during that occasion. Vinayaka was successfully and lovingly installed and, from that moment, he would overlook and facilitate all the wedding preparations and arrangements.

To get back to my story: After a hurried *darshanam* at the Sweta Vinayaka temple, we drove to Tiruvaiyaru, the sacred seat of the Tyagaraja Aradhana festival each year. At Tiruvaiyaru, the car park was choked with cars and there was a bustling mass of people everywhere. Making our way through the crowd, we walked up to the stalls of Tanjore paintings and stood there debating whether we should have our dinner first or listen to some music and then eat. We could hear a powerful young male voice singing and wondered if it was TM Krishna. To hear even a fragment of one Carnatic composition was all that Ravi needed and he felt instantaneously recharged. I was hot and tired and longed for a bath. Although it was early January, the evening was not pleasant. Enjoyment of music was directly and inextricably linked to how fresh I felt. It was dinner time. We decided to eat first. The queue leading to the hall where the food was being served was long, unruly and interminable. Ravi introduced himself to one of the men controlling the queue and he guided us to an emaciated looking man with long bony legs. That person asked us to wait outside a wide entrance cum exit, meant only for the organisers. Two men were posted there to stand guard. People were straining and pushing to get inside the hall. So many people scrambling for food was a sight, both amusing and disconcerting. That back entrance, not available to the public at large, was right next to a series of taps. The ground was slushy beneath them and liberally dotted with grains of rice, some of them floating in little pools of water.

The thin man, with his veshti pulled up above his knees, came to our rescue. He took me by my arm and firmly shoved me in through the door. I was taken aback because that was a very unconventional way of escorting a woman. The low-roofed large hall with long tables and metal folding chairs had captured the heat during the day and trapped it. It was such a bare functional hall that, unless you were hungry, you would eat out of habit than out of any real desire for food. The man gave us corner chairs. I had no appetite after a long day and the absence of any possibility of freshening up dulled it further. At this time, I wanted to use the washroom very badly. Ravi requested the same thin man to escort me out of the hall. This man handed me over to a woman with pepper-and-salt hair. Dressed in a crumpled white cotton sari, she had an air of authority about her. She spoke English with reasonable ease. I asked her to show me where the toilets were. The area was ill lit and there were too many people waiting to barge into the eating-place. She asked me, 'Do you want to pass urine or do number two?' The crude directness of this question embarrassed me terribly. I mumbled a response. She led me to a row of unlit toilets. After I shut the door of one of them, I waited for a few moments so that I could discern the shape of the Indian style WC. The stench was overwhelming. It was filthy and clogged, to say the least. I rushed out as quickly as I could. I was angry with the organisers for grossly ignoring such basic facilities as clean toilets and lighting in a place where thousands thronged for a sacred festival and where so much money was being spent on doing up the place for the concerts and the religious ceremonies. How can a sense of the sacred be totally dissociated from a sense of cleanliness and hygiene in public places? How can the organisers' priorities be so lopsided? How can elaborate and expensive arrangements for the Tyagaraja Aradhana festival ignore such fundamental needs?

When I walked into the hall, the servers had placed the banana leaves and the water before each person and were just about to serve the vegetable. I placed my hand over the leaf and said in broken Tamil, 'I don't want any food. Thank you.' I was ready to puke thinking of the filthy toilet. Ravi looked at me and said with mild sternness, 'You are not going to get any dinner if you don't eat. We might stay on here until midnight and you will get very hungry. Don't make a fuss. Eat.'

Not wishing to make a scene or ruin Ravi's dinner, I relented. 'I will eat, but very little.' I fought back tears of helpless anger and tried to tone down my revulsion.

It was the toughest meal of my life. I pretended to eat the *rasam-saadam*. Mercifully, as Ravi was immersed in his own food and the conversation with Chandra between mouthfuls, he did not notice my painful struggle with eating. It was as if someone had capped my food pipe and nothing would go in.

Once out in the open air we walked towards the place where the musicians were performing. It was packed with *rasikas* sitting on the sand. Not an inch of free space was visible. After combing the area several times with our eyes, we found that a narrow passage of space was available, leading up to one side of the stage, from where we could only see the back of the vocalist and segments of the forms of other musicians. We stood in a single file and listened. Yesudas' son was performing. His voice was as melodious as his father's, but it did not have the same control or the same technical surety. I looked around. Everyone looked fresh and brightly dressed for this music festival. The women wore dazzling Kanjeevarams and had flowers in their hair. The men wore well-ironed shirts and veshtis with attractive borders. Some of them had flamboyant shawls with a liberal sprinkling of gold on them. I felt drab and obnoxiously unclean. It was as if I was not destined to enjoy this unique gathering of musicians in Tiruvaiyaru or I was incapable of relinquishing my excessive sensitivity to certain things. I heard the music half-heartedly and waited for Ravi to say that he was tired and we should go back to our guest house in Tanjore.

In the car, Ravi was in a nostalgic mood and reminisced about his experience of the Tyagaraja Aradhana festival when he was young.

> 'I had seen the Tyagaraja Aradhana on TV in Chennai in the late Seventies. By 1979, my friend and I had started planning for our cycling trip in Europe, which, as you know, happened in 1980-81. In January 1980, we had to go to Kumbakonam to meet someone who was to assist us in our cycling venture. We went there and then accompanied that gentleman to the Tyagaraja Aradhana inauguration in Tiruvaiyaru. It was early morning. The District Collector was the chief guest and we accompanied him to the pandal to the sound of welcoming *nadaswarams*. After the inauguration, the VIPs left. My friend and I stayed on and were promised some accommodation.
>
> The atmosphere at the festival was lively, filled with music and devotion. We spent the day listening to concerts and participating in the various kinds of social interaction going on all around us. I recall one heartwarming scene: A *nadaswaram* maestro was relaxing under a tree and a disciple of his approached with

folded hands after removing his slippers—a mark of respect. During the evening concert, KJ Yesudas sang beautifully. We listened to the concerts standing just outside the pandal. In the open area, a group of youngsters chatted with an eccentric old man who was witty and entertaining.

Wonderfully happy, we decided to stay in Tanjore with friends and commute by bus to Tiruvaiyaru every day. On the Aradhana day, we left Tanjore early and reached Tiruvaiyaru in time for the *Unchavritti*. Along with the *Unchavritti Bhagvathars* we started from Tyaga Brahmam's house and went around the village streets singing Tyagaraja *kriti*s. Women from various houses came out with their offerings, poured them into the sack of the *Bhagavathar* who stood for Tyagaraja Swamy that morning, replicating the latter's morning ritual. They also sought his blessings. After about an hour or so we reached the pandal of the samadhi and slowly settled down for the *Pancharatna kriti*s. The lead singers sitting in a concentric circle around the microphones represented the stalwarts of Carnatic music: Semmangudi Srinivasa Iyer, MS Subbulakshmi, Dr S Ramanathan, Maharajapuram Santhanam, KJ Yesudas, MLV, DK Pattamal, Lalgudi Jayaraman and several others. The *nadaswaram* maestros Kunnakudi Krishnan and Namagiripettai were also there. It is more than thirty years since that event. I may be missing out on some names or adding some due to lapse of memory. However, most of them were there. The atmosphere was charged and full of anticipation as we waited for the songs to begin while the instruments were being tuned. Then it began with the first notes of *Jagadananda Karaka* in *Natai,* slowly transporting the listeners to the sublime world of Tyagaraja Swamy's *Nada Brahmam.* By the time *Endaro Mahanubhavulu* started, the audience was mesmerised and some openly wept with joy. The composition rose to a glorious crescendo and finished with the *avartanam*s on the mridangams and thavils, raising bhakti to an ecstatic pitch. The moment the *kriti* ended, the priests of the samadhi performed the *aarati,* accompanied by the clashing of cymbals and ringing of bells. The *aarati deepam* was the brought out for the gathering of devotees to worship and take in its divine light and energy. It was an unforgettable morning.

That evening was our last evening in Tiruvaiyaru and we listened to a concert by MS Subbulakshmi. Sitting on the banks of the Kaveri at the samadhi of Tyaga Brahmam and listening to MS's divine voice was an elevating experience. All other Tyagaraja Aradhana festivals that I have attended after that, have only been tepid versions of the earlier one.'

Mysore and Nanjangud

Nearly two months later, our dear friends, Revathi and Group Captain Ravi, who had been with us in Paris, were in Mysore for a few days to perform their son Praveen's sacred thread ceremony and we were invited for that. Ravi and I decided to make use of this visit to Mysore to travel a bit in Karnataka, primarily visit a few temples.

The *upanayanam*, which was on 1 March, was performed with ardent attention to the form and spirit of the ritual. In a large hall, with a select gathering of close relatives and friends, it had the auspicious and profound atmosphere of a significant rite of passage in a brahmachari's life. It was followed by a sumptuous lunch. Seasoned with freshly-made ghee, aromatic, with the right balance and blend of spices, it was food meant for the gods. The next day, in a Vishnu temple, we were invited to the *kalyana utsavam* of the Lord and his consort.

I wasn't feeling good at all. My stomach had begun to hurt in the morning and, before the ceremony was over, my acidity went up dramatically. I was sweating profusely because of the intermittent stabbing pains and could scarcely hold myself straight. I barely tasted a few grains of the divine *prasadam*—sweet pongal, *pulihora* and *daddojanam*. After we left the temple, one of the worst migraines of my life had me in its thrall. So vicious and unbearable, with nausea and retching, that I felt only instant death would rid me of my pain. Ravi was terribly anxious. He called three doctors to give me injections to alleviate my pain and control the nausea. After four hours of explosive pain, I finally went to sleep after the shots, totally depleted of all strength and the will to live. I know it sounds dramatic, but that is how it was that day.

The next morning, I got up feeling slightly wobbly and weak but fine overall. Ready for a new day, I washed our clothes with zest, as if I had been injected miraculously with a fresh dose of energy, even for the most mundane of tasks. This spurt of energy was short-lived. I soon began to feel nauseous and tired. My energy flagged. While Ravi was hugely relieved that my headache was gone, he was concerned whether we would be able to go ahead with our Karnataka trip. I asked him for one more day to decide whether I would be well enough to continue. Whether we continued with our journey or not, I did not want to leave Mysore without seeing the Jaganmohan Palace, now an art gallery. It has a unique collection of paintings and artefacts that once belonged to the Wodeyars of Mysore. There is antique ornamental furniture, glass and chinaware, artefacts in sandalwood and ivory, sculpture, photographs, a collection of gravure prints, samples of Mysore gold leaf style of painting, paintings on grains of rice and antique musical instruments.

After entering the art gallery, I sat on a bench for a good ten minutes. It was warm and stuffy in the foyer. My legs felt terribly weak; however, I allowed myself to bask in the sensation of being free from pain and enjoyed the precious moments of relief. On the other hand, I was suddenly inundated with memories of all my visits to museums in Paris and needed time to emerge from them to enjoy the present one. Ravi was exhausted, edgy and anxious for me because of the previous day's ordeal. He was uncertain about going ahead with the planned trip, wondering whether it would be wise to do so even as I reassured him that I was feeling much better. I left him alone to re-gather his calm at his own pace.

We looked through the ground floor of the museum rather quickly and cursorily. Curious about the Raja Ravi Varma paintings on the first floor, we made our way there. Our visit to the art gallery was too short for me to recall clearly even those paintings that appealed to me. No camera was allowed inside, otherwise I would have loved to take pictures of the ones I liked as an aid to memory. Nonetheless, there is one that I can recall fairly well—*An Indian Lady of Calcutta* by BC Law. Done in different shades of cream and brown, it shows a pensive-looking woman holding a brass plate with an effulgent brass water pot, a *kalasam*. With warm brown skin radiating health, she is attractive. Her face is young, her skin smooth and glowing, but there are touches of grey in her hair that is parted along the centre. She is at a threshold and has just stepped forward. One can see the glowing deeper brown of her revealed left foot. The brass plate in her hand is a rich golden and so are her armlets. Each fold, each crease of her cream coloured sari with a gold zari border, can be seen and one can feel the fine texture of the fabric with one's eyes. There is great attention to detail—the intricate work of her oxidised silver necklace, the silver ring on her last finger, her dangling earrings and other rings in the upper ear. The woman wears no bindi. That is puzzling. Is she a young widow, I wonder, but widows used to have shaven heads in Bengal at that time. I would have to ask someone to get my facts right.

As I stood looking at SN Nadyal's painting, *Lonesome,* I heard the brisk thumps of several feet on the staircase. Until then it had been very quiet except for the occasional hushed whispers of the woman and man behind the desk selling postcards of Raja Ravi Varma's paintings. I flinched at that sudden intrusion of sound. Soon a troop of middle school kids marched in. Led by their teacher who was as clueless about the place and paintings as they were, they gazed curiously, puzzlingly, vacantly, at the paintings. Eventually, one of them came and stood next to me. 'Hello,' I said softly. 'What's your name?' asked the girl with two well-oiled thick braids. I looked at her and smiled, 'Priti. What's yours?' She smiled brightly and said, '*Teertha.*' 'A beautiful name.' She walked away shyly. After that, three or four of them walked up to me and asked me my name. I wanted to chat with them but they were hurrying through the whole display. One look at their dour-faced teacher discouraged me further. Otherwise, it would have been interesting to ask the four children if any one of the paintings had appealed to them and why. Their teacher was ill-equipped to be their guide, or motivate them to take an interest in what they saw. I am sure that for most of them, the paintings were an array of puzzling images, considering the haste with which they walked past them. I was sad. I wish they had an informed or inspired guide. Brushing away this thought, I turned to the painting once again where a woman sits in the doorway of her thatched hut. She has bangles on her right arm and her hand rests in a basket. Perhaps she has paused mid-way through her work to contemplate something or is waiting for someone, very likely her husband, to return. The light from outside illuminates part of the clean bare room of her hut. Executed in differing tones of brown, from subdued to deeper to sepia, it exudes a mood of unvoiced reined-in loneliness.

The first-floor attendant had noticed that I had stood before some paintings for a long time. He offered to explain the exceptional technical aspects and the artistic merit of Raja Ravi Varma's work. We agreed to listen to his commentary because an extra buck on the side was what he was after and we conspired to make it possible for him.

All of Raja Ravi Varma's paintings were exceptional pieces undoubtedly, but I couldn't relate to even one on that day.

I had scant interest in the Tipu Sultan and Anglo-Mysore war paintings that Ravi observed with minute interest. Back on the ground floor, we went to the long gallery that has the reclining marble Buddha. Feeling ill again, I had little energy for any of the displays there.

On my way out, a painting by R Sitaram, called *Rapture,* arrested me. It was like a musical dream in blue, from the splendidly clear to the misty, rendered in slow tempo. Or, a sedate entrancement composed in blue. A woman in a blue sari with a resplendent zari border is playing the tambura, sitting on a green mat with blue bands. She looks serene and absorbed in her music. Her loose-sleeved peacock blue blouse, *jhumkas,* and a string of jasmine in her hair, add to her quiet charm. The shadow of the tambura falls in front of her. Her rapture is contained, or veiled from a curious onlooker. There is a painting above and a blue organza-like fabric, suspended from an invisible roof, hangs down in uneven folds. We see her right profile with the gentle curve of her nose. Her bindi is barely visible. Strands of stray hair stick to her neck and pale blue shadows waft under her eyes. Her solitude is breathtakingly pervasive. It penetrates my being.

Ravi waited for me patiently at the exit door. We walked down the corridor silently, past two or three handicraft shops and into the glare of the sun. We saw three young women, one of them a young white woman with pink colour on her face, grinning from ear to ear, and suddenly remembered that it was a day before Holi. Really hungry, we headed for our usual eating place, where I allowed myself to have only curd rice lest my acidity should play up again.

After lunch, Ravi called up Dr Rajyalakshmi, our doctor and friend in Hyderabad, and asked for both allopathic and homeopathic medicines to deal with migraine and acidity. She gave us a precise list and reassured me that I would be fine if I followed her instructions to the dot. While she sounded warmly concerned, her voice was feeble and agitated. I wondered why. At that moment we did not know that she was speaking to us from a hospital bed and was herself quite ill. She didn't give us even a whiff of a hint that she was unwell. I am grateful for her medical help and her smiling reassurance, each time I have had a migraine attack and called her, seeking alleviation of my pain. If I could celebrate her kindness and selflessness in a hundred verses, it wouldn't be thanks enough for all her unstinted advice through our six-year stay in Hyderabad.

After resting at the Circuit House, we started for Nanjangud. Twenty-five kilometres from Mysore, it is situated on the right bank of the River Kapila. Shiva is worshipped here as Srikanteswara or Nanjandeswara. It is believed that sage Gautama stayed here and installed a lingam here. Nanjangud was not originally part of our itinerary, but since we were not absolutely sure of our further travel plans, we decided not to miss an opportunity to see a temple town so close to Mysore.

At six in the evening, it was warm when we set out in the car. It was not a long drive but the traffic was heavy. My headache was threatening to come back with the same severity and this did not augur well for the trip. Normally, I would have taken just a paracetamol, but I figured that this time I had to combat and suppress the pain by taking something stronger.

Our talk in the car turned to myths and legends as I was becoming increasingly desirous of collecting as many as possible. I spoke to Ravi about the one I had come across recently, about Brahma's fifth head. Since we were going to a Shiva temple and Shiva played a significant role in it, my thoughts had turned to it. I was becoming quite interested in the various forms of Shiva and it was a peculiar coincidence that we later saw the sculpture of Shiva as Brahmashirachedanamurti (Shiva as the destroyer of Brahma's fifth head), the one my story would refer to. Ravi was unfamiliar with the story:

> In the beginning, Brahma had only one head. He created a woman called *satarupa* (a face with a hundred beauties or one with a hundred beautiful forms). Since he had created her from a part of himself, she was considered to be his daughter. As soon as he saw his own creation, he fell in love with her. Enamoured of her extraordinary beauty, he followed her by sprouting a head facing each direction in which she moved. Thus, Brahma had four heads. Disgusted with his inordinate passion, she flew skywards to escape his lustful gaze. Unrelenting, he popped a fifth head on top of the other four to pursue her. When she cried out for help, Shiva appeared in the form of Kalabhairava and destroyed Brahma's fifth head...

I paused in my narration to get Ravi's response. 'It's a strange story, isn't it, Ravi, of the forbidden incestuous love of one of the trinity. What meaning can it have?'

'I guess it is a warning to human beings against indulgence in unholy desire or love—a warning against transgression of a social code.' He thought for a while and added, 'I am beginning to wonder whether this is another reason why Brahma worship is not popular at all.'

'I thought it had to do with the Lingodbhava story where Shiva curses Brahma because of his overriding ego.'

'Well, this could be one more reason. It is worth checking out.'

We were nearing the Nanjangud temple, which bears the architectural stamp of various dynasties that ruled the region. Built in the Dravidian style, it has been a major centre for Shiva worship for a long time. The sanctum sanctorum is attributed to the Ganga period and the *mandapam* to the Hoysalas. It was dusk by the time we got to the temple. In the fading light of the evening, it looked impressive. Some of the vendors were winding up their stalls and the large open space before the temple seemed bereft of active life. We walked through the splendidly carved massive gateway, heralded by two elephants in front. Along the outer corridor, there was a lamp burning before a pillar and the devotees who walked past would make sure to offer a prayer there, bend down and take the *aarati* from the oil lamp. Ravi asked someone if there was some special reason for this. He replied that the spot was consecrated to the Bhoomi goddess and people took her blessings before they visited the other shrines. We did an *archana* at the main shrine of Shiva, Sri Nanjandeswarar Srikanteswara. When we put our offerings of money in the plate, the priest chanted a small prayer by resting his right hand on each of our heads, in turn. That was unusual, because generally in South India, the temple priests try not to touch the devotees in order to keep intact their ritual purity for the puja inside the *garbha griha*. The extent or strictness of the ritual purity observance varies from temple to temple.

After our *pradakshina*, we came across a raised, covered gallery in the outer *prakaram* where there were several magnificently carved stone sculptures, as dark as ebony, with well-polished glossy faces. The workmanship was exquisite and the attention to detail worthy of celebration. The names of the deities were written in Kannada. Since Ravi can read Kannada, though with some effort, I had him read out their names. After we had seen six or seven of the deities and Ravi had read out their names, we discovered that all of them were different forms of Shiva. This was the first temple where I had encountered twenty-five different forms of Shiva, all in one place. It was a beautiful gift because I was longing to see Shiva in his different aspects and slowly grow to recognise each of them by looking at each distinctive form and connect it with the story associated with the manifestation of that form. Ravi slowly read out the names for me—Chandrasekharan, Uma Maheshwara, Rishabhadeva, Nataraja, Girijakalyanamurti, Bhikshatanamurti, Kamasamharamurti, Kalasamharamurti, Tripurasamharamurti, Jalandharari, Ardhanareeshwara, Brahmashirachedanamurti, Veerabhadra, Shankaranarayanamurti, Kiratarjunamurti, Kankalamurti, Chandikeshwaraprasannamurti, Vishakanthemurti, Viratamurti, Sukhasanamurti, Bhaktadanamurti, Vighneshwara Chandrasenamurti, Somaskandamurti, Dakshinamurthy and Lingodbhava.

The *apasmara* or *muyalaka* that Nataraja is crushing under his foot is a full-bodied figure, fleshy with a well-rounded sumptuous bottom. He looks large and invincible, just as ignorance, oftentimes, is. Bhikshatanamurti wears the slippers of a mendicant and his face glows with a beautiful smile. Many lamps were lit before Kamasamharamurti, an inward-looking seated figure. Kama is on a parrot, opposite him. I stood for some time before the Kalasamharamurti. In January we had visited Thirukadiyur, where Shiva as Amritaghateswarar or Kalasamharamurti is the principal deity. I had not been able to see the idol clearly as there was a heaving crowd of devotees in front of me. I had content myself with an unclear fragmented view. In the light of the lamp held in his hand, the priest had shown Markandeya clutching the lingam, the mark of *kaala paasa* or Yama's noose on the lingam, and Yama held captive, rendered powerless under the left foot of the Lord. I had to imagine it all as the priest described it. I also struggled to understand Tamil. I had felt cheated, frustrated, at that time. To see Kalasamharamurti or Mrityunjayamurti is a symbolic way of overcoming the fear of death. I am not afraid of death but I am afraid of ceasing to be before having acquired a sense of self-worth and a clear purpose in life. A tall order, perhaps.

Ravi turned to me and said, 'Now you can have your fill of this form of Shiva.' I nodded.

Nandi stood to the right of Veerabhadra with folded hands. Garlanded with bilva leaves, it was sprinkled generously with kumkum or vermilion and turmeric. I did not know the story behind this prayerful submission and worship. And Ravi was getting a little weary of my persistent questions.

In Vishakanthemurti, Parvati's left hand rests on Shiva's throat.

The Lingodbhavamurti looked rugged and rough-hewn compared to the rest of the sculptures, which were remarkably well-executed with scrupulous and pleasing attention to beauty of form and ornamentation. It was placed in a confined narrow space, which had portable gas cylinders, a basket, an iron tray and cardboard cartons. A small cot with exposed legs and a bamboo stick resting against the wall completed its interaction with the world of day-to-day affairs. The divine and the human, the sacred and the mundane, were casually juxtaposed here with comical effect.

In the gathering dusk when the artificial light illuminated

parts of the bilva tree, the *sthala vrksha,* it looked like something stolen from a magical world of enchanting forms. Its fruit, green apple-like, looked more like a fairy decoration than something solidly real. Later, I discovered that it is called wood apple or bael, a fruit that we as kids loved to smartly crack open with a stone. Several threads tied around its branches and moving wispily in the low breeze were the *sankalpams* and prayers of the devotees. For a few minutes we sat down in the courtyard, opposite the shrine of Nandi, with its proud head turned to the right—a virile figure in effulgent, regal black. A thick garland of marigold, rose, bilva and some small purple flowers adorned its gallant neck. On a brass plate before it was a small Shiva lingam with two Nandis on either side of it. It was mignon.

We stopped a priest to ask him the story of Nanjandeswara. He explained in Kannada. Ravi followed most of it and I followed the Sanskrit words and those words that closely resembled their counterparts in Telugu. And it is the story that we have all heard as kids from our grandmothers or our elders: As the Devas and the Asuras churned the *ksheerasagara,* the original venom, halahala, which had remained undisturbed under the sandy ocean floor, now rose to the surface ominously, colouring the waves dark and rising into the air like vile smoke. All of them realised that only Shiva, the Master of the Universe, could save them from the vile poison. They appealed to Shiva and he rose from Kailash to help. As he took in the poison from the sky and the sea, it burned his throat and stained it blue. Since then he has been called Neelakantha. And here in Nanjangud, he is Nanjandeswara. Nanjangud literally means the place where Nanjandeswara (god who drank poison) resides.

The stone-paved floor of the temple's outer *prakaram* was warm under me—the stones still retained the heat of the day while I longed for their cool touch. Had only someone splashed them with buckets of water, the evening would have been perfect. The roof of the small *mandapam* facing the main sanctum was decorated with flower patterns in low relief. Bulbs of different colours encircled each of the roof designs. The frontal section of the roof of this *mandapam* had a small temple arch motif with Shiva and Parvati on Nandi. Ganesha and Subramanya, on either side of them, completed the divine family—Ganesha representing intelligence, auspicious beginnings and worldly prosperity and the warrior Subramanya representing prowess, physical beauty and temporal power. In place of the customary replication of the image of Nandi, the outer temple wall was surmounted by sculptures of deities inside individual arches—so many mini shrines graced the wall and bestowed blessings on all those who came to seek them. Brick-coloured in the evening light, they had austerity and the power to move. I was glad that they had been left free of colour—not painted in all the dazzling clashing garish colours that we have such an irrepressible penchant for.

In the streets around the temple, all activity was in low key. The temple chariot was being dismantled and shorn of all its festive trimmings. We walked past an old house with blackened walls and a caved-in awning. On the broken awning, there was an unruly jumble of discarded household trash. On sand and pebble heaps next to it, children played with gusto, kicking an old plastic bottle gleefully between them. Very thirsty, we looked for a tender coconut vendor we had seen earlier, but he had left. The eating places we saw there didn't look very promising, so we headed back to Mysore, to the restaurant where we had become a familiar sight.

Talakaveri

Eating very little and cautiously, made me feel better. We were going ahead with our trip. In Mysore, we rented a car with a driver and drove to Madikeri, situated at an altitude of 3,781 feet above sea level in the Coorg district. As we reached close to dinner time, we decided to go to the nearest vegetarian restaurant suggested by our guest house manager.

The next morning we decided to head for Talakaveri, the place where the River Kaveri originates in the Brahmagiri hills at a height of about 4,500 feet above sea level. As we weren't sure when and where we could have lunch, we thought it wouldn't be a bad idea to have a filling breakfast. Disinclined to spend time looking for another reasonably clean vegetarian place, the previous evening's restaurant seemed to be our best bet. This time we decided to eat in the room that was at road level. If not more cheerful, at least it had more natural light coming in. The wall facing me, which was on the left of the main entrance, was a cream colour wooden partition divided into rectangular spaces by vertical and horizontal intersecting beams. These spaces were used for individual posters showing places of tourist attraction and religious interest in Karnataka. These posters gave some cheer and brightness to the room. The wooden partition was mounted by a black iron grille and there seemed to be a room or some storage space behind it. The windows facing the road had pale peach curtains with a floral design. To the right of the entrance was the manager's seat behind a reception-cum-cash counter desk. Above his head was an open wooden cabinet with a clock and a colourful Ganesha picture garlanded with fresh jasmine. On top of this cabinet was a Bisleri bottle with oil for the brass lamp next to it. For privacy, the right rear corner had two tables behind a low pink enclosure. It looked more cheerless and grimier than the rest of the place and, just as I was wondering as to who would wish to sit and eat there, it was occupied by a couple well past their prime. The need for privacy must have dictated this preference.

The two waiters there seemed to be in perpetual agitated motion, as if they were feeding a band of fastidious starving guests. I was impatient to be served. The burning sensation in the pit of my stomach was increasing and I needed to get a bite of something quickly to pacify it. A plate of idlis was slid before me. They were thick and lumpy and the coconut chutney was faintly rancid. Deciding not to make a fuss, I downed the idlis with the help of a lemon soda that was served at room temperature. It had a generous amount of salt but no sugar—I had asked for both salt and sugar. When I asked for some sugar and pepper, a small steel plate with three sugar-encrusted spoons was placed before me. They had no pepper. It intensified my disappointment with the breakfast. The driver had his breakfast in a jiffy and was waiting for us restlessly.

Talakaveri was forty-seven kilometres away from our starting point in Madikeri. As we drove up the hills, I saw wild flowering plants and their different colours enticed me. There were large long bell-shaped white flowers in bunches. Right next to them was a bush with small sparkling orange ones. Then, there were exuberant hedges with soft purple flowers whose Kannada name I failed to discover in spite of my unflagging efforts. Ravi thought I was off my rocker as I exclaimed at the beauty of those flowers. On the way we stopped at a spot, 3,700 feet above sea level, officially named as the viewpoint. It overlooked row upon row of hills and fields. Down below, a series of fields curved like a river and dissolved into the distance. As I looked at the heads of the densely packed trees, heard the birds and the insects, wondered at the different forms of life sheltering here, I was grateful for this magnificent respite from the city, with its quotidian life of prosaic practical affairs, its functional disagreeable structures and its aesthetically vapid soulless commercial centres.

The viewpoint seemed to be a congregation spot for insects – thronging hordes of them. On the inner side of the road, the rocks had been cut to widen the road and create space for the vehicles that stopped at this spot. Just below the outer edge of the road, so many rocks had either tumbled down or rolled off. They were squashing the trees below and I was afraid that one of these days they would hurtle down further in a landslide with disastrous consequences. However, as far as I could see, there was no road or human habitation in their trajectory in case they did fall further below. Also, they seemed to be well entrenched in the dense growth and trees.

The spot was littered with cigarette packs – there is irreverence combined with a compulsive need to leave behind undesirable signs of our presence even in the most beautiful spots. Mindless desecration of beauty – a carelessly-flung acknowledgement for a gift of beauty that we receive not with humility, but with overreaching pride and a sense of ownership. We appropriate spaces where we should seek nature's permission to inhabit.

The sun was strong at half past eleven. A busload of screaming tourists went past and we were on our way again. At Talakaveri, Shiva is known as Lord Agasteshwara. I asked Ravi why Shiva was known by that name. He said, 'Kaveri was born from sage Agastya's overturned *kamandalam*. The River Kaveri originally flowed in Kailasha, the celestial dwelling place of Shiva. On Shiva's request, she entered sage Agastya's *kamandalam* so that the sage would have an ever-available source of water wherever he went. Agastya crossed the Vindhyas and moved down south, which had been badly affected by a terrible drought at that time. An asura had prevented the clouds from giving much-needed rain to the parched earth. Agastya was doing *tapasya* when Indra requested Ganesha to help release the waters of the Kaveri. In the form of a crow, Ganesha overturned the sage's *kamandalam* and Kaveri was born from the water that spilt from the pot. Another version is that the sage himself contained Kaveri in his *kamandalam* in order to teach her a lesson in modesty.'

Ravi couldn't recall why the sage did that.

(When we returned from our journeys in Karnataka, I wrote to Chandra in Chennai and learnt the interesting details of the popular version of the story. Once, sage Agastya was on his way to the Podigai hills in South India to counterbalance the big congregation in the Himalayas, on the auspicious occasion of Parvati *kalyanam*, the marriage of Shiva and Parvati. Lord Shiva chose the diminutive muni for this task, because of his exceptional yogic powers. After crossing the Vindhyas, sage Agastya met a proud and wilful Kaveri playing with her friends. Generally, the Kaveri has more water than any other river in Tamil Nadu and the old saying is that even if the rains fail, Kaveri will not fail. Naturally, Kaveri is personified as a proud woman. When Kaveri and her friends tried to make fun of sage Agastya, he advised her to change her behaviour. Kaveri's arrogance did not allow her to make amends and respect the short muni. As a result the sage wanted to teach her a lesson. He shrank the whole river and gathered her in his *kamandalam*. The consequences were grave. The land had no water and the rains failed. Later, the drought-affected people prayed to Lord Ganesha who appeared as a crow, overturned the *kamandalam*, released Kaveri and made her flow freely.)

'Well, the latter is certainly not flattering to women,' I said to Ravi. 'I like the first version better. Anyway, how do you know all these little things?'

Ravi was curious. 'Why did you like the first version better?'

I thought for a while and spoke more to myself, trying to define something that was just an intuition or a spontaneous perception. 'Because it has the concepts of magnanimity, gift-giving, the fight of good versus evil, the river as a source of plenty, grace and blessings, all interwoven in it.'

He smiled at my seriousness. 'You have a point there.'

The temple was being renovated and enlarged; a lot of construction work was going on. There were heaps of stone blocks, piles of sand, trucks and a crane. We walked up the uneven path to the wide steps of the temple. I was about to remove my slippers when I heard a voice full of victorious self-defence and glee say, 'See, even these people have not removed their footwear.'

It took me some time to register this sudden comment from a faceless voice. I looked to my left and saw a slender, attractive woman in her late fifties nod to me cursorily and then look away in the direction of her three fellow travellers and the men from the temple. They seemed to have paused briefly in the middle of some argument or heated discussion.

'We are just taking off our slippers and shoes as you can see. I don't get you,' said I defensively.

'You are supposed to remove your slippers much before this spot. Apparently, there is a sign at the bottom which all of us have missed. This is what we are explaining to these two men from the temple. They don't seem to understand that it is very easy to miss the sign.'

'I didn't see any signboard. Anyway, we are still not quite inside the temple.'

'We have been arguing about this for the last ten minutes.'

'I see,' I replied and then joined Ravi who had already reached the top of the steps and was waiting for me to join him. Sometimes it is difficult to understand raised voices and arguments in places where, ideally speaking, we are supposed to leave our egos and all petty causes of conflict behind us.

We went up to the shrine of Lord Agasteshwara. It was a silver lingam with a face carved on it. Eyes shut, smiling face – that is Shiva's form there. I have always preferred the unadorned lingam without human features. It is austere and conveys the sacred mystery. On the outside wall, directly behind the shrine, was a stone door with knobs. The wooden sloping roof had little bells at the edges of the narrow metal awning. Surrounded by the Brahmagiri hills, it was a splendid spot for a temple. Till then I had not spotted even a small stream that I could name the Kaveri.

'Where is the Kaveri?' I asked Ravi.

'Can you see the tank over there? The river originates as a spring feeding the tank. In front of this tank is a *kundike* with a shrine. Can you see the small group performing some puja there? When we go down you will notice that in the *kundike* there is no *vigraham* or idol to show the presence of Kaveri. The holy water there is the *vigraham* and there is a *panchloha* arch that encircles idols to show that this is where the goddess Kaveri is present.'

'Should we go closer to see it?'

'Later. Let's go up the steps over there, leading to the Brahmagiri hill where Saint Agastya did penance.'

The steps were steep. Since I had just recovered from a nasty attack of hyperacidity and a vicious migraine, I wasn't strong enough to climb without several stops. I was also ashamed of myself as, after Paris, I had stopped taking long walks and my stamina was abysmally low. A taut old man and three other members of his family had climbed up to the hill very briskly and were already on their way down. The hill had scanty vegetation—one kind of a low bushy plant with glossy green leaves was scattered everywhere. It did not look like a wild plant. It may have been consciously planted to bind the soil. A single-petalled flower with a touch of pink, sprinkled the hill slope. These single-petalled flowers were gathered around a central cluster of buds. Although pale, these flowers gave the hillside some dots of colour. The other glowing surprise was a solitary plant with bright yellow flowers. I was desperate to find someone who would name these plants for me but that was a tall order. I was dissatisfied. My pleasure was incomplete, inadequate and fragile, as I couldn't name the plants.

The top of the hill was brown and barren—brown earth, pebbles and stones. It had a tall metal pole with iron projections to serve as footholds and a circular ring at the top with arched bars touching and going past its circumference at various points. What purpose did this serve? I couldn't tell. Was it some weather-related thing? We could not tell.

We had to walk barefoot to the top of that hill as it was considered a holy spot or so I assumed. The steps were not a problem, but on the hill one had to walk carefully so as not to hurt one's feet on the little sharp stones, the cached bigger ones and the coarse mud. Keeping the temple and the steps to my left, from where I stood, I could see a dirt path leading to another hill where a group of young men had gathered. It had what looked like an upright open-ended ladder fixed in the earth at the lower end. I could also see some windmills farther away. I suggested to Ravi that we should walk up to the other hill. Afraid of hurting his feet, he didn't seem very enthusiastic about it. 'It is just another hill. I don't want to walk barefoot. The path is full of pebbles, sharp stones, dry grass, broken jagged twigs and, who knows, even a treacherous hidden thorn. We will have to walk very slowly, very carefully. I don't think going there is worth all this effort.'

'After all, there are others who have gone there. It can't be that painful a walk and it is a short distance. Let's go. Don't protest.'

'Why do I have to give in to your foolish desires?'

'They are not foolish,' I protested, looking hurt. 'Come on, be a sport. I am sure the view from there is superb. Ample compensation for a little bit of pain.'

'Okay,' he consented half-heartedly.

Stepping cautiously and gingerly, we made our way to the other hill. It wasn't as bald as the previous one—dry plants, some wild ones, low pine shrubs and the same lovely green bush with glossy leaves. Here I could pluck the leaf and feel its texture—an adequate reward for our troubles. The hill had a rusty triangular ladder and another one lay prone in a state of pathetic dereliction. The hills towards the west that had the windmills were barer than the rest. The ones in the south were a misty grey. We were surrounded by hills and here silence spoke in deep subdued tones or lapped languorously around us in low limpid waves. I could see that Ravi was moved by the solitude and beauty. He broke the silence, 'I am going to call my friend in Chennai and tell him that we are in Talakaveri and that he must visit this place.' There was no signal. He couldn't call. Thankfully, the silence was breached only for a passing moment.

I turned to look at the other hill from where we had just come. From this distance, the upper portion of the tall pole there looked like a toy aircraft poised for take off. On the hill where we stood, there was an upright cylindrical moss-covered stone resting on a wide stone base. It looked abandoned and worthless but I wondered if it had served some useful or religious purpose in the past. There was a clump of ferns – some still green, others a fading orange and a weak yellow. The rest were different shades of grey – brown grey, bluish grey or a drab grey; there is colour even in the process of ceasing to be.

We retraced our steps and I sat for a few minutes on the steps, midway from the bottom of the hill and contemplated the temple. I was facing south. Once the renovation and building work would cease, the temple would have a different atmosphere, a more detailed and fuller story to tell and a different pervading spirit. The small hill behind the temple was a warm chocolate brown and a fence skirted its top curve. To the right, on a level higher than the temple, was a largish asbestos shed with stone slabs and other construction materials around it. I hoped that it was not meant to house the workers, who would get baked inside it very rapidly.

We went to the small temple tank. Ravi wanted to sprinkle the Kaveri water on his head since he had no change of clothes for later, after a proper dip. Two women and a man were in the water. They held hands and made their way cautiously to the other side of the tank. The women were wearing long baggy ankle-length dresses, in common parlance referred to as 'maxis', which clung to their rotund wet bodies. Religious faith and devotion have many different faces and I would get to see quite a few of them on that trip. The water was cold and refreshing as I dipped my hand in it. On the opposite bank of the temple tank, a priest was performing puja for a small group of people. Offerings of flowers and coins were made to the *kundike*. The Kaveri was the presiding deity—she was holy water, ancient and pristine. Her touch cleansed and blessed—her devotees journeyed to her with this touching faith. We would meet her again seven kilometres away at Bhagamandala at the Triveni Sangam, the confluence of the three rivers, Kaveri, Kannike and the mythical Sujyoti.

Bhagamandala and Triveni Sangam

On the way to Bhagamandala, we stopped at a makeshift shop to pick up some coffee. This mention of coffee reminds me of the many coffee plantations we saw on our way to Talakaveri. At one spot, at a wide bend in the road, I glimpsed a coffee plantation to my right on a gentle slope. However, I could get a clear view of only two or three plants and on top of their branches were perched an astonishing number of sprightly white butterflies. I gasped in surprise. How was such a thing possible? I was puzzled but did not saying anything to Ravi and did not ask the driver anything because I did not wish to disturb him on a high hill road. As I re-visualised that surprising sight in my mind and savoured its image, I chanced to see other coffee plants on the left from my car window. No, they were not butterflies but dense clusters of flowers emerging from the branches, together with the leaves—untainted white against the lustrous dark green of the leaves—sparkling and splendid.

'Can we stop right here?' I said urgently. The driver sensed the excited appeal in my voice and stopped.

'What is it?'

'Flowers. I want to see the coffee flowers. Just a little bit behind us.' Ravi was getting used to my trivial insanities and mini passions. He didn't say anything because this time he too wished to take a closer look at the coffee plants. As we got off the car and retraced our steps, we could smell jasmine, sweet and delicate. Soon we spotted the jasmine flowers and the coffee flowers that had made me pleasurably restive to see their untouched white against the deep green of the leaves. They sat so pertly and fairy-like on the branches that they had me in their thrall. As we entered the plantation, I bent closer to inhale their perfume – subtle and sophisticated. The coffee plants with their vertical trunks and branches that radiated from higher up on the main column looked like low, generous-sized umbrellas.

Coming back to our halt at the coffee shop: It was propped on tall pillars leaning against the hill slope to bring it to road level. It looked very inviting with its wide, open entrance and large bottles of local wild honey, visible from a distance. The open shelves were lined with jars of honey, cardamom, packets of long strips of cinnamon, cloves, coffee powder, bottles of mildly spiced honey with dried nuts, figs and dates. A charming, pregnant young woman was the only one managing the place. Large gold *jhumka*s in her ears, a big bindi, soft features, kajal-lined bright eyes, with the tender 'regard' of a mother-to-be reflected in them – this was our shop owner cum salesperson. Her fine cotton purple sari had large orange and pink flowers moving sinuously across it. She wore a daringly contrasting orange blouse and dainty silver anklets on her feet. A good and generous salesperson, she let us taste three different kinds of honey. Keen on seeing a coffee plantation, we asked her if anyone in that area would let us visit his or her plantation. She pointed to different kinds of plants, trees and cultivation on the slopes and said that all that was theirs. I could also see a nice-looking cottage in the narrow valley below. Even before

I could venture to ask her if we could see their varied plantation and walk down to her cottage, she said, 'You are welcome to walk through our plantation and see our house. The gate is about half a kilometre down this road, so you take your car up to it and park by the roadside. There is a wide winding path through our plantation to our cottage down below. If my husband were here, he would have shown you around.' I was a bit surprised because we were total strangers and she had not hesitated even for a moment to invite us to walk through their property. In fact, I had observed that the people in these parts were simple and trusting. After thanking her warmly, we got into our car and stopped at the first gate on the left. Just short of the gate was another shop selling the same local products. The woman standing outside her shop looked at us with a question in her eyes as we and our driver made straight for the gate. I told the driver to explain to her that we had permission to go inside. After the driver spoke to her in Kannada, she replied in broken English that the pregnant woman was her sister-in-law and that we were more than welcome to explore the place and walk down to her house. She took us to the edge of the slope and pointed to her house, which was pretty close to the other woman's cottage. Basically, they were the wives of two brothers.

Our driver was as keen as we were to walk down to the cottage through the unkempt plantation, which seemed lost in the tangled undergrowth and wild luxuriant irrepressible plants and bushes. We had barely entered the gate, where the gradient was steep, when my foot slipped on the loose stones and I slithered and fell, but managed to break the severity of my fall by thrusting my open palms on the ground. It was the second of my four falls during this trip and could have been a bad one, but I escaped with nothing more than a sore bottom and grazed palms.

On two sides of this stony and leafy path was a curious plant I had never seen before. There was something fatally attractive and forbidding about it. It was a low plant with a yellow fruit resembling a smaller version of a lemon. The leaves had thorns sticking out of them. I was about to pluck the fruit when I heard the driver's voice of warning. 'Don't. It could be poisonous.' Ravi who hadn't noticed my move, now pounced on me justifiably, 'Are you crazy? Do you have to touch every unusual plant? Don't the thorns tell you that it is not meant to be touched?' Guilty of being foolish, I did not reply but joined him. He shook his head in severe disapproval. 'Can I at least take a picture?' I asked hesitantly. 'If you want to,' he conceded reluctantly, still annoyed with me for being silly or thoughtlessly curious.

The wide winding path was stony, with small loose and larger entrenched stones. For the most part, it was covered with dry leaves from the trees on either side. Pale brown, rust brown and dusty pink leaves gave the path an autumnal visage. The misty pink leaves were from a tree that had green and red leaves. I felt frustrated because I liked the tree and wouldn't get to know its name. The extent and intensity of my desire to know a flower, a plant, or a tree would perplex Ravi. When it perplexed, amused, or exasperated him, I would begin to wonder if I was a little off. Just as we are happy to call someone we like by a known name, I guess I wanted to be able to identify the plants I liked. I wanted to call the plants I was curious about by their names. This would enhance my pleasure, make it more complete, better rounded and bring the process of discovery to some well-defined end. Or, so I felt.

Right along the left of the sinuous path was a narrow pipe, most likely taking fresh spring water to the two houses below. To the right of the path was a plant growing at regular intervals, with long and sword-shaped leaves yellowing at the edges. I asked our driver if he knew the name. He gave the name in Hindi, 'Elaichi'. 'Can I see the elaichi?' I asked. 'No, it is unseason,' he attempted a response in English. The cardamom was interspersed with coffee plants and there was a lot of confused entangled undergrowth on this hill slope, so I wondered how the workers would find their way through the plants to gather the cardamom and the coffee. What surprised me further was when the driver said that the pregnant woman would have to walk this path every day to the shop and back home in the evenings. That was admirable because it was a strenuous walk, uneven and tricky because of the loose stones and the thick carpet of slippery leaves. We reached the end of the path and were rewarded with a splendid display of at least thirty anthurium plants with their valiant upward thrust of thirty odd spadices with their colourful solitary spathes in white, rose, soft orange, and shiny red. The plants were still in their dark earth-filled plastic bags. The cottage stood in a large clearing in a narrow strip of flat land surrounded by gentle slopes. A woman, in a crumpled and faded cotton sari riding high above her ankles, who had been pottering among the plants looked up inquiringly as we drew closer. The driver explained to her in Kannada the reason for our visit. She relaxed and invited us to look around. She named some of the flowers for me in Kannada—mallige, sampige, sevanthige, madarangi. There were coffee plants, areca nut palms, pepper creepers which had deftly and effortlessly moved up the slender trunks of the silver oak, mango, orange and citron or bitter lemon trees. After ages, I had once again seen the bitter lemon tree and it pleased me greatly. Ravi and his family are great fans of the narthangai or naradapakai pickle and it tastes wonderful with curd rice. It stimulates and uplifts the appetite and takes care of nausea. I resisted the temptation to ask the woman for three or four unripe fruits. Apart from the fact that we were travelling, I did not want to abuse her hospitality. She pointed to a wooden box on a short pole, which was meant to attract honeybees to make honey. I saw a few of them lurking near the box. No sooner had I stepped forward to take a closer look than I felt a sharp tug at my arm.

'Are you insane? Can't you see the bees buzzing around?' I turned around and looked at Ravi, with a sheepish smile on my face. 'Why don't you plonk down on that box? Give you a much closer perspective, don't you think?'

When I did not respond, he continued, 'When will you learn to be a little more careful?'

'When you are not around,' I answered smilingly.

'Why then? Why not now?'

'Because, then I will have to fend for myself.'

'Don't give me this junk of a theory,' he said, half-serious, half-jocular. Fortunately, neither the woman nor the driver understood our petty verbal skirmish.

The domestic help invited us to sit for a while in the covered veranda in front of the house and offered us fresh spring water. It was the most delicious and strength-restoring water I had ever tasted. She was keen on chatting with us. Ravi asked her questions about the plantation in his halting and inadequate Kannada. In her naiveté, she told him that her masters, the two brothers, owned about eighty acres. He asked her the number of labourers they employed to harvest the various produce and the cost of land per acre. She answered readily. We were ordinary curious visitors, delighted with everything we saw but I wish she had been more discreet and guarded in her approach to us. Corrupted by city life, I found her simple and trusting nature very refreshing and surprising. The driver told me that the people in these parts were like that. Thanking her warmly for her hospitality, we made our way back to the main road and took off for Bhagamandala and the Triveni Sangam.

The driver was very enthusiastic about our visit to Lord Sri Bhagandesha and the Triveni Sangam.

At the entrance of the temple was a huge four-tiered brass lamp with a woman at the top holding a *deepam*. It was black and greasy and still had the wicks in each of the smaller lamps. When fully lit, the little flickering jyotis would dispel any gloom, physical or mental. Unlit, the lamp was still impressive, but without the power to evoke a sense of ceremony and thereby re-energise the viewer. The temple was being renovated, hence the feeling of dispersed energies or vibrations. It had shrines of Eshwara, Vishnu, Subramanya and Ganapati. Made in the style of a Kerala temple, each of the shrines had a steep conical roof, constructed of wood and covered with copper plates. A smaller second roof on top of the larger one was supported by various sculptures and small columns with arched gateways. The structure of the roof conveyed the impression of a mini temple.

On the western wall of the Subramanya Swamy Temple, there was a curious niche sculpture. It had two figures joined at the waist in a strange fashion. The upper half was a woman with full round breasts. From the waist downwards was the figure of an upside-down man doing a handstand on a horse and an elephant. The large feet of the woman also rested on the horse and the elephant. On the outer wall, in a doorway just above the sanctum, a human figure in the centre held a lotus in either hand. There were two elephants on either side of the figure and musicians playing different musical instruments.

A plaque behind the Sri Mahavishnu *sannidhi* read:

> According to the *Skanda Purana,* the Sri Bhagandeshwara temple is named after Bhaganda Muni who installed the Shiva lingam at this site. King Dodda Virarajendra renovated this temple, which was damaged in a bitter battle in 1790.

Stepping out of the temple, as we walked down the sloping path on the left we saw labourers cutting stones. Buffaloes squatted languidly in the fields ahead. It was too warm for those creatures to move, but the men, who had to make a living, had no choice but to do hard physical labour in that energy-sapping afternoon heat.

We crossed the road to see the place where the Kaveri, Kannike and the mythical Sujyoti met. A plaque there said that the Kaveri flows eight hundred kilometres from Talakaveri to Poompuhar in Tamil Nadu. Another sign warned visitors and pilgrims to keep the place clean but I was already beginning to see disagreeable signs of trash strewn here and there. In front of us, to the left, was a large concrete shed with a tin roof; it was supposedly a changing room for pilgrims who chose to bathe at this holy spot. A peepul tree before it was garlanded with strings of marigold and stone tablets with entwined serpents were placed against its massive trunk and ample overlapping roots.

We walked to the bank of the Kaveri or the meeting place of the three rivers. A small rough-hewn statue of Nandi faced the river. Subdued and restrained there, that spot marked the unostentatious beginning of the mighty Kaveri. On the opposite bank, four young men, with trousers rolled up high above their ankles, were playing cricket with a long flat piece of wood which they had managed to shape into something that could be called a very distant cousin or the crude prototype of a cricket bat. Their soft rubber ball would often find its way into the other shallow arm of the river and one of them would wade into it to fetch it. The batsman would whack with such gusto that I wondered if the poor ball would survive the bashing of that afternoon. One of them was barefoot and the others wore ordinary bathroom slippers or flip-flops. They were calling out to each other in Hindi. One of them teased the other, '*Apne aap ko bada khiladi samajhta hai.*' Curious, Ravi asked them where they were from. One of them replied, 'We are from Madhya Pradesh.' Surprised Ravi asked, 'What brings you here? Are you students?' 'No, we are doing the repair work at the temple.' I could sense that they resented this interruption. Clearly, they were not happy to be distracted from their game.

Desirous of dipping our feet in the sacred water we walked further to the left bend in the river where the water was shallow. That March afternoon the sun was blazing bright. Our faces and arms were hot but our feet tingled pleasurably in the cool water. I would have loved to sit on the steps for some time if the surroundings had been more pleasant. I could not help feeling that modern man's intrusion had spoilt the atmosphere and the physical appearance of the place. The deserted functional concrete structure with rain-streaked walls and the scattered trash contributed substantially to this unpleasant feeling. Not being fortunate enough to ignore the first impressions of the spot, I could not rejoice in the awareness that I was standing at the sangam or confluence of three rivers. Incapable of being oblivious to my immediate surroundings, I was disappointed.

A bridge would give a different perspective of the place so we walked up to the bridge and walked along it to get another image of the place. The bridge had pats of dried cow dung. Facing east, I could see a road curve up an easy slope. That was attractive—it held the promise of a trek to more picturesque spots. Towards the south, at the other end of the bridge, was a trail through a dense mass of trees—a promise of new places to discover. The air was filled with the excited and jubilant shouts of the four young zealous cricketers, sans even the basic equipment.

Famished, we turned back. Not far from where we were, was a restaurant run by Karnataka Tourism. This was our only hope of getting something to eat until we reached Madikeri. Getting off the bridge, I saw several disgusting heaps of paper plates in a high clump of grass behind a narrow ridge of earth and whatever pleasure I had experienced in looking at the rivers from there evaporated completely. I was appalled and angry but all such strong feelings are impotent and futile unless they lead to something concrete. One has to help create awareness in people that all of us are personally responsible for the appearance and upkeep of all the spaces that we inhabit, visit or frequent.

Madikeri: Mother Kaveri and Méditerranée

The next day was the last day of our stay in Madikeri. Ravi had fallen in love with the hills and wanted to prolong his stay here. He asked me, 'What do think? Should we forget about the rest of the trip to various temples and just stay on here for three to four days? We could visit a coffee plantation, even stay on one, go on treks—basically, just enjoy the hills. I can check with the tourism office about the interesting things one can do here. Give it a thought.'

I continued to pack our things, choosing not to respond immediately. He waited patiently while sipping his cup of tea. I had heard of the benefits of pilgrimages but I had not given it serious or conscious thought. For me it was an attractive concept, an emotionally comforting thought but not the impelling force behind my need to see the temples we had decided to see. I just hoped that as I visited these temples something would change within me either imperceptibly or noticeably—that I would learn to look within myself for strength and solace in times of distress and loneliness and not yearn to find it elsewhere, in the ever-shifting bewildering realities of life. I hoped that my restless search for a remarkable transforming experience would cease and I would learn to focus on the present moment. Absorbed in my thoughts, I did not answer for a moment or two.

'What are you thinking?' asked Ravi.

'Let's do this when Ananda visits us. He might enjoy this kind of thing. Let's stick to our original plan if it's okay with you.'

'It was just an idea. So are you ready to leave in a couple of hours?'

'Yes.'

'If you are all packed, let's take a walk although it's beginning to get bright and warm already.'

We stepped out and the air was fresh and invigorating. It was around eight in the morning. Our guest house had two lovely enclosures with a variety of plants and flowers, some of which I had never seen before. I had spotted a splendid white hydrangea the previous morning and I stopped to take a picture of this beauty. I had first become acquainted with this flower in Paris and ever since it had never failed to delight me whenever I saw it. I was both thrilled and startled to see it in my home country, as if it were a surprise foreign guest and not a native of this soil and climate.

Our guest house was at an elevation. This gave one a good view of some parts of the town of Madikeri and the surrounding hills and valleys. As we stepped out of the gate, I once again saw the creeper with purple flowers spreading across the entire length of the rock face that bordered the left side of the road. I wanted to pluck one flower so that I could look at it closely but all of them seemed high and inaccessible. As I reached out for one that seemed nearer than the rest, Ravi reached out and got it for me.

'Don't you wish you were a little taller?' he said with a laugh. 'The way you were stretching out, you could have grazed your arm or fallen into the ditch. When is this silliness going to end?'

'Not very soon. Aren't you glad that it is a colourful silliness? Thanks.' I took the flower from his hand.

'Now don't stick your nose into it,' he admonished. 'And throw it away before it wilts. You know that I hate dried or wilted flowers.'

'Don't worry. You won't see it wilt. I'll press it between the pages of a book you will never open.'

'Why would you want to do that?'

'A souvenir from Madikeri.' I could sense his irritation wax now. 'Enjoy the walk. Don't focus on this flower and its wilting,' I appealed.

The flower, a jaunty purple with five delicate petals fused together, had to be held carefully because it threatened to droop from careless touch. The underside of the petals was streaked with fine pink lines, which gave the flower an additional chaste charm that could not be perceived from a distance. It was like discovering more things to appreciate in a person as one gets to know him or her better. I was holding the flower in my left hand and balancing my notebook on my left arm while making notes. In a moment of stupid inattention, I tore a part of the flower. I was miserable at my shabby neglect. Ravi would have been annoyed with me had I asked him to pluck another one. I bent down by the side of the road and hastily, but tenderly, covered the purple beauty with two fallen leaves. I was grateful when Ravi did not notice that I no longer had the flower in my hand. At the end of the road, which joined the Field Marshal Cariappa circle, we turned right, onto the main road that led to our eating joint. We had barely turned the corner when we heard vicious barks. Close to the hedge and iron fencing of a house, which retreated from the road, were two strapping restive German Shepherds. Drawn by the stunning overflow of orange bougainvillea, I had walked too close to the fence. Ravi gripped my arm firmly and yanked me away from it.

'Are you mad?' he screamed. 'Those dogs are ferocious!'

'But they are on the other side of the fence. Be reasonable,' I protested weakly.

'I want you to look where you are going,' he said, with some exasperation. 'You are behaving like a child today.'

'Sorry. Let us walk up to the enclosure there. It has a statue—very likely that of Field Marshal Cariappa.'

The house adjoining the one with orange bougainvillea had pink bougainvillea and right next to it was a bushy creeper with the same purple flowers but in a calming pastel mauve. A few freshly fallen flowers lay unheeded on the ground. I picked up one of them and carefully flattened it between the pages of my notebook. I felt like a thief but this act subdued my inordinate desire to possess the pretty flower. Ravi had already entered the enclosure. He connived with my silly move.

The traffic was picking up, I noticed, as we crossed the road. A children's park was at a level lower than that of the road. Attracted by a bronze sculpture of a woman with a pot, I wanted to see it more closely but I had missed the entrance. Seeing Ravi's mood to walk along the quieter hill roads, I decided to postpone my desire to enter the park.

On our way back from our short walk, across the road, I saw the office of the Urban Development Authority of Madikeri. It was a poorly maintained structure—ratty, a dump. I wondered how it could prevent ugly structures from coming up, wholly incongruous with the physical landscape and native architectural wisdom when the office itself was such an eyesore.

Now, I could not resist entering the children's park, or what used to be a park. Ravi was not interested in rundown or seemingly abandoned places. Finding the gate, which I had missed earlier, I walked down the few steps leading into it. Jungle gyms, slides, see-saws, a frame for the swings with the swings missing—it had everything that could attract kids to come and play, yet there was something derelict and sad about the place. The play area needed a fresh coat of paint. The long narrow park had a cheerless deserted air about it. There were no flowers to liven it up. The grass was brittle, a discoloured lifeless brown and the ground had ugly black patches where the grass had been burnt to check its wild growth. I walked carefully through the grass, sharp and spiky in parts to get to the sculpture—the only redeeming feature of this pitiably neglected park. Perhaps the children did play here in the evenings and on holidays but I would not get to know since we were leaving shortly. The sculpture, very likely in bronze, pleased me instantly. Called *Mother Kaveri,* she is a soft-featured benign woman pouring water from a water pot held in both her hands. The gesture is graceful and generous. She wears a small crown and her hair is tied in a bun at the nape of her neck. Her two additional arms rest at the back of her head. She is holding something in each hand but I could not figure out what it was. Two mermaids with hands folded in prayer, stand at a lower level behind her, touching her. In my haste to get to this sculpture, I had left the camera with Ravi who was already slowly making his way back to the guest house. The sculptor was KK Muthanna. This was my second significant experience of sculpture in India—the first one having been at the Chennai Museum where I had seen a heart-rending depiction of poverty and howling hunger. *Mother Kaveri* took me back to Paris and the Jardin du Carrousel at the border of the Tuileries where I had seen Aristide

Maillol's work for the first time. For some reason, at that moment, I thought of his *Méditerranée*—a maternal-looking woman with a body that exudes quiet strength and promises comfort. She is self-contained, reflective, as she sits with the right leg folded and the raised left leg bent at the knee. Her left elbow rests on her left knee and her hand rests on the side of her head in a gesture of pensive self-absorption. Her stretched right hand grips the rear right edge of the metal slab on which she is seated. Whenever I had visited that garden, I had often wondered at the need in people—tourists, young men and women, children—to touch Maillol's sculptures and have some tactile experience of them: Grip or feel or 'take' the hand of a statue, place a hand on its shoulder, encircle its waist, or touch its belly. The children did it more unselfconsciously and with an innocent claim on the bodies or forms of the sculptures. The others did it more surreptitiously and tentatively, afraid of being chastised by the security guards. But among all the images of this tangible contact with sculpture, there is one that stands out: One spring evening, I was standing on the left side of *Méditerranée*, contemplating the thoughtful incline of her head, when I saw a young woman stroll up to her, look at her with touching wonder for a few moments and then move her hand tenderly along the statue's right arm till she reached the strong muscular shoulder. Without attracting her attention, I silently moved a few paces behind the sculpture. Clasping the shoulder firmly, she rested her head against *Méditerranée*'s neck and upper back. This gesture lasted barely a few seconds but in those moments I saw the naked and heartbreakingly simple need in her for ungrudgingly given, no-strings-attached touch and the need for the kind of enduring comfort which only a lifelike lifeless statue can give. From a sculpture, there is no expectation of reciprocity so there is no disappointment and no betrayal.

It was a willing receptacle of all the things she had projected onto it. Although unresponsive and motionless, the energy and life breathed into *Méditerranée* by the sculptor had evoked a spontaneous delicate response from the young woman in consonance with her own strong personal longing and led her to look for something human and giving in the bronze figure and connect with it unselfconsciously for a brief moment. I felt that I had witnessed something I was not supposed to, but was secretly grateful all the same that I had. I was a trespasser. I had caught a glimpse of an intimate moment forbidden to the unsympathetic. My heart had warmed to this young woman who looked very vulnerable and childlike. That evening I sent her a silent message of my best wishes and walked away unnoticed. It connected me to her in some way although I knew that I would never see her again.

(Long after writing this page, it struck me that I had already fictionalised this *Méditerranée* episode in my novel. I had completely forgotten about its inclusion. That this scene should come back to me with such a sense of novelty and vividness as if I were talking about it for the first time, is what amazed me about the trick my memory had played on me.)

Murudeshwar

From Madikeri, we drove to the Kukke Subramanya Swamy temple and then moved to Dharmasthala where we visited another temple and spent the night. The next day we proceeded to Mangalore and stayed there for the night.

The following morning we left for Udupi which is fifty-eight kilometres north of Mangalore. It was nearly noon when we got there, so bright and hot that one couldn't stand outside beyond a few minutes. After Sri Krishna's *darshanam* and lunch inside the temple, we stepped out to stand at the *kanakana kindi,* a small window, to have another *darshanam* of the deity.

This window has a touching story. Kanakadasa, a great bhakta of Krishna, was not allowed into the shrine by orthodox Madhvas as he was not a Brahmin by birth. Unperturbed by this, he began to sing praises of his beloved Lord Krishna and became completely immersed in his bhakti as he stood in a corner outside the temple. Suddenly there was a breach in the wall where Kanakadasa was standing. Moved by his devotion, Lord Krishna offered unhindered *darshanam* by turning towards his ardent singer-devotee. A small window now stands in the erstwhile gap in the wall.

After leaving Udupi, around three in the afternoon, we stopped at the Maravanthe beach. At that hour, there was no one except for the vendors in their stalls selling coconut water and soft drinks. As the heat was getting to the driver in his non-air-conditioned car, he was glad to have this respite. Under the roof of a stall made of dry, deftly interwoven palms, we enjoyed the welcome shade. Facing the Arabian Sea, we sat on the long backless bench thirstily guzzling the coconut water. The gradient of the beach was sharp as it plunged into the ocean. The water looked inviting. I would have loved to stretch out on the bench and take a nap but we were short of time. A brief halt at Murudeshwar and then we were heading for Kollur where we wanted to reach in time for the evening *aarati*. Across the road was a stretch of trees with tall slender trunks and long fine pine-like grey-green leaves. I asked the driver the name of those trees. He gave me their Kannada name—*gaali marra,* which, literally translated, is wind trees. Used for fencing, they serve as wind breakers. To see their pliable trunks submit to the wind's whims is an interesting sight if one is fascinated by trees, their forms and their messages for us humans. Later, I was delighted to discover their botanical name—Casuarina equisetifolia L.

A few kilometres down the road, from the place of our brief halt, I could see the hills of the Western Ghats to my right. It was a beautiful tree-lined drive except for the heavy traffic—trucks and tankers with gas, crude oil and cooking oil. Around thirty kilometres away from Murudeshwar, we climbed a low hill and found a truck ahead of us piled high with huge logs of wood jutting far out of its posterior. It laboured its way up like a monstrous beast of burden, at a moaning pace, and I was afraid it would soon pack up.

For a short stretch, our drive was not very green. Shrubs, dried plants, scattered trees—that is all. A little later, I saw many trees that looked like jackfruit trees but I could have been mistaken. When we entered Uttara Kannada, the vegetation became thick and abundant again. A little short of Murudeshwar, we left the main road. This smaller road was a great disappointment. The sides were littered with empty plastic bags and packets of chips. To ruin things further, laminated Janata Dal S flyers, which had been strung together and hung everywhere to promote their candidate for some local elections, had come apart and were now omnipresent like strips of discarded colourful unsightly linen. Such carelessness towards physical surroundings that lead to spiritual and sacred sites is an unforgivable sin. It marred my enthusiasm to visit a temple whose approach road had been desecrated so inexcusably. As soon as we reached the parking lot, our driver gently warned us not to take too long if we wanted to catch the evening puja at Kollur.

Ice cream vendors and other vendors in their temporary stalls lined either side of the path to the temple. A very tall new *gopuram* was under construction. It looked abnormally high, incongruous with the rest of the structure of the older temple with steps leading up to it. It gave the impression of being compressed or flattened and did not have the well-rounded, full-bodied appeal of the temple towers I had seen. The reason could be that it was still far from finished. A large statue of Shiva loomed behind the temple—its size was impressive. That is about it. It was modern and un-alive—a formed stone without vital life. I wasn't inspired to take a closer look because, for me, a sense of the divine can only be experienced if the deity rests in the sacred space of the *garbha griha,* illuminated only by the flickering light of the oil lamps and enveloped in an atmosphere redolent of incense, camphor, sandalwood, ghee and sweet-smelling flowers – bathed in an atmosphere invoking the divine mystery.

It was nearly four in the afternoon and the air was warm and humid. It moved around me in suffocating, closeting swathes. We were sweating profusely and in that state I did not wish to enter any shrine but we had no choice. Desirous of freshening up for a meeting with god, I looked for a water tap at the lower level of the temple, but there was none. Hot, sweaty and irritable, I entered the temple, which had two other people apart from us. After a brief *darshanam* and an apology to Shiva, 'Forgive me, I feel too uncomfortably hot to pray,' we walked around the temple enclosure, looking at the sculptures on the *vimanam*. The south side had several Dakshinamurthys, placed one above the other in diminishing sizes. There was also Shiva and one other figure I could not place. I asked Ravi what the story depicted there was.

He said, 'That is Shiva giving Ravana the *atma lingam*.'

'I am sorry, I don't understand.'

'I don't remember the story very well.'

'Disappointing. I remember seeing a small temple bookstall at the bottom of the steps. They might have a book with the *sthalapuranam*.'

'Yes, worth checking.'

The west side was dedicated to Vishnu. Garuda in human form carried Vishnu on his shoulders and above that was Vishnu with his consorts, Sridevi and Bhudevi. Right at the top was Vishnu with Adisesha. Brahma figured on the north side.

On our way out, I picked up the slim booklet, which gave a brief story of the temple. Its English was replete with Indianisms and some awkward expressions that made comical reading. Extremely thirsty, we walked up to the second level of a restaurant next door that gave an exceptional view of the sea and the beach. While we waited for our fresh lemon sodas and bhelpuri, I read the story of Ravana and the *atma lingam*. The sea breeze was calming and the view gorgeous. My mood improved. I now understood the driver's insistence that we stay for the night in Murudeshwar. Unfortunately, we could not change our plans so easily.

I told Ravi the story:

> Ravana wished to get the *atma lingam* from Shiva so that he could become extremely powerful and immortal by worshipping it. For this reason, he went to Kailasha and did rigorous *tapasya*. Pleased with his devotion, Shiva appeared before him and offered him a boon of his choice. Extremely happy, Ravana asked Shiva to give him the *atma lingam*. Shiva was concerned when Ravana expressed this wish but he could not go back on his promise. Granting him the *atma lingam*, Shiva placed a condition: He should walk home carrying it and never place it on the earth. If he failed in this exacting exercise, the lingam would become eternally fixed in the spot where he might chance to place it.
>
> After Ravana got the *atma lingam*, the gods were very apprehensive that he would become invincible by worshipping it, so they appealed to Mahavishnu for help. Vishnu came up with a very smart plan and deputed Ganesha to carry it out. Vishnu knew that Ravana was very particular and scrupulous about performing various pujas at specific times of the day and he had to use this quality of Ravana's to trick him into placing the lingam on the earth. Ravana was nearing Gokarna when Vishnu eclipsed the sun with his *sudarshan chakra* to make it seem like evening. Ravana was in a dilemma. Should he place the lingam on the earth and perform the evening prayers and rites or should he forgo them for once? At this moment, Ganesha in the form of the Brahmin, Vatu, came to that place. Ravana sought his help.

Ganesha agreed to hold it but on one condition: He would call Ravana three times and if he failed to come, he would place the lingam on the earth.

Choosing an auspicious moment, Ganesha placed the lingam on the earth even before Ravana could complete his prayers. The gods celebrated this moment with showers of flowers. Vishnu withdrew his *sudarshan chakra* and, as soon as he did that, there was bright sunshine. Ravana realised that he had been duped into giving up the lingam. Extremely angry, he tried to uproot the lingam from its fixed spot but it was an impossible and futile task. In insane anger, he threw the various things associated with the lingam in five different places, which became the panchkshetras. When he threw the cloth wrapped around the lingam, it fell over the Kanduka hill and took the form of the Murudeshwara Linga. At first, it was without a base, so Lord Parameshwara asked Vishwakarma to create one.

'Yes, now I remember the story. Interesting,' said Ravi.

'What is interesting for me is that Ganesha was sent to help out here and he was also selected to help release the Kaveri. I am sure there are other stories where he initiates good things. Guess that is why he is the god of auspicious beginnings.'

Our plates of bhelpuri came. The first spoonful, the first mouthful, and I was disappointed. Since I had asked the waiter not to make it spicy, he had added a generous pouring of ketchup and sprinkled the whole thing with sugar. The exaggerated sweetness was very inconsistent with one's concept of bhelpuri—it was inedible. There was no trace of either the tamarind chutney or the green one with mint and coriander. It was a travesty. I pushed my plate away while Ravi tried to eat his.

'Don't you want to eat it?' he asked.

'I am not too hungry,' I lied.

I did not wish to ruin his appetite and changed the topic.

'Do you remember the art and crafts emporium we went to in Mangalore?'

'The same place where you picked up the *uruli* for good luck?'

'Yes.'

'What about it?'

'I was thinking of the bronze Ganesha we saw. A strapping Ganesha is pulling a handcart in which the rat, his *vahanam,* sits comfortably and regally. He does it with great alacrity and grace in spite of his corpulence.'

'I do remember that curious piece. It brings in humour.'

'It is an interesting piece because I think the craftsman was just enjoying himself reversing the roles of the two, Ganesha and his *vahanam,* but I don't think he was aware of the other implication of his creation.'

'Which is...?' Ravi asked, spooning the bhelpuri into his mouth.

'I read somewhere that the rat represents the intractable problems of life that Ganesha keeps in check by riding him. Here the problems have a royal ride.'

'Just enjoy the contemporariness of the Ganesha image and forget about the rest.'

'It is just a passing conjecture, nothing to do with the craftsman's real intention.'

'Ganesha is such an accessible and likeable god that the artists and craftsmen like to play with his image. Don't you remember seeing Ganesha with a keyboard in the stalls of Mahabalipuram on the way to the *rathams*?'

'I do. Since Ganesha is a scribe and a scholar, it does not come as a surprise. It makes him even more accessible.'

'I like those Ganeshas where he is made to look like a playful chubby child and not where he looks mature and sagacious.'

'I see. I don't have any such preference.'

We watched the sea and the beach as we sipped our fresh lemon drinks. The sea was calm and the beach was clean and not crowded. A boat called Sea Star was anchored there. No one seemed interested in a joy ride. A few young men were swimming close to the beach and a group of women had waded into the water, fully draped in their saris. The water looked cool and inviting. It was soothing even to look at. It was lovely to watch the water wash over the uneven heads of the smaller rocks, retreat, once again move over them from two sides or swirl around them. It was like a ceaseless *abhishekam.* The advancing and retreating waves created a little whirlpool around the rocks or rose up zestfully in a small fountain. A jeep was speeding along the beach. At the other end of the long rope tied to it was a large colourful parachute-like air umbrella and a man was suspended from its lower end. He was getting his adrenalin fix for sure. We made our way back to the car park. On the way I bought myself a vanilla-and-chocolate stick ice cream and then looked around desperately for a proper dustbin to throw the wrapper in. The roadsides and parking area were evidently nothing but uncomplaining trash receptacles and would have magnanimously received my pathetic offering. The tea stall owner thought I was behaving strangely when I dropped the wrapper into his cane waste basket. Ravi was amused and exasperated, but kept his counsel. The driver observed me curiously as he waited with some impatience to drive us to Kollur.

Kollur

The guest house where we stayed for a day looked like a chawl. Dimly-lit reception area, long corridors with innumerable rooms for devotees, made it look drab and very functional. Its only redeeming feature was that it was away from the centre of the town and had a very spacious front yard and parking area. Our air-conditioned room on the first floor was at the end of a dark passage. A musty draft hit us as soon as we entered. I rushed to open the door at the other end, which opened onto a small sit-out or balcony murkily speckled with dead insects. Three or four winged insects sailed in. Ravi pulled me inside and slammed the door shut. 'Twilight is not the time to air the room. We will have a host of insects barging in.'

There was a fine layer of dust on the furniture. After wiping the coffee table with a paper towel, I arranged our tea things on the table: A small travel-sized immersion rod for heating water for a cup of tea, steel glasses, two teaspoons, tea bags, small plastic bottles with sugar, regular milk powder and soy milk powder. I was ready with my mini portable chai shop. Tea outside would be thick, milky and sickeningly sweet. Not desirous of spending a moment longer than necessary in that large, unventilated room, we took super-quick baths in a small bathroom with cheap slippery tiles. The white plastic bucket was woebegone with wear and the tap sputtered out its contents each time it was opened.

Glad to be out of the room, we hastened towards the temple for the evening *aarati*. We were grateful for an escort from the temple; he would help us get an unhurried *darshanam* without a long wait and help us with the *archana*.

While waiting in the temple administrator's room before being called for the *darshanam*, I thought of a dear friend who had a lot of faith in Sri Mookambika. I wished to make an offering and do a puja in her name. Since I did not know her *nakshatram* and *gotram*, I tried to call her from the temple office. After several failed attempts to get through to her at home or reach her on her cell phone, I gave up. In all these months, after my return to India, it was the first time that I had not been able to contact her. I grew increasingly anxious and concerned. Ravi felt that I was worrying unnecessarily. Perhaps she was travelling or just busy and did not wish to be disturbed, he said. For some reason, his explanation did not reassure me that day and I had an inexplicable sense of unease with respect to her. Later, when we got back to Hyderabad, we learnt that the time at which we were trying to reach her desperately she had been in hospital with a sudden illness. If I had known that she was ill, I would have offered special prayers for her. All the same, I thought of her as I took the kumkum *prasadam* for her.

The priest who helped us get a *darshanam* of the deity Mookambika and did the *parivar puja*, the puja for the well-being of our family, was tall, fair, with a lean and taut body. Wearing a red silk veshti and an angavastram, he looked singularly striking. In a deep resonant voice, he explained the significance of the devi who was breathtakingly radiant with her jewellery and adornments. This is what he explained in good Hindi while pointing to the beautiful large emerald adorning the goddess (That his explanation was in Hindi was not all that surprising since this temple attracts pilgrims and visitors from all over the country):

> The goddess Mookambika includes in herself both Shiva and Shakti and represents all the three forms of Shakti—Lakshmi, Saraswati and Parvati. Adi Shankaracharya consecrated the *panchloha* image of the goddess. In *padmasana* posture on a lion, the Divine Mother has four arms. In two of her hands she holds the *shankha* (conch) and chakra (discus). The other two hands are in the *abhaya* and *varada* mudras. The former gives assurance of freedom from fear while the latter grants boons or holds the promise of fulfilled wishes in this life.

Two or three months later when we met our friend Chandra, he asked us if we had seen the spheroid jyotirlingam in front of the idol. This lingam, he explained, is the repository of very potent mystic energy.

'I am sure I missed it because the priest hurtled through the explanation. I wish I had seen it.'

Chandra explained further, 'The jyotirlingam is divided into two unequal parts by the *suvarnarekha* or the golden line. The left side, which is larger than the right one, stands for Shakti or the dynamic energy aspect of the Divine. As Shakti is more powerful and predominant here, the Divine is embodied in the female form of Sri Mookambika.'

The priest took us to the Shankara Peetha where Adi Shankaracharya had meditated. The small room, which was locked, was opened specially for us. It has a seated figure of Adi Shankaracharya in a state of eternal repose. The atmosphere in the room is very restful and conducive to calming a troubled mind. We could not linger there.

The atmosphere in the temple was festive—it was the fourth day of the Brahmarathotsavam, the festival that falls in March. After the evening puja, the temple procession was in place. Two sturdily-built priests carried the two *utsava murti*s of goddess Mookambika on their heads. The bronze idols rested on rolled and coiled fabric, shaped like a thick ring. Two priests fanned the goddess. They were followed by other devotees and priests carrying the replicated models of the attributes of the deity mounted on long sticks—the conch and the discus. The spear and the trident were also included. Musicians and men bearing lighted torches formed part of the procession. There were *nadaswaram* players, a *kanjira* player and others who clashed cymbals and played different kinds of drums.

Near the *bali* stone, the acharya or the chief priest and his assistant performed the ritual of *bali* or sacrificial offering to the deity. Symbolically, he lit the *homam* or the sacrificial fire. With elaborate stylised movements, the chief priest shook some rice and bilva leaves onto the stone. He pretended to pound something in a silver bowl. Each of these gestures had a deeper meaning, but there was no one close at hand to tell us what was being enacted and what was being offered as a sacrifice and why.

The playful or folk element in this temple procession was the Tattiraya, the oversized hollow legless dolls. Fiercely mustacheoed, these dolls with popping out eyes looked comical when two men got inside them and only their thin legs were visible as they danced, skipped and swayed gaily to the music. The children joined in the fun, clapped and danced with the dolls. They were greatly entertained by these huge puppets with fixed expressions, brought to life by two pairs of incongruously thin legs. After three *pradakshinas* in the outer *prakaram*, this colourful celebratory procession moved out of the temple. The priests placed the *utsava murtis* in a small *ratham* or chariot that the devotees took turns to pull through the main temple street. To light the way, some of the men had tied neon lights to bamboo poles, which they held upright on either side of the procession. I thought that was very innovative.

We walked barefoot with this motley procession. I walked on my toes for the most part, suspicious of every dark stain and wary of each wet, greasy or sticky patch on the road. I was the odd one out. Ravi implored me to become oblivious to what my feet were stepping on and to soak in the atmosphere.

The main street was brimming with life. The shops and small eateries were open but there was no business. Along with their families, the shopkeepers stood before the shops to welcome and propitiate the goddess who had graced and blessed the street with her presence. She was in their midst and they rejoiced on seeing her. It was not an occasion to be missed. At several spots on either side of the road, men, women and children stood with offerings of flowers, incense and *deepams* arranged on a plate. Each person's offering was taken by the priest, offered to the goddess and the *prasadam* given to the person concerned. On the way back the people offered fruit to the goddess, and each person's offering, whether less or more, was given the same priority by the presiding priest. To the reverberating beat of the drums and the full-blown sound of the *nadaswaram*, the goddess returned to her resting place. The doors of the shrine opened. There weren't too many people around. At this point, I caught a glimpse of Sri Mookambika. Without her golden face-mask, precious jewellery and other adornments, she looked awe-inspiringly austere and more approachable. To witness her sublime form in a state of beautiful repose was a blessing. We waited for the last puja and got to have the *kashayateertham*, a slightly sticky liquid concoction that is beneficial to health. Mildly flavoured with pepper, other spices and herbs, it was sharp on the tongue and soothing to the throat.

We were deliciously tired when we headed back to the guest house. The shops were winding up for the night. A few people were going about their last-minute purchase of an image of Sri Mookambika and haggling over the price. The tired shopkeeper ignored the insistent appeals for a better price by a family of three. Many of the Mookambika images were in cheap plastic frames—one of them was a glossy tawdry pink interspersed with shiny black. I wanted something simple and sober in a chaste frame, but as the shopkeeper was running out of patience, I decided to wait until the next day and not purchase any picture in a hurry.

A long, low moan from a cow tethered in the front yard of a house made us stop for a few moments. The cow was straining at the girdle around its neck and moving restlessly in the narrow circumference provided by the rope. The gate was locked from the inside and there was no one on this stretch of the street to whom we could report the helpless creature's panicked movements. Guilty of ignoring its agitation, we quickened our pace to the guest house.

Small groups of teenaged boys were lingering near the streetlights in front of our guest house. At that late hour, it came as a surprise. Four of them sat on the low parapet wall talking to each other in hushed excited voices. There was a lull as we neared them. They looked at us curiously. Ravi greeted them cheerfully and asked them if they were into exams because they had books in their hands. One of them replied, 'We are intermediate students.'

'It is very late. Where do all of you stay?' Ravi asked in a concerned voice.

'Our hostel is there,' the youngster said, pointing into the darkness. 'We study. We have exams,' he said, explaining their presence there.

'Do you have an exam tomorrow?' asked Ravi.

'We have English tomorrow,' said the same boy.

'That should be easy,' said Ravi encouragingly.

'Yes,' he replied hesitantly and timidly. They exchanged embarrassed looks. 'Well, good luck to all of you.'

If Ravi had tried to talk to them in Kannada, they would have been less awkward and unsure. We left the boys and walked into the guest house with its long silent corridors and staircases. There were closed doors and more closed doors but not a sound from behind them at that hour of the night. I was so tired and so rested in my mind that I just wanted to hit the deck as soon as we entered but a petty ludicrous drama was in store for us. I had barely rested my head on the pillow when Ravi, who was just about to turn off the lights, let out an angry yelp, 'Priti, get up, quick.'

'What is it?' I said, startled and peevish.

'Get off the bed. I just saw a big cockroach disappear into the bedclothes.'

I groaned, 'There goes our sleep.'

We launched a futile mission to hunt down the cockroach with vengeful zest. This mood was totally at variance with the spirit of devotion we had witnessed, and been a part of, at the temple.

We pulled off the bed sheet, threw the blankets onto the armchair, tossed the pillows off the bed, yanked the mattresses half off the bed, thumped it, prodded it, peered under the bed, tapped it with the handle of an umbrella, but our slippery culprit was nowhere to be seen. With the major hullabaloo we made, it had a million warnings to secure itself in an inaccessible dark spot.

Grumpy and tired, I said to Ravi, 'Let's sleep. I am sure it has scurried miles away from here or is hidden under something, the heavy almirah for instance. It's not going to come out.'

'How can you be so sure?'

'I can't, but if it crawls all over you, you can get it,' I said, with gentle mockery. This comment did not go down too well. He was fully awake now and fuming.

'I need to sleep. I am tired. Stop saying ridiculous things.' I realised that Ravi was in no mood for my ill-timed humour. To pacify him, I remade the bed carefully and coaxed him to rest. He slept fitfully and managed to catch an hour of good sleep only around five in the morning. He woke up, grouchy. It was only the thought of the morning *darshanam* of Sri Mookambika that kept his irritability in check.

I opened the back door to let in the morning light. The air was fresh and cool. The trees and the hills in the distance were a welcome sight. After an hour or more, there were signs of life and movement in the girls' hostel diagonally behind our building. Two of them sat against a pillar in the corridor and chatted. Two others had cups of their morning coffee or tea in their hands. They sipped it while strolling in the open courtyard. One young woman had washed her hair. She wiped her thick black tresses, flowing down to her hips, gently and lovingly with a handloom towel. Others had books in their hands and memorised something as they walked up and down in the corridor of their hostel. To my left was the roof of a house crammed with all kinds of junk: Crushed scrap metal, the battered door of a car, deflated tyres, rubber tubes, entangled plastic pipes, weather-beaten tarpaulin sheets, dented tin cans and a host of other trash. I turned away from it to gaze on the hills once again. They reassured me of the presence of a different world of experience.

A chill in the air invigorated us when we stepped out for our morning visit to the temple. The open drains clogged with rubbish marred the pleasure of the walk temporarily. The small businesses were happily oblivious to their immediate surroundings to which they had partly, or largely, contributed. We have de-sensitized ourselves to filth, even that which is in close proximity to us as long as it leaves our last doorstep untainted. All the guest houses were eyesores.

After the morning *darshanam*, we walked along the outer *prakaram* of the temple. The temple has two *dhwajastambhams*. One of them is eye-catching because of its workmanship. Its base rests on a tortoise. A little higher up, an elephant with a lotus bud in its trunk, stands on a *kamalam* pedestal. A man or mahout seated just above the elephant's tail has an axe in his right hand. Why? I couldn't guess. Above the elephant is a shrine with four deities for each of the four directions. Vinayaka faces the goddess Mookambika.

At the Saraswati Mandapam, a religious ceremony was in progress. The bronze *utsava murti* of Saraswati was resplendent in a white and gold sari. Two young girls in silk blouses and long skirts were sitting in their fathers' laps and tracing something in brass plates covered with rice grains.

Ravi said, 'This ceremony is *vidyarambham* or *aksharabhyasam*. The girls are forming the first letters of the alphabet with the help of their respective fathers.'

'Yes, I understand. It is a ritual initiation into learning. It's a beautiful concept and practice. I wonder why we did not do this for Ananda.'

'I guess because we were not in India. Amma's frail health

must have also contributed to this neglect of observation of significant ceremonies in our child's early life.'

A little behind the Saraswati shrine stood the Tattiraya. I could get a closer look at these dolls now. A metal frame formed the basic inner support or skeleton. A big bindi on the forehead, wide popping-out eyes, pitch black eyebrows fringed with yellow, fierce moustaches, arms proudly akimbo, elaborate green and red or pink and red turbans, a long turban cloth hanging behind, frilly-edged robes with bands of gold and red, concentric circles of red, gold and glittering green paper pasted onto the front of the robes, wrists encircled with candy pink ribbon—these were the theatrical-looking dolls with their fixed stares. They had a square hole through which the folk performer could see. The previous evening, the men inside the Tattiraya had infused them with a peculiar prancing life. This morning they looked lifeless, lost, awkward and uninteresting in spite of their colourful garments and large staring eyes.

We walked past several shrines—of Prana Lingeshwara, Partheshwara, Panchmukha Ganapathi, Chandramouleeshwara and Nanjandeshwara. The Nandi in front of the latter was draped in flowers. Next to the shrine of Anjaneya carved in low relief on a stone slab, a man sat on his yellow angavastram immersed in *dhyanam*. Pausing before the Sri Veerabhadraswamy shrine, I noticed that his gaze was potent. It radiated a kind of fierce energy that was difficult to take beyond a moment or two. The *bali* stone was opposite his shrine.

A boy was selling newspapers in the outer *prakaram* of the temple. I wondered at the way the profane world penetrates and exists alongside the sacred world. Commerce and monetary transactions are an integral part of the temple, as all ordinary and special pujas and sevas can only be performed if you pay for them.

It is acceptable as long as money is a means to an end – to serve the devotees, help the priests make a living, help the temple fulfil its ceremonial sacred functions, sustain its various charitable activities and maintain its premises.

Around a quarter past nine, the two *utsava murtis* of Mookambika were taken in a procession. One priest fanned the deities and some others followed with large-sized attributes of Sri Mookambika. A modern band with trumpets, drums and pipes, played two or three devi-based Carnatic *kritis*. The band players were dressed in maroon veshtis with a yellow border. The modern band was followed by musicians playing traditional instruments – *nadaswaram, kanjira* and *thavil*. The two made strange companions – incongruent and dissonant at moments.

Ravi did a *sashtanga* namaskar or full prostration before the goddess and we headed out of the temple. At a very minimalist-looking tiffin place not far from the temple, we had our brunch before leaving for Sringeri. The sight of the crispy hot dosas on our battered plates eclipsed all else from our sight – the small room with its ramshackle chairs and tables. *Annadaata sukhi bhava.* I regretted not having enough time to visit the banks of the Sauparnika river where an eagle called Suparna had performed penance and attained salvation.

Rivers attract pilgrims, holidaymakers, travellers, adventure sports enthusiasts, people dependent on them for sustenance and their livelihood; hence rivers have great stories to tell, songs to share, messages to gurgle, splash or stormily churn in times of spate. For me, to observe people on the banks of a river and all its plant life, its birds, its fishes, its rocks, stones, pebbles and sand banks, is to touch and trace the contours of life's myriad faces and read its changing expressions. I missed this experience on that visit to Kollur.

Sringeri

After breakfast, we walked down the main market street to the two small bookstores adjacent to each other in the hope of finding something on Sri Mookambika and discovering stories about the significance of this kshetram and the surrounding Sanjeevini hills and forests, which are replete with shrines. It is also believed that they are frequented by siddhas and yogis in their *sukshama sharira* or subtle forms. We found a little booklet *Om Sree Mookambika,* which, apart from giving the significance of Sri Mookambika, had something on the quintessence of the cosmos. The latter was too condensed and too brief to be of any interest to me. In addition, the style was too jerky and unsure to leave any impression on me.

It was late morning by the time we left Kollur for Sringeri. It was getting to be quite warm. The sun had decided to be unsparing. Our driver told us that we would go past Agumbe, the Sunset Point. He wanted us to get to Sringeri in the afternoon, rest for some time and then come back to Agumbe to view the sunset, which is spectacular. He was very enthusiastic and our non-committal response was a dampener. The winding road through the forest had some uncomfortable dicey twists. Under repair in portions, there were piles of earth, which narrowed the road further and made it more taxing for the driver to negotiate his way. Though it was adventurous for us, it strained the driver's nerves and demanded his utmost alertness. When Agumbe was nearly eight kilometres away, we climbed a hill and the road became darker and shadier. As we neared Agumbe, many monkeys charged into view and, at first, Ravi refused to get off the car to see the view from Sunset Point. A man was selling roasted *chana,* peanuts, sev and some other savouries. A family had descended from the car and was leaning against the parapet wall skirting the outer edge of the road and eating some of the snacks they had bought from the lone vendor. Lurking dangerously near them, the monkeys were interested, watchful and cunning spectators. Absorbed in their chatter and the pleasures of the palate, they were oblivious to the monkeys waiting to grab their eats in an unguarded moment.

Nothing could persuade Ravi to get out of the car. It was only when the driver laughed genially at his unreasonable, exaggerated fear that he relented hesitantly. The driver offered to escort us to the projecting concrete promontory. He even offered to take our picture. The three monkeys who had temporarily occupied Sunset Point scampered away when they saw us enter through the narrow passage between two stone posts.

'They are equally wary of us,' I told Ravi.

'No, they are waiting for a good moment to pounce on us and take our camera.'

'I don't think so. Anyway, we should have offered them the *prasadam* from Udupi Sri Krishna since we have quite a bit of it.'

'Are you mad? And risk being scratched by them?'

We stopped there for barely half a minute. There was no time to take in the view. There was no time to reflect on how glorious and unique the sunset from there would be. There was no time to move out of the mundane to experience something memorable. The monkeys and Ravi's fear of them had usurped the present and limited its possibilities.

As we neared Sringeri, the forest area abounded with bamboo. Before this trip to Karnataka, I had seen only the young and green bamboo that always seemed so pliant and so elegantly decorative to me. For the first time, I saw giant clumps of bamboo which filled me with a nameless fear and awe. They seemed like monstrous, treacherous traps with the intricate knotty interlacings of woody arms and wild grass that draped their tall forms in a maze of dizzying webs.

We reached Sringeri a little before two in the afternoon. We were given a room in the temple guest house. Located within the large serene area that housed the temples and other structures linked to the temple, it was very basic and ordinary, but thankfully, it was free of any dank smells or stale air. Two single beds, with blankets and a thick bedspread, separated by a bedside table, open stone shelves covered with yellowing dusty newspaper, four plastic garden chairs piled one on top of the other, a small eating table with chewed edges—this was the room. One window, divided into an upper and a lower half, opened onto the covered corridor in front of the rooms. The other window faced a back corridor skirting a courtyard full of potted plants. If one walked to the end of this corridor and cut across the small stretch of open space, one could see the unassuming flow of the placid Tunga.

It was nearing the end of lunchtime, so we hurried to the dining area of the guest house. The district-level official (a DRO) took us to the dining room meant for special guests. He refused to eat with us because protocol demanded that he maintain this decorous distance. I felt bad that we had delayed his lunch. A short pot-bellied gentle-looking man served us the simple fresh meal with dignified deference. He filled up large cups of *payasam* to the brim and was disappointed when we told him that both of us could not digest milk.

On our way back, Ravi asked me if I knew the story of why Sringeri was chosen by Sri Shankaracharya as a spot for a math.

'No. Do tell me.'

'No doubt this is a beautiful spot by the Tunga river, on a plateau in the Western Ghats. Surrounded by densely forested hills and the Rishyasringa mountain ranges, it must have appealed greatly to Adi Shankaracharya.'

I was looking at the flowers in the flower beds while listening to Ravi. Suddenly some flowers caught my fancy. 'Just a moment, Ravi. I want to take a couple of pictures of these lovely flowers.' They were very pale blue in colour and grew in close clusters. Four-petalled like the white Nandivardanam, they were charming in a contained way.

'When will this obsession end, Priti? I am just about to tell you a story and you go chasing flowers,' he said good-humouredly.

This will end when I end, I said to myself.

After I had taken several shots of the pretty flowers, I turned to Ravi and said, 'I am ready for your story.'

'Are you sure?' he asked doubtfully.

'I am all ears.' The DRO didn't know what was happening.

'On the bank of the Tunga river here, Adi Shankaracharya saw an unusual and heartwarming sight. A pregnant frog that was in labour was being shielded by a cobra. It had opened its hood over the frog to protect it from the harsh light and unbearable heat of the sun. A place which could bring two natural enemies together was no ordinary place, so he decided to establish a math here to spread the philosophy of the *Advaita Vedanta*.'

'Interesting. Is this the original Sri Sharada temple?'

'I don't think so.'

Ravi addressed the question to the DRO who answered in English, interspersed with Kannada. I got fragments of the brief explanation. Ravi re-explained it to me more clearly, 'Adi Shankaracharya installed a sandalwood image of the goddess on a Sri Chakra, carved on a rock by the side of the River Tunga. The temple, at that time, was a very basic structure with a thatched roof. The present gold *vigraham* of Goddess Sharada was installed by Sri Vidyaranya, the twelfth acharya, who was also responsible for its renovation and improvement.

Looking back now, I realise that I had forgotten to ask if the original sandalwood image of the goddess was still there. Later when I opened the book, *The Greatness of Sṛingeri*, which I had bought that evening, I saw a picture of the sandalwood Sri Sharada in it. I wondered if it was the original image or something created later in harmony with the original and sanctified with pujas.

The meal, the travel and the afternoon heat had made us lethargic. We decided to rest a bit before going to the temple. The DRO told us that the acharya usually gave an audience to visitors around half past five in the evenings. He suggested that we could meet him first and then visit the temple. I suddenly felt a bit anxious about this meeting. I knew that I should get into a sari if I wanted to feel more at ease in front of the acharya but I did not feel like doing anything out of the routine with my appearance and mode of dress in that unfamiliar ordinary room. 'It's better for a traditional married woman to not go before the acharya in a salwar kameez,' said Ravi's eyes. Something in me protested. I resisted his silent appeal. 'It's too much of a bother. I have bathed and changed. That should suffice,' I thought to myself. The DRO was waiting for us.

We walked on the bridge across the Tunga and paused to take in our surroundings. Long black fish cruised smoothly just below the river surface. Some of the devotees had left puffed rice on the submerged steps for the fish. Some jet black crows swooped down to deftly pick up the grains scattered on the steps. An exposed rock looked like the back of a motionless crocodile. I turned around and looked in the direction of the temple of Kala Bhairava visible in the distance. Ravi asked me if I wanted to see the temple. I told him that I had no desire to see this fierce aspect of Shiva.

Walking to the other end of the bridge, we entered the peaceful and beautifully maintained Narasimhavanam. The hall where the acharya gave audience was very spacious with a high ceiling. Silence presided there with unchallenged authority. There were around fifteen of us waiting to meet the acharya. We stood in a single file at the very head of the line, next to an unusually large veena. Called Mahasarvabhowma Veena, it was placed inside a glass case and had been made by C Natarajan and family from Bengaluru. There was a description of the veena, but I was too nervous and too afraid of making even the slightest sound while pulling out my glasses. The veena was an example of exquisite and devoted workmanship. It had carved images of some gods and the musical trinity. A line of some *kriti* was also carved on it. We soon became aware of the acharya's entry and his appearance on the stage before us. He made his way to the edge of the stage and sat down. I had imagined him to be austere and formidable-looking. He was quite the contrary. Although I had seen his picture elsewhere, I hadn't made the connection that he was the present Sringeri Shankaracharya. A roly-poly man with a benign round face, he looked learned but approachable. Ravi and I walked up to him and offered the fruits. Ravi introduced himself and told him that he was from the East Godavari district of Andhra Pradesh. I stood on his left, a little behind him. He introduced me as his wife. I did a namaskar and the acharya offered me an apple as *prasadam*. The acharya asked Ravi one or two questions about his community and then indicated silently that he was ready to receive the other devotees. The meeting went so smoothly that all my apprehensions and Ravi's concerns seemed exaggerated.

We made our way back to the main temple complex and walked inside the Sri Sharada temple. The *koti kumkum archana* to the goddess had just started and there were quite a few priests seated on the raised platform of the *mandapam* before the deity's shrine. There was a small mound of maroon-red kumkum before each priest. Two or three of them were standing and directing the invocation to the goddess. They were praising the goddess, using her innumerable names from the *Lalithasahasranamam*. The temple resonated with the charged and powerful chanting. The whole atmosphere was auspicious and celebratory. It gave hope to the listener to face life's challenges and its untoward twists and turns. We could see Goddess Sharada only from a distance. Ravi described her to me: 'She has in her hands a jar full of nectar, a book and a rosary. One of the hands is in *chinmudra,* signifying the identity of the *jiva* (the soul) with *Brahman*.'

I had to be content with the *utsava murti* of Sri Sharada which was not very impressive.

The night air was fresh and cool. I slept with the top half of the windows open although they opened onto the front corridor and that awareness cut into one's sense of privacy. I had set the alarm for half past five but I never really moved into deep sleep. However, it was the deepest rest I have known. To sleep in a guest house room within the temple premises was a unique experience for me. I felt as if I had gathered all my worries and concerns and placed them in a heap before the goddess. I also felt profoundly reassured and comforted as I left the various deities to keep night-long vigil while we slept. I have never felt as light and carefree as I felt that night. I heard the temple bells at midnight and also heard them every hour, on the hour, through the curtain of sleep. Very early in the morning, as I drifted in and out of sleep, I heard the Sharada suprabhatam and then some chanting. I finally woke up at six, very fresh and energetic. As our bathroom had no geyser, I stepped out of the back door of our room to look for the odd-jobs young man who had promised to give us hot water for a bath. The door opened onto a covered corridor which skirted one part of a small mud courtyard liberally covered with potted plants. If one walked to the end of the corridor and cut across a part of the adjoining yagnasala, one could catch a glimpse of the river Tunga, the hills and the thick forest beyond. It was a very uplifting and spirit-restoring sight on a clear morning. When I stepped back into my room, I could see the inside gate of the temple complex and the devotees moving in and out of the Sri Sharada temple.

The DRO had promised us that he would try to get us a local guide to explain the architectural beauty of the Vidyashankar temple there. He was waiting for us outside our door and told us that the guide would join us later. Built in the first half of the fourteenth century, this stone temple combines the Hoysala and the Chalukya Dravidian architectural styles. Standing on a layered high plinth, it offers a splendid view of the surrounding hills and the forests. When we stepped inside for the *darshanam*, it was dark and peaceful in there. The Vidyashankar lingam in the *garbha griha* was adorned with garlands and sported a silver face. When lingams and stone statues of deities are given silver or gold face masks it displeases me because it takes away from the solemn beauty, the deep mystery, the engaging gravity of expression, the wonder-enhancing play of light and shade, that only stone can manifest. On either side of the main sanctum are shrines of Vidya Ganapati and Durga. We waited for our guide at the *mandapam* with the magnificent twelve pillars and the central ceiling with lotus and parrots, wondering if the number twelve had any special meaning. A small-made, wiry man with a furrowed brow and a high-strung walk soon joined us and introduced himself as our temple guide. Without wasting a moment, he launched into an explanation of the twelve monolithic pillars: 'These twelve pillars are marked by the twelve signs of the zodiac and are so placed that the rays of the sun fall on each of them in the order of the twelve solar months. Let us walk around and look at each of them.' Each of the pillars had a representation of a *rasi* and its ruling or governing planet. We started with Mesha and then looked at Vrishabha and Mithuna. When we were near the latter sculpture, the guide pointed out that there was no scope for going around the pillar, which was a deliberate and planned decision of the architects of that period. The reason is that the mating couple should be left in peace to enjoy their moment of togetherness. The guide explained this with a poker face in a matter-of-fact flat voice. I forgot to make a mental note of the planets that ruled the first three *rasi*s. The rest were as follows: Karkata—Chandra; Simha—Surya; Kanya—Budh; Tula—Shukra; Vrischika—Mangala; Dhanus—Guru; Makara—Shani; Kumbha—Shani; Meena—Guru.

Then the guide led us outside and started naming the amazing plethora of sculptures on the outer wall. He rattled off the names and a sparse explanation at a breakneck speed as we paused for a split second before each sculpture. There was no checking his impatient pace. Halted mid-stride once, he frowned disapprovingly.

I decided to let him be and see the sculptures later at my own pace but I doubted whether I would succeed in naming even half of them, although I was getting more familiar with the distinctive features of the deities, their attributes and defining characteristics.

Horanadu

After Ravi had his substantial breakfast of puri and potato curry and a plain dosa at an unassuming restaurant, we started for Horanadu, which has the Sri Annapoorneshwari temple. The name of the goddess means 'one who feeds one and all or she who fills with food'. I was very interested in visiting this temple, primarily because of Ravi who, in the past, had to accept severe dietary restrictions because of a very sensitive and touchy gut. I also loved the shloka: *Bhikshaam dehi, krupa valamban kari, Mata Annapoorneshwari* (O kind and compassionate mother, please give me alms...). The devotee prays for the boon of plenty and blessings so that he may never feel any want in his or her life. It is believed that Sage Agastya installed the deity in this temple. Generally, she is represented as a fair woman, either standing on a lotus or sitting on a throne. In one hand she holds a rice bowl and, in the other, a spoon. The temple has an image of Adi Shakti now, hence the name Adi-Shaktyatmaka Sri Annapoorneshwari. We did not know this until much after the *darshan*.

Around half past ten, we entered the Kudremukh national forest and I spotted many areca palms with their bunched up cache of areca nuts. The road was very serpentine and the air fresh and cool as we neared the Hanumangundi Falls. We passed Gangamoole, the origin of the Tunga river. After Bairikal, the forest gave way to tea estates and coffee plantations. The tea plants draping the hills were spectacular. In the late morning light, their rejuvenating green uplifted our spirits. Attracted by a small, cabin-like shop, which was selling tea, different kinds of forest produce, spices and dried fruits, we stopped to take in the view and sample their tea. They had a stove in the basement where one of the salespersons was making tea for the customers. One could not get the true flavour and aroma of their brand of tea because the tea leaves had been boiled along with milk, to taste like *kashayam*, or something far worse than that. No, I am giving a false impression of *kashayam* because a decoction, made for a sore throat or a cough and cold is aromatic, soothing and tasty, especially when one adds honey to it. This tea was a thick golden-brown liquid defying charitable description. I had a few polite sips and left the rest. Anyway, it was a minuscule cup.

It was nearly half past noon and the heat was beginning to pick up. I was concerned that the shrine would close by one and it would be very disappointing not to see the deity or have time to do a simple *archana*. I do not know whether it was the effect of the tea or the breakfast but I could discern uncomfortable signs of rising acidity. Little stabbing pains had started just below the diaphragm and my throat felt as if something was stuck there. I did not say anything to Ravi, praying that a visit to Annapoorneshwari would rid me of these symptoms and calm my stomach.

At a quarter to one, we reached the temple and rushed up the steps, our feet scorched by the sun-baked stones. To our immense relief, we learnt that the shrine was open throughout the day. The temple was dark and peaceful. Its atmosphere was very different from that of any of the temples I had seen. Its benign energy permeated one slowly and unnoticeably. Ravi walked into the temple office, introduced himself and managed to get an angavastram. We were taken directly to the shrine where a priest performed the *kumkum archana* for us. The standing deity was tall, gold-hued and dazzling. There was a smaller *vigraham* at her feet. At this point we did not know that the larger figure was that of Adi-Shakti and the smaller one that of Annapoorneshwari.

As we were doing the *pradakshina*, the pain and discomfort in the stomach got worse. My stomach was burning and I could feel strong waves of heat coming out of it as I rested my hand there to subdue its fire. I was concerned as we had a long day ahead of us. We were going to stop at Belur and Halebid before heading for Bengaluru. We did not hope to reach Bengaluru before midnight. After circumambulating the temple thrice, when Ravi went to the temple office to return the angavastram, they asked him to have lunch in the temple.

He turned to me and said, 'I am not really hungry. What do you suggest we do?'

I did not tell him that I was in no position to eat. I also stopped myself from saying, 'It doesn't seem right to reject food offered or blessed by Sri Annapoorneshwari. I am in a fix. What do we do since I won't be able to eat even a single grain of rice?' Instead, I said, 'I am not particularly hungry. We have the *prasadam*. Let's go.'

We had barely crossed the threshold of the temple when Ravi exclaimed, 'Priti, this is absurd. How can we refuse food in a temple dedicated to, and blessed by, Annapoorneshwari? I wasn't thinking when I turned down the offer of lunch. Why didn't you stop me?'

'I had the same thought.'

'Now, this even more ridiculous. You should have voiced your thought. Come, let's go and eat.'

I did not tell him anything about my physical state but prayed that I should not be sick there. We were led to a long rectangular room where a few people were sitting on the floor on long low *peetas* (wooden seats) and eating. The other side of the room led to a covered corridor with huge boilers for rice. We were given steel plates and as the server was already in the process of serving rice to the others, he served us rice first on our empty plates, which is unheard of in most places. It is an improper meal practice. Even a token serving of some form of dal or a vegetable preparation, a sweet, some chutney or a pickle is considered appropriate before serving rice. I asked for very little to be served on my plate and I prayed fervently to Annapoorneshwari that I should be able to eat and retain whatever little I ate. For someone who was feeling intense unease and an inability to take in even a single morsel, I managed to eat a little bit of everything. For as long as I sat in that room and ate, there was neither a burning sensation in my stomach nor any nausea. It was little short of a miracle. The symptoms came back only after we had left the temple. They returned with such distressing intensity that I had to take Digene tablets to keep them in check. The goddess had been kind to me. By and by, I was better and we reached Bengaluru without me creating any dramatic difficulties for Ravi.

Marudamalai

In early July, Ananda came home to Hyderabad from Montreal for his summer vacation and his cousin's wedding. We wanted him to experience a bit of his own country and have a relaxed time in Ooty. For nearly three weeks we had an eventful time, packed with different kinds of ceremonies linked to our niece's wedding, an *upanayanam* and my father-in-law's three day *shraadh* ceremony. All of us needed a break from social events, a bit of solitude. We decided to visit Ooty with Ananda. The plan was to fly to Coimbatore and then hire a car and a driver to reach Ooty.

After a comfortable flight to Coimbatore and after dropping off our bags at the Circuit House, we looked for a restaurant for a filling snack. Our search took us to Annapoorna. The early evening tiffin was a very relaxed affair. The ghee masala dosa was an appetising crisp golden and each mouthful was a comforting and pleasurable experience. The room was large, spacious and cheerfully lit. I hate air-conditioned middle-level eating joints with their strange dim lighting that can make one's spirits plummet to murky depths in the middle of a bright day.

We lingered over our food. We were deliciously full. The coffee was fresh and steaming hot. Its mildly heady aroma revived us.

The plan was to rest for an hour and then head for the Marudamalai hill temple, dedicated to Murugan. It is about ten kilometres away from Coimbatore and more than eight hundred years old.

It was around half past six when we started for Marudamalai. The evening was very pleasant. In the fading light, a host of crows congregated on a young banyan tree in the garden – their shelter for the night, I suppose. Their dark forms made the tree look denser and fuller than it really was. Although the traffic had picked up in the evening, it was not half as bad as it is in Hyderabad during peak hours. A man drove past us while glancing at a small TV screen fixed next to his rearview mirror and I said to myself, 'Lunatics people our roads.' It was the acme of irresponsible road behaviour.

We passed several small shrines on the way to Marudamalai. I regretted not having started earlier because we could see nothing in the dark except the hill road illuminated by the car headlights. As we neared the temple, Ravi told me that Marudamalai is associated with the mystic Tamil siddhar called Pambatti Siddhar. A snake charmer by profession, he was initiated into the world of philosophy by another siddhar called Sattai Munivar. Ravi added, 'Pambatti Siddhar's shrine is in a cave. A forest abounding in herbs and trees of medicinal value skirts the steps and the pathway leading to the cave shrine. There is a Shiva linga and a snake sculpture in low relief on an overarching rock. Lord Muruga is supposed to have granted *darshan* to Pambatti Siddhar in this form. That is why people with sarpa dosha come here to pray and be healed.'

The car park was practically deserted. We climbed a series of steps to get to the temple. On the right side were small brightly-lit shops. At one such shop, we picked up a small plate with a coconut and other offerings for *archana* at the shrine. A large spreading tree, which was basically five trees that had moved into each other, caught our attention at the base of a flight of steps. It sheltered the shrine of Panchavriksha Vinayaka (literally, the five-tree Vinayaka) – one prayed to this deity before going to the main shrine. On a closer look, I could see the different shaped leaves of the five trees. I was curious why the five trees had been planted so close together, but the one or two priests in the vicinity did not have a clear idea. However, on my way back I managed to get the names of the five trees from the corner-shop girl. She named them in Tamil: arasa maram (Ficus religiosa; peepul), athi maram (Ficus glomerata; Cluster fig tree), korakkatai, vanni maram (Prosopis cineraria; shami tree) and vembu (Margosa; neem).

The Dandapani form of Murugan is enshrined and worshipped in the sanctum here. He is without his consorts, Valli and Devayani. He stands with his *vel* or spear which symbolises true knowledge. As we stood before the shrine, I saw that the deity's face was an unnatural chalk white. It seemed as if he was wearing a mask. I was disappointed. He seemed distant and inaccessible. Ravi explained that it might be the sacred ash *alankaram*. After the *darshanam* we walked along the outer *prakaram*. The south wall of the main temple had niche figures of Nritya Ganapati and Siddhivinayaka, the west wall had Dandapani and the north wall had Senani, Chandikeshwar and goddess Durga. Near the water taps at the back, there were steep steps leading to the cave and spring of the siddhar but at night it did not seem like a very encouraging prospect to go down the steps. I stood at the head of the flight of steps and looking over the parapet found myself staring into a bottomless well of darkness. It was both mysterious and scary. In addition, Ravi had told me that Pambatti Siddhar had written songs addressed to snakes. At eight in the evening it did not seem such a good idea to walk down the steps that seemed to hurl themselves into a gaping smoky black hole.

After the *pradakshina,* I sat on the edge of the low raised platform, which had the main *mandapam* and the main shrine, facing outwards to the east. The lights of the city liberally sprinkled the deepening dark and shone like innumerable minute golden beacons. Just then the loudspeaker gurgled and blared into life. The speaker started narrating stories of Subramanya from the *Skanda Purana.* The narration was in Tamil. It was impossible to decode the entire text as I could only gather the names and the Sanskrit expressions. After some time, I gave up trying to make sense of the expressive dramatic narration and was content to just listen to the powerful voice as I took in my surroundings. In front of me, the dark hill silhouetted against the night sky, soon merged into the advancing darkness and became indistinguishable from it. A stone spear or *vel,* the attribute of Subramanya, rose prominently from behind the low background wall. Very likely, it was visible during the day from below, the wide level clearing near the foot of the steps. One could see the road winding down and a structure under construction—an extension of the present temple premises. At the moment, under the cover of the creeping dark, it seemed like a detached independent creation although it was connected to the main structure by a jutting limb of level land on the same hill—accessible by jumping over the parapet wall. A cockroach appeared and scuttled away from view. Behind the low wall were scraggy bushes and wild plants, some of them growing through a discarded half-reclining grille door. A metal grille barrier punctuated with spearhead shapes on its upper margin lay discarded across a beaten path leading to a temporary platform, supported by a sturdy framework of bamboo poles. At this point in the narration, I managed to understand the story of the battle between Tarakasura and Subramanya. I looked at the tall shapely coconut palm in front of the Navagraha shrine and rose from my stony seat to see the last puja of the evening. The *puliyodarai prasadam* was divine.

We walked down the temple steps past the shops with their colourful wares to attract the kids—stuffed purple giraffes, plastic dolls with flashy purple hair, little rattles, wind chimes with small dangling balls, plastic toy pianos, xylophones, guitars and so on. I had been intrigued by a set of small black flat circles inside a plastic wrapper, hanging like a chain from the awnings of some of the temple shops. I knew that they were something edible and was curious about their taste. Eager to taste at least one of them, I stopped to ask what it was. I gathered that it was made from some berry to which salt and some spices had been added. As I pulled out some change to buy three pieces, Ravi said, 'Why must you wish to try out anything unfamiliar? It may not be hygienically prepared. Worse still, I don't recognise it.' I persisted.

'It's so cheap. I'll throw it away if I don't like it.' I bought three of those. It took me some time to peel off the plastic wrapping clinging to the black edible circle. I put half of it into my mouth. It was more sour than sweet; it had salt, sugar, pepper, chilli powder and was full of coarsely-ground little seeds. I allowed my tongue to experience the taste of the added ingredients and then spat out the seeds, which must have been smaller than the seeds of grapes, as soon as we reached our car. I felt as if I had eaten something very gritty. The black stuff began irritating my throat and my tongue felt funny and slightly coated.

'How is it?' asked Ravi.

'You won't like it.' He looked at me, searching for further explanation. I didn't offer him any. Ananda piped up, 'Please don't offer me any of that nasty black stuff. I saw the face that you made while eating it.'

'Yes, it was an anticlimax after that glorious *prasadam*.'

'You asked for it,' said Ravi with jubilant gloating delight.

'Two is company. Why don't you share my experience of it?' said I, teasingly.

'Sure, some other time.'

Isha Centre and the Dhyanalingam

The next day we saw the Patteeswarar temple in Perur, very close to Coimbatore. In the afternoon we decided to go to the Isha Foundation and see the Dhyanalingam. I had heard of Sadhguru Jaggi Vasudev, the founder of Isha yoga, but hadn't heard of the Dhyanalingam. It would have been a waste of time to go back to Annapoorna in Coimbatore just to eat, so we lunched at a minimalist eating joint not far from Perur. To our pleasant surprise, the South Indian meal served on plantain leaves was very reasonable and palatable. The waiter was deferential and eager to be generous with extra servings of everything. Not being big or voracious eaters, we had to decline.

We drove along the Perur-Siruvani road to get to the Isha Centre, which is situated against the backdrop of the Velliangiri hills. As we neared the place, there was a strong smell of cow dung and organic manure in the air. It invaded our nostrils. At the entrance to the foundation, we were welcomed by a young man dressed in a spotless white kurta pyjama. He had noticed our curious gaze and the avid interest with which we were taking in the surroundings and guessed that it was our first visit. He gave a brief description of the *Teerthakund*, the subterranean water tank, and the Dhyanalingam. To illustrate the potent glorious energy of the Dhyanalingam, he said helpfully, 'When you sit in meditation before the lingam, you don't have to recite any specific mantras or chant any special prayers or hymns. Just sit before it silently and allow its divine energy to fill you. Be open and receptive to its positive energies.'

We entered through the main doorway. The place where we left our footwear was unlike any other that I had seen. I was familiar with shoe racks or the loosely demarcated dirt areas outside temples where someone guarded your shoes for a small fee. Two young men were in charge of the open shed-like room where the footwear of the visitors and devotees was kept. They gave us pale sand-coloured cloth bags or *jhola*s to place our shoes in. These were then hung from hooks driven into wooden beams. I can't remember the last detail very well. What I do recall observing is that the footwear was hidden from view. Here the disagreeable sight was averted, thanks to the novel idea of using *jhola*s. I have always disliked the sight of so many pairs of shoes, sandals or slippers outside any temple. There is something unclean, ugly and chaotic about the accumulation of used footwear in one spot.

We walked past the gift shop and the coffee-cum-snacks canteen that looked clean and efficiently run. To the right of the pathway that led to the *Teerthakund* was a large impressive brick dome. Unaware at that moment that it was the home of the Dhyanalingam, I wondered what it housed and enclosed. The shape reminded me of an igloo.

Another young man dressed in a sparkling white kurta-pyjama stopped us in the corridor that went past the *Teerthakund*.

Our hesitation and wondering glances in the direction of the water tank must have told him that we were in need of some guidance.

He addressed us, 'I think this is your first visit here.' We nodded.

He continued, 'Then let me tell you something about this spot. The *Teerthakund* is located in the northern perimeter of the outer *parikrama*. This rectangular water tank, enclosed by large granite stones, is embedded 30 feet in the earth. The water gets its special powers and energy from the submerged Rasalinga, a lingam made of solidified mercury weighing over 660 kilograms. Ellipsoidal in shape, this mercury lingam was solidified using the ancient science of Indian alchemy.'

Ravi asked, 'Why isn't the tank made closer to ground level and why is the lingam submerged in water?'

'When the water is so deep in the earth, it retains its special energy better. Closer to ground level, open to the air and sky, the energy will get diffused.'

'Would you like to take a dip in the tank?' He noticed our hesitation. 'I forgot. This is your first visit here so you may not have a change of clothes.'

'We didn't know. We didn't bring a change,' Ravi explained.

'If you like, we can give the two of you lungis.'

Ravi debated for a few seconds and said, 'Next time. This time we will just dip our feet in water.'

Before leaving us the young man pointed to a table, 'We sell *vibhuti* here and a copper ring, shaped in the form of a snake. In our daily lives, we tend to lose a lot of precious energy. When you wear that copper ring on your left ring finger, it helps to harness and retain the precious energy.'

'Why is it shaped in the form of a snake, though?'

'Our kundalini is in the form of a snake. When it rises, it rises just like a coiled snake, uncoils itself and raises its hood.'

'I see. We will take a look at what you have to offer later.'

'Okay. Please buy tickets for entry to the tank and wash your legs and feet.' He pointed to the separate bathing areas and washrooms for men and women.

We descended the steps to the tank. At the top landing was a large brightly polished brass *uruli* with water and floral offerings floating in it. On the last broad step, which was partly submerged under water, there were two lit brass lamps at the extreme ends of the step, close to the wall. I stepped into the water. It felt cold. A young man with dark shoulder-length hair stood in the tank embracing the lingam. Then, clasping it with both his hands, he stretched himself out on the surface of the water in a *sashtanga* namaskar pose and stayed like that for nearly half a minute. At this point, a man and his wife stepped into the water. Their son hesitated near the brink, his hands clasped tightly in front of him. The father held out his arms and the son leapt into them with confidence and alacrity. The parents waded to the lingam and stood there clutching it. With heads bent in earnest prayer, they remained like this for a minute or more. They seemed to enjoy the cold feel of the water and the silence. The water reflected the colour of the granite slabs lining the walls and the hand-painted ceiling mural. Painted with vibrant and nature-reminiscent vegetable dyes, it depicted the Maha Kumbh Mela. The reflections on the water undulated in several tints of brown. Uneven splashes of red-brown, sandy brown, pale brown, bluish grey shimmered in the water and made the tank a theatre of ever-shifting, colour-enriched scenes and playful delightful water sounds.

The mercury lingam is 2 feet tall. Under water, it seemed smaller—more compressed. The *avudaiyar* or the rock on which it rests is five or six times bigger than the lingam but I couldn't get a clear picture of its form or size. Perhaps I did not look too closely. I was more interested in the four people apart from us and their ways of connecting with the Rasalingam and receiving something from it.

Water streamed down through apertures from the left wall. With his back against the wall, a slender young man stood erect under the water with cupped palms to receive it. He seemed lost to this world. I envied him his pleasure and his repose. I watched him unashamedly, curiously, hoping to get a peek into what he was experiencing in those moments. The water looked very inviting and calming. I wished we had brought a change of clothes.

'Next time,' our guide had said. I wondered how far away that was. The *Teerthakund* was a place like no other. Its deep stillness and energy would trickle into one, gradually and unnoticeably, if one remained there for a reasonable length of time. Since no large group had invaded it yet, it seemed reserved for just the seven of us.

Before we moved towards the Dhyanalingam, Ravi bought the little copper *kalasam* with *vibhuti* and the coiled snake copper ring. I asked him if he felt confident about wearing it in public. Someone unfamiliar with its metaphysical meaning could easily misconstrue its significance and presume that Ravi belonged to some dubious Tantric sect. He shrugged off my anxious concern and brushed it aside brusquely.

Descending a flight of steps, we reached the outer entrance of the dome, which houses the Dhyanalingam. Before that, in a wide corridor, two volunteers were selling *deepam*s and lotus bud offerings that we could place in an *uruli* filled with some water. Everything was neat and orderly; it was most unlike the fully-stacked shops lining the streets outside temples with their heady spread of colourful wares. The other visitors and we were shushed all the way. I walked gingerly, afraid that my slender silver anklets that barely gave out even a tiny tinkle would suddenly sing out all the seven notes.

At the entrance to the Dhyanalingam was a stone structure with the symbols of all religions etched on it. The message: People of all faiths are welcome here. A stone image of a sun adorns the pinnacle of this white granite pillar that, I discovered later, is called the *Sarvadharmastambha*. I wonder what it signifies: The dawn of enlightenment, the awakening of consciousness or the beginning of a new phase in one's inner life, or the beginning of a new phase in the history of humankind. Ravi failed to notice that granite pillar. The cuffs of Ananda's jeans were touching the floor. Someone walked up to us soundlessly and motioned to him to roll up the bottoms.

We entered the open pathway and saw the shrine of Patanjali, the author of the *Yogasutras*. That black granite sculpture, which combines the forms of man and snake, was impressive. On the right was Vanashree, a sculptural relief of the peepul tree with a gold leaf in the centre. What does it symbolise, I wondered. Plenitude? On either side of the pathway, along the aisles, were six granite panels with low-relief stone sculptures depicting the lives of six South Indian saints or Nayanmars: Kanappa Nayanar (it was the second time during the day that I had encountered his name and, at that time, I wasn't very clear about the story of his devotion to Shiva), Akka Mahadevi, Poosalar, Meiporul Nayanar, Sadashiva Brahmendra and Sadguru Parabrahma. Except for Sadashiva Brahmendra, I was unfamiliar with the others. I recalled one of the extraordinary or miraculous incidents linked with his life. Ravi had told me this story:

> Sadashiva Brahmendra used to wander about as an *avadoota* in Karur and, during those wanderings, children would seek him out because he would give them the food that he had received as alms. One day, the children who would gather around him fondly expressed a wish to go to Madurai. Brahmendra promised to take them. He asked the children to get onto his back and close their eyes for some time. When he asked them to open their eyes, they discovered they were in Madurai. They rejoiced to see the *utsava murtis* of Lord Somasundarar and Goddess Meenakshi that were being taken around in a procession at that moment. Their wish fulfilled, they were again transported back to Karur on Sadashiva Brahmendra's back.

The atmosphere in the walkway was solemn and quiet. Stillness walked sagely. We entered a vaulted tunnel that led to the dome of the Dhyanalingam. I entered the brick dome and, for a few moments, stood in puzzled wonderment. I wasn't expecting to see a very tall lingam in polished black granite. I discovered later that it is thirteen feet and nine inches high. I remembered my experience of the Shiva temples in the Tanjore region. There, one crossed several thresholds before one could behold the deep interior of the *garbha griha* where the lingam always seemed encased in awe-inspiring mystery. Only illuminated by the lamps framing the doorway and the lamps suspended from the ceiling or placed before it, the lingam was suffused with a powerful aura of sacred mystery. Oil lamps, camphor, incense sticks, *vibhuti*, coconut water, flowers, bilva leaves, the rush of people and the eagerness and urgency of the devotees gives these temples a special charged atmosphere infused with intermingling fragrances and smells. The chants of the priests and the prayers and footsteps of the devotees visiting it over hundreds of years has endlessly energised and sacralised these shrines. All this flashed before my mind's eye as I entered the dome. The harmony and serenity of the Isha Centre had certainly prepared me for the Dhyanalingam. On the other hand, as I recalled the Tanjore temples and replayed the experience in my mind, I found myself slightly unwilling to accept the pervasive silence inside the dome and allow myself to move into it. To my uninitiated immature self, it felt artificially created and sustained.

The circular wall of the dome has recesses or niches for meditation all along it. Initially, for the first few moments, I sat at the edge of the ledge of the niche and looked around. People walked in on padded feet and selected their niches to pray in or meditate. I observed a white man in a snowy kurta pyjama direct the visitors silently or gesticulate frantically as a woman dipped her fingers into the narrow water channel around the lingam and sprinkled the water on her head. My mind was alert and active. I was observing things instead of trying to withdraw from the external world. I was a curious observer whereas I was supposed to meditate and benefit from the sacred energies in this hallowed space. I wondered if Ananda would remember to pick up his wallet that he had kept beside him. It had all the money that we would need in the next few days of our travel. I noticed that the lingam had seven copper rings—the *avudaiyar,* in the form of a snake coiled beneath it in seven circles. Why seven? In a book on numerology that I had read in my teens, number seven had been called a mystical number that denoted harmony and perfection. My mind wandered along other paths. I began to think of the number seven in folk tales, fairy tales, myths, religions, astronomy and listed these mentally: Seven dwarfs, seven seas, seven skies, seven planets, the game of seven stones, the seven horses pulling the sun's chariot, the constellation of Sapt Rishi (the Great Bear), seven rungs of perfection, seven deadly sins, seven hills of the Roman Empire and the seven hills of Tirupati. (Later, a helper-guide told me that the seven rings referred to the seven chakras in the body. Then everything fell into place—the copper ring in the form of a snake symbolising the kundalini and the seven rings on the lingam and the seven coils of the snake.) I jerked myself back from that train of thought, closed my eyes and began to chant '*Aum Namah Shivaye*', yet my ears remained alert to the slightest sound. I was acutely aware of the people who entered the dome: The scrape of feet, the brush of someone's foot against the floor, the swishing sound of trouser legs, the tinkle of a child's anklets, the muffled thump as someone sat cross-legged on the floor and the muted patter of tiny feet. Each sound was distinct and visible. It had a substantial life, dimension and presence of its own. A crow cawed in the distance, a sparrow twittered, two other bird calls trailed through my mind. Why was I keenly receiving all these insignificant impressions from the space around me when I was supposed to ignore the outside world, gradually release all thought and become receptive to the energy pervading that place? I was losing an opportunity given to me on a platter, to re-energise myself. However, I did not leave the place impoverished. I took back with me an ever-fresh memory of courtesy and serenity and a keen desire to return and know more about Isha Yoga.

Just outside the dome, in the aisle to the left, one of the volunteers sat behind books meant for display and a basket of sesame *laddoo prasadam*. We spoke in whispers and I was amused at the contrast between that place and a shop outside any temple. In the latter, the shopkeeper calls out to the devotees and urges them to buy things for *naivedyam*.

There is bustle, commotion and the anticipation of *darshanam*. The sesame *laddoo prasadam* was the best I had ever tasted. The taste of freshly roasted, coarsely ground sesame with jaggery uplifted my mood.

On our way back to Coimbatore, Ananda asked me, 'What are your impressions of this place?'

I thought for a while and replied, 'The place is replete with earth colours. The signs directing you to specific spots are quaint or reminiscent of those I would find in a nature resort or woods in the west. At the gift shop, the emphasis is on handcrafted, hand-woven and hand-embroidered stuff. The colours of the things are warm, sober and pleasing. The whole place is clean, restful and gentle on the senses. Everything in the environment, philosophy and architectural design of the structures has been packaged tastefully to appeal to the upper-class educated Indian (or the NRI of a certain propensity: One who wishes to experience tradition or the distilled essence of perennial philosophy in a novel form) or the Western seeker who desires spiritual experience in a reclusive, pleasant retreat.'

We stopped at the Coimbatore Golf Club as we had heard a lot about how fabulous it was. Sitting outside the clubhouse, we enjoyed the beautiful green course. It was a cool evening, a bit on the nippy side. Against the horizon in the distance were hills behind hills, the smoky grey of the last merged with the smoky grey of the clouds. Looking at the hills through a horizontal rip in the clouds, Ravi said, 'These peaks look like an ECG graph.' Surprising comparison, I thought.

Ravi and Ananda enjoyed their beers in the gathering dusk and the cool breeze. My tea was strong, bitter and barely warm. The first two sips and then I spotted a fly in it. It was a disgusting anticlimax to a fulfilling day. The golfers returned from their play, two of them so rotund and heavyset, I wondered how they managed to move at all. Surprisingly, even after hours of play, they were not sluggish. They settled down to their drinks and avidly watched golfers on TV, the viewing punctuated by expert comments. I looked at the darkening sky and arrayed the different realities of the day in my mind. Just above the horizon, it appeared as if someone had dipped cotton wool in a watery pink colour and daubed it lazily on the sky. Right before me the pink hibiscus flashed brightly against the deep green leaves of the low bushy tree. The tree gradually merged with the spreading darkness and the pink hibiscus continued to smile—mysterious and dreamily attractive. I gathered their smiles and saved them for a rainy day.

The next day we left for Ooty armed with eager curiosity for new experiences with ginger candy for motion sickness during the winding drive.

For the first few days, we stayed in a privately-owned guest house, imbued with old-world charm.

Ooty's Thread Flower Garden

Our visit to Ooty's Thread Flower Garden and its handcrafted flowers and plants made me think of art and illusion; it made me deeply grateful for its gift of a beauteous memory. I had not heard of the Thread Flower Garden until Ananda read about it in a travel guide on Ooty and told us that it was certainly worth a visit. I dismissed it casually, assuming that it is one of those places that is given exaggerated mention to attract the undiscerning tourist.

After my ludicrous attempt to row a boat on the Ooty lake, we walked to the large rectangular shed-like room that housed the Thread Flower Garden. Irrationally, I had imagined it would be outdoors and was completely unprepared for the unique indoor floral world that I was going to experience. The entry ticket was very reasonable—₹10, a little over the price of a milky, syrupy cup of tea. The ticket for using the camera was ₹15. Foolishly, I left the camera at the counter. The man who issued our tickets did ask me, rather surprised, whether I really did not wish to take my camera inside. I was not expecting anything remarkable so I said I was sure I wouldn't need it. He looked at me, unconvinced.

Ananda was happy. 'You have far too many pictures of flowers already. How many more before you stop? This is madness.'

'It is beautiful madness, you must admit. I am just going to look at the flowers this time.'

As soon as we entered, I was dazzled by the profusion of colour and struck by the stillness of the verdant world. Soon, a voice intruded jarringly. A man at the entrance began to explain the salient features of the garden in an elocutionary voice, reeling out the facts in a booming, breathless and declamatory tone. There was just the three of us. It seemed unnatural to talk to us as if he were addressing a large gathering of people. This is what I gathered from his lecture-like introduction to this singular artificial flower garden with its plants, creepers, vines, patches of grass and lotus ponds. Antony Joseph was its creator. It had taken fifty specially trained artists more than twelve years to complete this visual delight. Stiff pieces of cardboard were cut and shaped into leaves and flowers. With meticulous dexterity, these were then wound with thread. Steel or copper wires were used for the stems, which were then wound with the appropriate colour of thread. No needle or mechanical aid was used. Nearly 400 shades of plain embroidery threads, sixty million meters long, were used to create 150 varieties of flowers. Within myself, I praised the loving attentive workmanship, flawless patience and devotion to beauty of the artists. Walking along the railing, I took in this fairy tale world of undiminished colour. I tried to identify the flowers that would neither fade nor wilt—time would pass them by and visitors would marvel at this charming defiance of the imprints of the footsteps of time. Any moment I expected diminutive fairy tale creatures to trip nimbly among these flowers. Three more visitors entered the garden. The guide's voice blared out the information and a Tamil song played loudly from a nearby shop. These auditory assailants ruined the atmosphere. I wish silence were a necessary fee for entry. I also wish the lighting could be improved to enhance the ambiance of this world. As I walked out, I saw samples of these flowers for sale. At the counter, encased in transparent plastic boxes, these flowers did not look life-like. They were bright and lovely—a tribute to the artist's patience and industry but unmistakably artificial. I selected a plant with three flowers—a flaming orange, a warm yellow and a jubilant red. I did not recognise the flowers. Were they daisies? Immaterial. I brought back a handful of ageless colour into my home. Precious material.

Mudumalai

The next day I woke up to a very wet morning—a heavy downpour and then a drip, drip, drip kind of rain. The living room in our guest house in Ooty felt cold and damp and bleak; it felt colder, damper and more depressing as I watched the rain from inside. As there was no fire to cheer things up, I stepped out into the garden and walked in the rain. I was wet but felt revived. I walked towards a covered archway with a rose creeper. Pink and white cosmos grew wild and swirled around it in small smiling waves. Narrow stone steps led from the garden to a clearing below. It would be a pleasant retreat in summer for reading and dreaming. On the inner edge of the clearing was a small temple with no idol. A trident rested against a stone painted yellow. It had three horizontal white lines, reminiscent of Shiva, hence I assumed that it was a spot dedicated to him. Coniferous hedges bordered the outer edge of the clearing. A single honey flower plant made tiny funnels of soft orange colour against the green hedge wall. Closer to the stone steps, rose cactus and wild yellow flowers held sway. Two erect blue gum trees (Eucalyptus Globulus) shot through the two dark cypresses and asserted, 'We are the masters of all we survey.' Who would question this claim? Pleased with the seclusion and tranquility of this retreat, I would have loved to linger there but we were leaving for the Mudumalai Wildlife Sanctuary in the forenoon and I had to pack our bags. We were also moving into the Tamil Nadu Circuit House, where we would stay the remaining three days of our trip.

After a prolonged breakfast and a round of goodbyes to the guest house staff, who had taken good care of us, we hit the road for Mudumalai. We would be staying at the Tamil Nadu Electricity Board guest house at Masinagudi. At the start of our journey, we took the West Lake Road from Ooty, crossed a bridge across a swamp oozing out nauseating odours and entered the shabby, filthy town of Talakunda by the straight road. The smell of some pungent chemical and that of rotting vegetation assaulted our nostrils. The road on the left led to the Pykara Dam. Mudumalai was thirty-four kilometres from there and the driver would have to negotiate thirty-six hairpin bends. I was glad I had eaten a light breakfast, for the dizzying curves would make even the hardiest of stomachs churn. All of us popped sugar-coated ginger pieces into our mouths to forestall nausea or motion sickness.

Sprawling bushes covered with tiny clusters of orange and pink flowers made our journey bright. I had seen these flowers in Hyderabad and I also remember that as kids, we used to take a head of flowers and then very patiently and intently suck the nectar from behind each minuscule stem. Although these flowers are quite common and grow in untamed profusion, I did not know their name. I also saw my phonogram flowers, which were a delicate lavender shade.

We reached Masinagudi at lunchtime and checked into the guest house. Our driver was relieved that it was no longer wet and cold and so were we. '*Nalla* climate,' he said, beaming. He meant that it was good weather. Away from the town, the guest house was peaceful. If one stood at the head of its long driveway that gently sloped towards the gate, one had an uninterrupted view of the Nilgiris. A lone temple *gopuram* dominated the foreground. One of the highest hills in the distance had a flat summit with just three or four erect conifers crowning its crest. It was like a balding scalp with three or four upright strands of hair. Because of this distinguishing feature, I followed its random appearances as we drove back to Ooty the next afternoon and discovered pleasantly that it was somewhere in the neighbourhood of Ooty. The hill was like a guiding beacon whenever we sighted it on our way back.

The caretaker-cum-cook of the guest house gave us a simple but satisfying meal. It was the closest to a home-cooked meal that I had eaten on that trip. After the meal we left for Mudumalai. It was late afternoon by the time we got to Teppakadu, the headquarters and reception centre of the Mudumalai Sanctuary. Ravi got in touch with the forest department staff hanging around there and that ensured that we got the first two seats on the bus taking the visitors along selected routes of the sanctuary. The walls of the office complex and waiting area had pictures of the wild creatures and birds that we could hope to see in the area: Tiger, elephant, gaur, spotted deer, mouse deer, four-horned antelope, the Nilgiri tahr, bear, wild boar, wild dog, hyena, the Malabar flying squirrel, bat squirrel, the Nilgiri langur and some birds.

The bus rattled along its way on the circular route demarcated for visitors. Its surly throaty engine warned the animals to keep away, although I am sure they were all familiar with its noisy harmless inroads into their territory and did not feel threatened by it in any way. We kept our eyes peeled for the animals and were delighted to see an elephant family, a peacock, a porcupine, the half-hidden tail of a flying squirrel, the disappearing-into-bushes rears of wild dogs and pretty picture-perfect groups of spotted deer. For the rest, I was content to observe the forms and the reach of trees, and their different shades of green and brown. I am sure they had plenty of stories and 'awful' secrets to tell of the various creatures that moved in and around them, but we were not equipped to hear their fantastic and fear-inspiring tales. The many small castle or fortress-like anthills were rare works of art.

After the bus ride, as we headed to the canteen for a cup of tea, the forest department chap suggested that we see the elephants being fed at 5:45 pm. He also told us that we could see a nine-month-old orphaned baby elephant. Now that was more compelling than the first suggestion. We had to retrace our steps, walk across the bridge over the river Moyar to get to the elephants' feeding area and the forest museum. Ravi and Ananda went ahead while I finished my cup of tea. A small group of young men and women stood outside the canteen, speaking boisterously in Tamil. They had bought themselves ice cream cones. I saw them remove the paper lids, nonchalantly peel the wrapper and throw the uneven bits of paper on the road. The road and dirt sidewalks were cleaner than any I had seen in a tourist area. In fact, they were trash-free. As they continued to litter the clean spot outside the canteen, something exploded inside me. I was angry, angrier than I had been in a long time. I think the sight of trash and filth in tourist places was beginning to get to me, and this seemed to be the last straw as the place was otherwise wonderfully clean. Hence, their act seemed like one of desecration. It was not merely an instance of uncivilised behaviour. Controlling myself, I walked up to them briskly and addressed them in a cold, peremptory tone. I was surprised at myself. I do not speak Tamil and didn't care if they understood English well. My tone would serve the purpose.

'What are you doing? Is this road a dustbin? Do you see

anyone else throwing bits of paper on the road?' They looked at me blankly as if I was talking to someone invisible behind them. I pointed to the strips of paper and ordered, 'Pick these up right now.' They looked at me, shell-shocked, as if I was being exceedingly unreasonable or imbalanced. I bent lower, pointed once again to the trash and said, 'Pick these up.' 'This very minute,' I added, enunciating each word slowly and clearly. I pointed to a large blue trash bucket, just behind them, in one corner of the entrance to the canteen and said, 'Here is a dustbin. This is where you throw this rubbish, this paper.' They understood. Silently, glumly, they obeyed me. From the looks they exchanged with each other, I could see that they considered me a freak or felt that I was off my rocker.

There were still a few minutes before the elephants' feeding time. This gave me a chance to see the baby elephant. I had imagined that he would be in a secure enclosure in the open but he was within a bamboo enclosure in a room. I pressed my face against the sliding glass windows to see him better. His skin was dark, jet black, with hair sticking up like a porcupine's. He was moving restively in circles, without pausing. He really looked like a child, vulnerable and cute. Three kids huddled near the window to get a closer look at the over-sized child and tapped the glass pane to attract his attention. The guard saw their eagerness and slid the window open partly. The baby elephant promptly put his trunk out. The children stroked it and said in surprised voices, 'The skin is thick. It is hard.' One of them tried to poke his finger into the elephant's nostrils. The elephant baby seemed to enjoy company — he didn't mind the touch, the fondling. The guard closed the window, scared of being hauled over the coals by his superiors who were obviously concerned about the baby catching an infection. The children exclaimed in disappointment at the very brief meeting. Their playmate of barely a minute was denied access to them. He began to circle the room ceaselessly again. Although he was extremely well looked after, I felt sad and wondered how he had become an orphan. I asked the forest department official for his story. He said, 'He was a month old when we found him by the roadside, very close to the sanctuary. He was very weak and lay in a faint. We took care of him, and when he was strong again, we tried to find his parents. When we couldn't trace them, we tried several times in various ways to help him move into an elephant herd and merge with it. He showed no interest in, or capability of, being with his own kind and felt lost. Fearing for his survival, we brought him back here to take care of him. After all, he is very young and unfamiliar with the ways of the forest.' I asked him how he came to be separated from his parents and whether elephants desert their young if they are frail and sick. I was surprised to learn that a mother elephant will not forsake even its dead child and carries it with her trunk for as long as a week. Seems like an instance of attachment and grief. My eyes filled with tears as I heard this. My thoughts were with the baby elephant as I walked unenthusiastically towards the elephants' feeding area. Ananda called out to me, 'Hurry, it's time. You don't want to miss this. They are all here.'

The twelve elephants were waiting behind bamboo railings for their evening meal. On aluminium-top tables, under a shed, expert hands were mixing and preparing their food. Huge square cubes of steaming rich brown stuff, topped with something white, were put on the table. Then that was mixed with other ingredients. It looked soft, mushy and disgusting, but the onlookers watched, fascinated. I asked the forest department chap what it was. He said it was raagi, horse crap (I was aghast), rice, jaggery, cane sugar, coconut, minerals and salt. Their work diet was different from their rest diet. The diet chart and the calorie intake was prepared very meticulously and shown on a table drawn on a wall display board. To my immense relief, I discovered that the forest official had meant horse gram. Either his pronunciation or my hearing was awry.

Mudumalai, the elephant in front of me, had dysentery. The feeder took the huge lumpy mass of food and tried to shove it into its mouth. It let the whole thing fall to the earth. They had mixed some medicine with it to alleviate his problem but he could discern something unfamiliar or distasteful and refused to eat. The feeder succeeded in the third attempt. I looked at the elephant next to Mudumalai and discovered how different their faces were. I had thought that, except for some distinctive marks on their bodies, it would be difficult to tell one from the other. How stupid I was! Mudumalai was handsome, with a very proportionate, pleasing face, while the elephant next to him had a very long face with nothing particularly singular about his visage. He was plainly plain. A host of wild boars had gathered not far from the elephants; they moved around keenly and cunningly, eager to pick up any scraps of the mushy mounds of food, that had fallen to the earth, either by accident or because these were rejected by the pampered elephants. I had not seen such expert and tenacious scavengers. Every evening the boars showed up at the precise feeding time, alerted by an unfailing internal clock. A NRI family near me was wondering what the elephants' food consisted of. I sensed their curiosity and told them. We got talking and the couple told us that they had taken the bus ride the previous afternoon into the forest and spotted a tiger. It was around half past three in the afternoon when they saw a tiger on a high branch of a tree with a small animal trapped in its jaws. I was surprised since the bus's engine was cantankerous enough to warn away the most docile of creatures. I suppose the animals were quite familiar with, and scornful of, these noisy excursions into their territory. The moment Ravi and Ananda heard that these people had seen a tiger the previous afternoon, they decided to come back the next day to try their luck, or better still, take a jeep ride late at night on the Teppakadu-Bandipur road. I am glad that someone dissuaded them later from doing this as the people running these night trips, occasionally into prohibited areas, were doing this illegally to make easy money. The gullible visitor is lured by their glamorous promises of showing the fierce felines. I am terribly scared of tigers and leopards even on-screen, so the mere mention of a possibility of seeing them in flesh in their natural habitat is enough to scare the daylights out of me.

As we sauntered out of this place, a lone peacock strolled in regally with its magnificent tail feathers stroking the earth; it seemed to taunt the wild boar behind it for its lack of colour and grace. It ate the tiny specks of the scattered remains of the elephants' dinner, but with dainty disdain for its hulking competitor, the boar.

We returned to Teppakadu the next afternoon to try our luck once again with the animals. On the seat directly behind Ravi was a couple who spoke both Kannada and Tamil. The man was big-made, barrel-bellied and had heavy pouches under his eyes. Loose flesh seemed to ooze out of him. With sagging balloons for cheeks, he looked unhealthy. Behind this couple sat three hefty young men. They had squeezed themselves into a seat meant for two. Although these men did not know the couple, they struck an instant friendship that was based on inane exchanges of ridiculous comments on the sanctuary and its administrators. Within five minutes of boarding the bus, they were impatient to spot animals. They were loud and uncouth. Fearing that their noisy talk and raucous laughter would scare away the animals and cancel our chances of spotting any creatures, the driver warned them to be quiet. However, they did not seem to understand that their unruly obstreperous energies could scare away the animals. After ten minutes, we spotted a family of elephants in the distance. The driver stopped the bus. As soon as we saw the elephants, these men started squealing and laughing mockingly. The elephants quickly moved deeper into the forest. The four men had denied the other visitors a chance to take pictures and get a good look at the elephants. Remorseless, they continued their unseemly behaviour. The bus driver once again warned them to be quiet. Another ten minutes and no animals to be seen. They continued whining and complaining loudly as to how unfair the tour was. Bored, they called out, '*Puli, puli*' (tiger, tiger) and then yelped at their own pathetic joke. Then they pestered the bus driver with questions and demanded to see the animals. They insisted that he take a different route. 'Turn right, turn right!' they shouted. He shushed them at first but when they got out of control, exasperated, he rebuked them in Tamil, 'I am not a zoo bus driver. Do you understand? This is a sanctuary.' They wished to understand nothing. I could see that their behaviour was getting on Ananda's nerves.

The obnoxious behaviour of the four men had ruined the pleasure of the other visitors who sat mouse-like, without protesting, throughout the ride. For us, it was the third ride. For the other visitors, it was very likely the first and only ride. I am sure they were disappointed but understood that spotting wild animals is a matter of chance and luck. I am also quite certain that the loud and vulgar cries of the four men had shooed the animals away. Our driver, too, was taken aback by the four men's moronic nonsense. There had been a large group of young men on the bus ride into the sanctuary the previous day but they had not behaved like this. They were fun-loving, but civilised, and knew the rules of visiting a sanctuary.

As soon as we got off the bus, our driver whispered to us, 'They are drunk, I think.'

Ananda said to us later, 'I don't think they were sozzled. They were as sober as the day on which they were born.' I agreed with him.

Later, our driver told me the name of the pink and orange flower clusters. He had asked the sanctuary bus driver. 'Madam, pink and orange flowers you like, name lantana.' The restless desire to name these flower clusters was sated. These flower shrubs are so persistently invasive that they overtake entire areas. The forest staff considers them a nuisance but for me the orange clusters were beautiful. In one cluster, you can see so many colours—a flushed red, a charged orange, a proud peach, an incandescent yellow. It is a delightful palette.

Early evening when we drove back to Ooty, I recalled our drive towards Bandipur the previous evening. We had been approximately five kilometres away from Mudumalai when I had seen a thin old man with stick-like legs walking on the dirt side of the road, in the direction of Teppakadu. He was wearing a weather-smeared shirt and a veshti folded above his legs and gathered around the waist. A long piece of cloth, its four edges meeting in a knot over his right shoulder, hung down like a U-shaped cloth cradle or mini hammock. It had some of his basic worldly possessions, I presumed. He was carrying something in both his hands. I cannot recall whether he had a walking stick, a *kamandalam* or an eating bowl in his hands. He was walking at a steady pace on his bony legs. Our headlights had caught his emaciated figure. When we drove back nearly two hours later and were heading towards Masinagudi, we saw the same old man walking at the same steady pace. He was four to five kilometres from Teppakadu, so he had walked approximately nine kilometres in less than two hours. His tenacity and stamina surprised me. He seemed oblivious to the passing vehicles, the gathering dark and the thick forest. Our driver remarked, '*Manas sari illa.*' (He is not in his right mind.) Ravi responded to the driver in Tamil, 'Who knows, he could be a siddha.'

The shadowy form of a bison in a ditch by the road loomed before us. Face turned towards the road, it looked large and scary. I rolled up my window cautiously, fearful of, and fascinated by, the dark, silent forms of the trees, bushes and shrubs. I wondered what mysteries they guarded and what menaces they harboured in their heavily tangled secret interiors.

My First Experience of Art in Hyderabad

November in Hyderabad is a very agreeable month with a pleasurable hint of winter which used to be very short and mild till a few years ago. In the preceding few weeks, I had seen the Kalakriti Art Gallery mentioned in *The Hindu*. I had read that the works of Sisir Sahana, a celebrated artist, were on display. I regretted the fact that in the last year and a half, I had made no active attempt to see any art. I had also been keen on learning at least the simple forms and motifs of the folk art of Madhubani, but hadn't found any teacher. Then I read in the papers that this art form was being adapted to express contemporary themes, in particular women's issues. My desire to experience art in Hyderabad gathered strength and intensity. For two days the name Kalakriti Art Gallery circled in my mind like a tireless winged insect. I wondered whether I would be able to go there any time soon.

My father had suffered a major heart attack in October and wasn't his usual energetic self. Hence I didn't feel good about going to the other end of town to see paintings. We were invited for a dinner and I was going to turn down that invitation when Ravi persuaded me to accept it as he felt that meeting people would do me some good and I would be able to get out of my over-anxiety about my father's health.

At the dinner party, I met several people for the first time, but the most beautiful coincidence of the evening was that I met Prshant and Rekha Lahoti, the young couple who own the Kalakriti Art Gallery. That such wonderful coincidences are possible is very reassuring. It is both surprising and not so surprising. If we are all connected, as the book *Reinventing Medicine* claims, then there was nothing all that amazing about my so-called chance meeting with the Kalakriti couple.

We send out imperceptible subtle messages to each other about our desires, wishes, emotional and mental proclivities and our deep yearnings. While there is something called destiny, our deep longings and prayers also shape the course of events and bring into our lives those people, who we've been looking for, either actively or subconsciously. Everything needn't happen by conscious design or planning. If we really want something sincerely and wholeheartedly, we attract all those possibilities that will make our desires a reality.

The next morning we received a text message from Rekha Lahoti that on Sunday they were going to have a private viewing of the painter Aditya Basak's work, followed by a brunch. It was followed by a phone call that they were keen we join them for this event as we had expressed an interest in art and in seeing their gallery. I could hardly believe that an opportunity to see the art gallery would materialise so quickly and so unexpectedly without any deliberate move on our part. Of course, we seized it and spent a lovely afternoon with art and four artists—all very accomplished but unassuming and down-to-earth. The good food added considerably to the rich and varied flavour of the afternoon.

Quite unfamiliar with contemporary Indian art and artists, I took my time to take in the paintings while most of the others chatted and socialised. I was struck by the masterly interplay of light and shade in Aditya Basak's paintings and their powerful invitation to journey beyond the familiar world to another realm that is full of mystery, haunting images and some unsettling truths. Apart from his other works on display, I paused for a long time before his paintings *Globe, The Performer, Icarus, Black Rainbow* and one other work which shows a mountain goat poised to leap over an obstacle.

The Performer reminds one of a Thai version of the Dancing Shiva. He emerges from the inky blue-black background of the painting, a bronze-yellow figure whose form is not a clear luminous golden-yellow. His form reminds one of a bronze piece tarnished or marked by time. His left cheek is in shadow and the right one is brighter. The dancer's left leg is half bent at the knee and the other is folded at the knee horizontally. One has the impression that the performer's left foot is not placed firmly on the ground. There is a slight impression of the dancing figure floating in bluish-black space; he doesn't seem to be performing on any fixed stage. The hands and feet are not well formed and the right foot is lost in something flowing around and behind it. Is it the loose end of a loin cloth? Difficult to say. Something that streaks out and shoots upwards from the right hand, contains within it an image of a ghastly face—in fact, near-demonic. The performer's form carries the images of many faces. With the exception of one, as far as I could make out, the rest are either unhappy or fill one with apprehensions of painful life experiences. Above the left shoulder of the performer is a face, with lips curved in a grotesque grimace and a left eye that bulges out. Their forms crisscrossed with tiny lines, three seated featureless spectators watch the ambiguous dance of this mystifying dancer.

I turned to my left to take a second long look at Basak's *Black Rainbow*. The title of the painting filled me with foreboding and despair. The image of the painting that remained with me was this (it may not be entirely accurate or do justice to the complexity of the work as I rely on memory to recall its visual impact): The right half of the painting (when I am facing it) is dominated by the large smiling face of a woman with a prominent nose and full lips. Below her torso is a dancing figure with six arms and long-lobed ears (a deity?). Opposite this face is the outline of an animal standing on its hind legs with raised forepaws. The left side of the canvas is given over to a dark rainbow. It is eclipsed by, or smudged over with, black paint. Something flows out of the lower half of the rainbow—a crisscrossed misty pink-brown stream. It has dark zigzagging lines with an uneven pink lining—a dark version of lightning. I see something resembling a horse and an antelope at the edge of the pink-brown stream. The upper left of the canvas has a dramatic narrative contained in an uneven yellow cloud. Three tiny humans appear to be running. Are they fleeing from a scene of conflict as there is a swirling funnel of smoke rising from the earth not far from them? Is the black rainbow and this scene of human unrest something that the inward-looking face is aware of, but remains unperturbed by, because it recognises it as a passing reality and hopes or knows that the black rainbow will appear in its clear lovely form sometime in the future? The painting is visually powerful, engages your mind and draws you into its challenging, intriguing narrative.

I was reminded of my days in Paris when I would take off alone to spend time in some of the smaller museums. The significant difference was that my experience of art there was not part of a social event and my interaction with a work of art was more complete, more solitary, and therefore, more rewarding. I could be myself—brood, frown, or smile; gaze long and deep; give a curious or cursory glance; be moved, be elated, be pensive; feel nonplussed, bewildered, or astonished, by all that I saw.

Ganesha Doing Linga Abhishekam

The first week of December didn't bring much cheer. I was anxious about my father's health and concerned about what the cardiologist would suggest for my father—a bypass or an angioplasty.

Whenever I am anxious, I either embroider or listen to music. While in India, the desire uppermost at such times was either to visit a bookstore or a handicrafts emporium. Hating the idea of getting caught in traffic, I decided to go only up to Secunderabad's main shopping area. On Sarojini Devi Road, the choice was between Lepakshi and the Cauvery Arts Emporium. Since I spotted a parking spot right in front of Kaveri, I settled for that place. As soon as I walked in, a man in his mid-fifties, I presume, (I later learnt that he was the manager) asked me if I was looking for anything in particular. I told him that I just wanted to look around and had nothing specific in mind. Then I asked him for a *panchloha* Ardhanareeshwara, although I was certain, for no good reason, that they wouldn't have it. The brass and the bronze idols were arranged on a large table-like place, a little to the left of the main entrance. They caught your eye as soon you entered.

I lingered there for a long time unable to decide whether I wanted something in brass or bronze. The bronze pieces were very few but the workmanship was far superior to that of the brass ones. Of course, there was a considerable difference in price too. A 20 per cent discount on the quoted price made the bronze idols even more attractive. I looked at the two bronze women with a lamp for a long time, wondering if I should pick up just one of them. On the display shelf opposite, Rama, Sita, Lakshmana and Hanuman looked large and impressive from a distance but a closer look was disappointing. Sita's form was stolid and her face had no *kala* or charm. The reclining Buddha was satisfactory. The Nartana Vinayaka or the dancing Ganesha was well-made but too small. The manager stood nearby waiting patiently for me to make up my mind. He remarked a few times, 'Madam, this is a very good price. If you order a piece like this, it will cost you more than double. Don't hesitate to buy it.' I wished he would stop breathing down my neck and give me time and space to make up my mind. I wandered away from the spot and went to the first floor to look at their export section. Downstairs again, I looked long and hard at the brass and bronze statuettes and idols, trying to select one that appealed to my eye and pocket both. Then I suddenly spotted a piece that had escaped me altogether. It was a seated Ganesha doing *abhishekam* to the Shiva lingam. I picked it up and was struck by its beauty. I hadn't seen this form of Ganesha before and, although it may not be unusual, for me it was singular because I had never come across Ganesha doing an *abhishekam*—a son's ceremonious offering of devotion to his father. I knew that this was the piece that I wanted. After discount it would cost me a little less than ₹3000. It was an extravagance I could ill afford at that time but I didn't want to let go of the magnificent piece. I had also discovered it at a very propitious time. It was the month of Kartik or Karthika masam, as

Ravi says it in Telugu, and, at that time of the year, it is considered good to visit at least one of the well known Shiva temples. I hadn't been able to accompany Ravi on his recent visit to Draksharama, a Shiva kshetram, because I didn't want to leave my parents alone. That bronze idol of Ganesha doing an *abhishekam* was an auspicious sign, a vicarious unexpected fulfilment of an impelling need to visit a Shiva shrine. I was thrilled to hold the beautiful shrine in my hand.

The Ganesha was an exquisite piece made with splendid attention to detail. Let me describe it:

It is a work of love and reverence. It is an uplifting prayer in bronze. Adorned with different kinds of jewellery—necklaces, waistband, armbands, bangles, anklets, chains around the ear, tika, intricately designed band for the forehead, an elaborate hairdo, a thick braid reaching down to the hips just like the Kuchipudi and Bharatnatyam dancers have, a sacred thread, an angavastram and a veshti whose fine folds can be seen individually—this is Ganesha. He is seated with the left leg folded under him. The right foot rests firmly on the floor, its heel touching the inner thigh as the leg is bent at the knee. The back arches inwards at the waist and this gives the hips a very attractive filled-out curve. The deity has been given a very shapely form and so it is aesthetically pleasing apart from its religious dimension. Thus seated, Ganesha is doing *abhishekam* to the lingam. With the help of a pot or *kalasam* held in his right hand he is bathing the lingam in a devout manner. He exhibits the grace of a dancer while doing this. Going by the thickness of the liquid poured, it could be honey. With his left hand, he holds the front end of something like a *kavadi* that rests on his left shoulder. From the rear end of this *kavadi* is suspended a rope holder or a woven frame that holds a pot of some sort. Ganesha seems to have stopped during the course of his journey or pilgrimage to do this *abhishekam*. It is a piece resonant with rich meaning and engaging beauty.

It was stolen from my home sometime in January 2008. The piece was precious and dear to me for several reasons. When it left me I was miserable. It stayed in my home only for three to four weeks after I had bought it. I miss it not just as a work of art, of intricate craftsmanship, but as something that enhanced the meaning of my moments each time I looked at it. I still wait for it to reappear on my shelf miraculously.

Paris: A Very Different Journey

For three months we had been toying with the idea of going to Paris during the Christmas and New Year break to meet Ananda there. Ananda was in Montreal, doing his undergraduate studies in Economics and Management from McGill. He didn't want to come all the way to India for his ten-day break. The idea took definite shape in September. When we had firmed up our minds to go to Paris, the trip was riddled with challenges. As I had mentioned earlier, my father had a major heart attack in October and didn't do too well initially. Given this scenario, I was nervous about even contemplating leaving him and my mother by themselves. Then he improved gradually and also became more positive about his recovery. My cousin and his wife offered to come and stay with my parents for the fortnight that we were planning to be away in Paris. I had a free air passage as my father had served in the Indian Airlines and we, his family, could use the free staff tickets. We were under the misconception that the privilege extended to the spouses of his children also. To our dismay we soon discovered that Ravi would have to buy his ticket. Our savings were touching rock-bottom. The only option was to encash our National Savings Certificates which would pay for Ravi's ticket, the medical insurance and our stay in Paris. I was concerned and insecure because I didn't want one trip to completely deplete our resources but Ravi was composed, or at least not visibly ruffled. He had formulated a definite plan to make us more financially comfortable in the coming year. I felt mildly relieved.

The second irksome obstruction was when I learnt that Ananda had been refused a visa to France, a country he had lived in for three-and-a-half years. The official at the French Consulate in Montreal spoke no English or claimed he didn't. He refused to look at the two documents which were in English – one, a letter of invitation from our friend in the Indian Embassy in Paris saying that he was going to host Ananda for his period of stay in Paris and the other which certified that he was a student of McGill. The official brusquely waved the documents aside and asked Ananda to come back in the first week of January because there weren't any appointment slots free until then. Or, he would have to spend time online, monitoring like a hawk, when someone would cancel a visa interview appointment and grab that free slot. Ananda was in the middle of exams and this meant an awful waste of time. To add to our problems, Ravi's friend who had given the letter of invitation was on home leave in India. Ananda had already bought his air ticket and was scheduled to reach Paris on 24th morning. Would his visa work out? We hoped foolishly that it somehow would. Actually, something told me that this entire affair was a nuisance, an irritant, but eventually he would make it to Paris. Fortunately over the following weekend, Ananda spotted a freed-up visa interview slot for the coming Monday. He asked his friend to translate Ravi's friend's letter into French, attached it to the original and got a letter in French from McGill saying that he was a student of their University. Determined to take his chances, he told me that he was going ahead with the visa interview. Ravi was away, visiting his ancestral village in East Godavari and there was no way he could use any of his contacts in Paris, at such short notice, to help Ananda out. Ananda was in a huff over the rejection and was in no mood to wait for another free slot which might clash with his exam day or happen too late to serve any purpose. On the 'fateful' Monday, the official who looked at Ananda's papers spoke perfect English. A quick professional glance at the papers and without any fuss, he gave our son a three-month validity visa to France.

The next hurdle was totally unforeseen and absurd. The whole mini drama could've been lifted out of some third-rate slapstick comedy. Ravi had sent our French visa application forms to the MEA by Blue Dart. Someone there was going to take charge and help us speed up the procedure. While we were waiting to hear that our visas were through, we heard that a messenger had swept away the forms as trash and then burnt them along with the rest of the discarded paper in the concerned office. We didn't know whether to grin and bear it, grind our teeth in annoyance, or explode into laughter at this ridiculous scenario. We had less than a week before our scheduled date of departure. Of course it was another matter that Ravi had not yet bought his ticket; he had merely blocked his seat on Air India. The last annoying bit was when we learnt that Ravi's ticket would cost far more than what the travel agent had indicated earlier. She had forgotten to include the tax. Anyway, we did get our visas in time and were scheduled to take the flight to Mumbai on 20 December to take the Air India flight to Newark via Paris. The previous year, Ananda had taken the same flight to Newark on the same day.

It was a comforting coincidence for me—a coincidence that augured well.

On 21 December, around four in the morning, we sat in the executive lounge of the International Airport in Mumbai, waiting to take the morning flight to Paris. That I was going for a brief holiday to Paris seemed too good to be true. Our friends Sreedhar and Aparna had made plans to drive us to Mont Saint-Michel the same afternoon. They were quitting Paris for good on the thirtieth and had very little time to spare before the packers came in and started winding up stuff in their apartment. It was very gracious of them to offer to take us. I had missed seeing Mont Saint-Michel during our stay in Paris for some reason or the other, and the longing to see it had become sharper and more acute with the passage of time.

I remembered the previous instances when our plans had been thwarted repeatedly. I was grateful for the wonderful opportunity in December 2007. On a certain weekend, a month and a half before we left Paris on 4 August 2006, when Ravi had suggested that we drive down there, I had responded, 'Not this weekend. It's okay if it doesn't work out.' My lack of enthusiasm hadn't surprised him as his father was quite ill in Hyderabad and we were becoming increasingly anxious about his health each passing day. I also have a very clear memory of the executive lounge in the wee hours of 5 August 2006. It had smelt faintly stale. Mustiness and the smell of spices diffused through the air-conditioning had put me off. The low lighting had accentuated the dank and heavy atmosphere. A year and a half later, it felt so different. The air was fresher, the general feel more cheerful, more wholesome. Had the place been refurbished? At least, that is how it felt. Had the sofas been reupholstered? They were beige with a flowing floral pattern—large olive and brown flowers lounged luxuriously. The marble floor was a warm shiny reddish-brown. Had it been carpeted earlier? Couldn't recall.

My state of mind on 5 August 2006 and my mental and emotional state on 21 December 2007, were poles apart. In August, I had left Paris for good. I was very sad as the link with Paris seemed to have been broken for good. The enforced rupture seemed final, definitive. I didn't know when I would get to see my friends again or even hope to have a temporary home there. It felt as if a part of me would continue to sit day after day late into the night, on the long sofa in our former apartment's drawing room, looking at the rooftops of the buildings on Rue d'Andigné, observing the minute shifts in the tone of the light in the night sky. A divided self, I would mentally and emotionally live in Paris and Hyderabad at the same time, inhabiting two contrasting worlds that could never meet.

Checking my emails on Ananda's laptop, while sitting in the airport lounge that August morning, I had seen a message from a dear friend that she had read the first seven-and-a-half chapters of the manuscript of my novel and had really liked what she had read. While praising my writing, she had said that the problems in the text were technical, to do with the narrative voice. I hadn't expected her to get a chance to even glance at my work because I had handed over the completed manuscript to her barely two days before our departure. On the evening of 4 August, she had meant to read only the first chapter but had found herself impelled to read on, late into the night. I had felt tremendously encouraged, elated in fact. That some publisher would accept my work and I would get to see it in the form of a book was a vision I didn't have the courage or confidence to see. I was content to revel in the feeling that a writer-friend had found my work good – well, at least the first few chapters. A year and a half later, I had the good feeling of knowing that Penguin had accepted my novel and would publish it sometime in the near future.

I was very excited about going back to Paris. However, when I learnt that two of my dear friends would be away from Paris during the winter holiday season, it diluted some of the charm of going back to that city which had once been home. I looked around me at the executive lounge. Next to my sofa, the square side table with a marble top had a painted wooden peacock on it—not graceful but stout and squat, with mild wonder in its guileless eyes. The wall above had a Tanjore painting on glass—Hanuman paying homage to Lord Rama, Lakshmana and Sita. Several others were also assembled there to pay their respects. Rama was green, with thick arms and a benign smiling face. A winged horse and a cute smiling elephant were part of the retinue of devotees. All this time, while I was contrasting the two days of my life in that airport lounge associated with Paris, I intermittently heard the disagreeable peremptory complaining voice of a man in his early fifties. A tall heavyset man with a broad face and bullish attitude was complaining to a fellow Indian and a black British national about Air India and its 'don't give a damn attitude' towards its passengers. He had experienced some problem with his flight to Chicago and that meant that he wouldn't make the connection to some other place in time. Air India seemed to be responsible in some big way and he was peeved with the airline and its abysmal service towards its clients. It was not the complaint, legitimate or otherwise, which irked me. It was his bulldoggish superior air, his loutish attitude, his vulgar loudness that got me.

He shouted at the receptionist-cum-waiter, 'Why can't you keep some decent snacks? I want *pav bhaji* for breakfast. *Kaheen se* parcel *leke aao*. Give me vodka.'

'You already had two, sir.'

'Is there a rule that I can't have another drink? Call the manager,' he said threateningly. 'You make me wait for so many hours. Then there is no breakfast and a limit on the number of drinks. Is this how you treat your business class passengers? I could have flown economy.'

The waiter heard him out with apparent meekness and mock servility, while the 'wronged' man roared and raged, and then he slid away quietly to stand behind the reception desk.

I went to the next room which had a computer and an internet connection. A half-eaten plate of sandwiches and a glass with the last dregs of some drink rested sloppily on the computer table. I shoved it aside gingerly and distastefully. I looked up and saw an old Tanjore painting of Kartikeya as Shanmukha and felt good instantaneously. I typed an email to the friend who had read my novel over a year ago, thinking it would bring the associations with the lounge to a pleasurable culmination, with reference to my book and my nostalgia about Paris, but the screen froze briefly and the message didn't go. Although I had the time to retype and send it again, I felt I had lost the original words, the delicate emotion that had formed them and my pleasure in wanting to share those moments with her. I stood away from my annoyance and saw it dissipate slowly.

I had nearly two weeks of stay in Paris ahead of me. I was determined to make the most of it and enjoy my son's presence there.

Guimet: A Truncated Visit

On 22 December, a few hours after we reached Paris in freezing weather, our friends Sreedhar and Aparna and their twins drove us to Le Mont Saint-Michel, where we spent a night; the next day they took us to Saint-Malo; both, pilgrimage centres in my mind, for intensely personal reasons. After our return from Saint-Malo, Ananda joined us in Paris. We were thrilled to see him. We said our goodbyes to Aparna, Sreedhar and the affectionate kids. After thanking them warmly for their hospitality, we moved into our friends' apartment, Chitra and Alex's apartment, which was vacant, since they were away in India. It was a beautiful gesture on their part to allow us the free use of their lovely apartment, located close to UNESCO in the quinzième. It made our Paris stay affordable and very comfortable.

27 December was our Musée Guimet day. I woke up feeling very weak and sapped of all desire to get out of bed. My throat felt raw and painfully dry. I dragged myself out of bed, swallowed a paracetamol, gargled with warm saline water and made myself some herb tea with honey. By early afternoon I had put together a basic lunch for Ananda and his friend, who was also visiting Paris, and the two of us. Ravi looked at me and

said, 'You don't look too good. We can do Guimet another day. Just rest the whole of today.'

'No,' I protested, 'Time is short. I can't afford to lose even a single day of our stay here.'

'Fine. Rest for some time and then we will move.'

It was nearly three in the afternoon by the time we got to the museum. I felt quite feeble but was determined to not let that come in the way of the visit. We had a little over two and a half hours and it just wasn't enough. With a packed schedule for our stay in Paris, I knew that if I didn't see Guimet that afternoon, I wouldn't come back to it another day.

The Buddha that I had used in my novel *See Paris for Me* was right at the entrance of the visit, in the extreme right of the large room. I walked up to it at once with desperate urgency. Something told me that I must hurry and see the two or three exhibits that had to do with my novel, as I wouldn't have the energy for anything else. I was beginning to feel that I would collapse if I didn't hold myself up straight through sheer effort of will. In addition, I didn't want to ruin Ravi's visit. This was his first time in the Guimet Museum.

As I stood before the Buddha of the sixth or the seventh century from the Mekong Delta of Vietnam, I could hardly believe that I was getting another chance to look at it—the simple yet impressive figure that I had used in my book. I had never imagined that I would get an opportunity again to encounter him and gaze upon him. I observed: He stands on a low dual plinth; his right arm is missing; his face looks as if someone has smashed it in. On the left foot, some toes are missing. His robe clings to his body, accentuating his slender form, verging on the emaciated. The left arm is lost inside the folds of the long robe. The neck and a small part of the face are of a lighter colour than the rest.

The Buddhas in burnished bronze and granite have either a magnificent or a deeply grave presence, but this Buddha, in ageing, time-marked, bark-like segmented wood, had an austere grace that was singular. The simple form spoke a silent eloquent language. His sober, dignified form touched a deep chord in me and I walked away from him with his image ever-present before my mind's eye.

Soon I began to feel too ill to focus properly on anything. When Ravi stood before the *Head of the Buddha* in red sandstone from Mathura in Uttar Pradesh, I stood close to him for comfort. 'Isn't it impressive?' he asked. 'Yes, it is,' I said abstractedly and then looked at it with more interest. In a shapely, well-rounded face with full lips, the eyes are half-closed and the long gently curving eyebrows meet at the centre. The head tilts forward slightly and the hair is arranged in tightly coiled curls. The *usnisa* is half-broken. The large forehead, the slightly forward bend of the head, the prominent nose with large nostrils give the figure a majestic dignity.

An overwhelming weakness was beginning to overtake me. My legs felt boneless. They would crumple under me suddenly, I felt, and I would fall. I couldn't understand why I felt so drained and lifeless and why I had aches and pains all over. Was I coming down with viral? I sat down on the chair near the Nataraja in the Tanjore bronzes section and closed my eyes. I knew then that I just wouldn't make it through the museum and would not be able to see even a small part of its exhibits on that visit. I just had one desire at that moment and I held onto it tenaciously: To see the sculpture of Ananda from China that I had used in my novel. A cup of something warm might revive me, so I asked Ravi if we could go to the museum café. I took another analgesic with my coffee and that proved disastrous on an empty stomach.

Sharp stabbing pains of acidity started in my upper abdomen. I fought my intense physical discomfort so that I could make it to the China section and at least see Ananda.

Going up to the first floor, I followed my memory to lead me to Ananda. At one corner of a long room dedicated to works from China was a figure of a monk with a small plaque that said *Moine debout (Ananda)?—9th or 10th century*. It did not really look like the Ananda figure I had used in my novel nor was it placed in the centre of the room where my sculpture of Ananda had stood. He was placed next to a corner glass case which had the head of Kashyapa, 'le grand disciple de Buddha'. I was puzzled. The monk Ananda stood on a low plinth and held himself erect with stiff dignity. His sandalled feet were visible under the long robe. Round cheeks, a round jawline and hands clasped in front of him, he looked alert and worldly wise.

Still unsure whether I had really spotted my Ananda, I moved to the centre of the room. I found him just opposite the exit door of the room. I was thrilled and relieved. The sign said: *Disciple de Buddha, Ananda (Dynastie Sui)*. It belonged to the end of the sixth century and the beginning of the seventh century.

I was beginning to shiver violently in spite of two sweaters and a shawl. My forehead felt congested and frozen and my nose was blocked. Another bout of crippling weakness threatened to overtake me. I asked Ravi if he was cold. He said he found the place overheated. To re-gather my strength, I sat on the long leather-covered double-seat diagonally behind Ananda, to the right. Ravi wandered away to see the exhibits in the next room. I closed my eyes, leant back against the wall and rested. I recalled how disappointed I had been to see Ananda the previous time. The sculpture didn't correspond to the image of a youthful naïve devoted disciple of the Buddha that I had conjured up in my mind. I stood before him and observed him with detached curiosity. His slender form was draped in a long robe. A dome-like shaven head, a slender nose, a well-formed tiny mouth and a strong neck were his distinguishing physical attributes. His slit-like eyes seemed to veil the deep truths from a casual gazer. His feet were visible from under the long robe. The right hand was missing and his folded right arm touched the right shoulder. He held a narrow-necked pot in his left hand. With his lowered gaze, he didn't look as shrewd as he had looked earlier when I had first seen him during our Paris posting. All-knowing, all-comprehending, mature and still—that is how he seemed now. Earlier, I had perceived him as clever, astute, in the worldly sense. I wondered why.

To Ananda's left was Buddha's disciple, Kashyapa, in marble (Sui dynasty). He folds his hands before him in prayer or as a mark of respect. Two upper front teeth protrude and bury into the lower lip in a toothy smile. The jutting out forehead with three frontal bumps makes the deep-set eyes seem more recessed. Behind Ananda and Kashyapa, in the centre, is *Le Buddha Cosmique, Vairocana* from the *époque des Qi du Nord (550-577)*. His right hand holds the lower end of the robe. His left hand is missing.

The sobriety of his form is impressive.

There was a lot more to see in the museum but I had no energy for it. Garnering precious impressions of those Buddha-related sculptures, I left the place with a little stab of realisation that I wouldn't come back to it for a long, long time.

Museum of Modern Art on Avenue du Président Wilson

At the beginning of the New Year, I recovered fully from my viral fever. However, I had been forced to stay in bed for three days towards the close of the previous year and had lost three valuable days of our stay in Paris.

3 January was Ravi's birthday and he had planned to spend the day with Ananda and chat with him about various things. Ananda had spent most of his time catching up with old friends in Paris, hence our time with him had been limited. He was flying back to Montreal the next morning. Time was short and precious. I had visited the Museum of Modern Art on the second and decided to go back to it in the hope of getting something more out of the art displayed there and to take a second look at the paintings I had liked the previous afternoon.

The year had begun with some irksome plumbing and water seepage issues in the bathtub of the bathroom. The problem of not being able to take a shower still persisted and I hated stepping out of the house without a good shower. I debated, should I stay at home just because I haven't had a proper shower and miss a precious day of my stay in Paris? Or should I move out of this hampering mental state of feeling unclean and immerse myself in a visit to the museum? The latter seemed the more sensible thing to do. One doesn't travel thousands of miles to a city like Paris after spending so much money to lose days of one's stay for trivial reasons, I chided myself.

I took the metro to get to Iéna station. From there, the Museum of Modern Art was a very short walk. I remembered the times I had walked from our apartment in the Consular building of the Embassy to Iéna. I recalled all the occasions that I had seen movies, Indian classical music concerts or a dance performance in the auditorium of Musée Guimet. All that was a thing of the past now—nostalgia hit me head-on. Not good.

I walked into the museum but suddenly felt very alone. I wished I had chosen to spend the afternoon with Ravi and Ananda. Gloomily lost in thought, as I handed my coat to the man at the vestry, he smiled at me brightly and said, 'You are from India.' I nodded.

'Which part of India?'

'Hyderabad.'

'I am from Pondicherry. Have a nice visit,' he said kindly, handing me my number token.

'Merci.'

He had a nondescript face with thinning stringy hair but I accepted his genial warm smile and pleasant manner as an unexpected gift at that moment of loneliness and it dispelled my gloom for some time. I thanked him within myself.

I wandered from room to room, identifying the paintings and other pieces of art that had interested me the previous day and stopped to take a longer look at them. I appreciated those without understanding much and knowing next to nothing about them. Hungry after a while, I went to the cafeteria and bought myself a piece of dark chocolate cake. For the first time in Paris, I sat by myself at a table, eating leisurely and reading Hemingway's *A Moveable Feast.* I felt comfortable being alone and was surprised at myself. Unthinkable earlier, I had never been able to do this during our entire Paris stay. After this, I walked into the museum bookstore and found *A History of Modern and Contemporary Art,* published by Larousse. It was reasonably priced and detailed. It would give me the necessary overview of the various art movements, their pioneers and artists, but I hesitated because I felt that it would be a bit of a struggle to make my way through all that French. I did not pick it up and I regret it now. Sometimes it is best not to debate too much and make spontaneous decisions based on gut feeling.

After my little break, on resuming the museum tour, I entered a large room. It had several works on display by proponents of the Fluxus movement. I had never heard of it. The room also had a large number of black and white photographs of children. Were they taken by Christian Boltanski? I wasn't sure. But there was something about them which was riveting, compelling. Each picture was like a story, but not a readymade fixed story. It invited your participation. You were drawn into it and impelled to weave your own narrative. There was something vulnerable and tender about each child. They were engaged in ordinary routine activities, yet the photographs seemed to have captured a unique moment in their lives and made each one special. Each photograph focused on a single child doing one of the following things: Playing darts, hopscotch, climbing and jumping over a fence or railing, playing a memory game, playing with toy animals, climbing a jungle gym, cutting paper, pasting stamps, reading a children's newspaper, turning on the television with fist on screen, doing a crossword puzzle, making a paper plane, fiddling with a fork and knife on the table, walking on a stone-paved street carefully avoiding the margins where the stones are joined. These were so many commonplace activities that children engage in and yet one felt as if there was something extraordinary about these scenes because they changed the way you perceived a child and his or her world. You wished you were aware of how special each child is; you wished you were aware of them as individuals; you wished you were more attentive to their needs, more tuned-in to their little worlds, more observant of how they relate to the world around them and the kind of delicate handling and assured support they need.

I wandered around a bit, looking at different expressions of modern and contemporary art, understanding little but curious and foxed a great deal. While there were several paintings that interested me, I spent some time before Jacques Monory's *Velvet Jungle*. Ignorant as I was, the artist's name meant nothing to me. That composition in blue and white fascinated me. It had different shades of blue—dark blue, ultramarine blue, midnight blue and cobalt blue.

The painting shows a very still paradisal world, but soon, one gets the feeling that its loveliness is cold and illusory. Among the dazzling heads of sparkling white flowers in the foreground lurks danger—a tiger is concealed there. A father and child walk on the grass on the banks of a body of water and one feels uneasy for them as if some danger is imminent. Everything is too still for comfort. Two short lines with a single number at their ends streak out from the father and the son. Two other lines dart out from elsewhere in the painting. Now I can't recall from where. Are the father and child marked people? But marked for what? On the other side of the stretch of water, sheer slanting rocks jut forward threateningly. I looked at them closely and discerned three human heads there with belligerent faces. Were my eyes playing tricks on me, I wondered. In the upper corner of the painting, outside of it, yet attached to it, is a bluish black square with six bluish white keys or buttons. The forefinger of a hand with slender fingers rests on one of the keys. If the key is punched, will it blow up the marked figures in the painting or is it a means of controlling the dynamics between the numbered figures? Foxed and apprehensive, I walked away from that painting with its fantasy world and cold imperilled serenity.

I made my way to the stairway leading to the *salle noire* (Dark Room) and *salle* Boltanski (Boltanski Room) in the basement. As I walked down the steps, I was intrigued by a black mural design on a white ceiling and wall. It was like a wave of connected cells with over-sized nuclei or a moving cluster of cells, each infected with a large insect, swarming above and past you. Or, as the description on the plaque on the wall said, '*Du mur au plafond, le motif, compire d'une paire d'yeux répétes à la infinis...*'.

The silence in the basement was profound, endlessly renewed, and pregnant with untold stories and closely guarded secrets. It beckoned you into a world full of things that belonged to the familiar, yet their presence there had some other dimension, evocative and poignant, some other resonances which were far from commonplace.

I entered the first room to the right. The museum attendant stepped aside quietly to let me pass. The floor of the room was grey and the lighting subdued. The room had open shelves heaped with children's clothing in a range of colours. There were shirts, sweaters, jackets, tops, trousers, scarves, sweatshirts, frocks, party dresses, and so on. I stood there for a long time wondering, 'Who do these clothes belong to?' It felt strange to see piles of well-worn, used clothes in such a hushed atmosphere and not be able to see even a single child in flesh and blood, or read in a book about some of the children whose clothes were there. I was overawed and restless—overawed by so many personal histories both revealed and concealed there, and restless because I wouldn't get even a passing glimpse into any of them. I was reminded of death; I was reminded of how uncertain life is and how fleeting each cherished moment. The clothes made me feel protective towards the kids to whom they belonged. I thought of how fragile and vulnerable each child is and how full of grievous lapses memory is; we forget when we should remember and cherish and remember with morbid intensity when we should release.

This room led to a narrow rectangular room, more like a connecting passage to another room. It had black and white photographs of the faces of children and one of a newborn baby. Who were these kids who had been immortalised here? What kind of lives did they have? Where were they now if they were still around? And what was the purpose of those pictures? I was perplexed, troubled, and curious. What was I supposed to take with me from there? Each child there had a life story, a destiny that I would never know. I was fascinated by those faces and uneasy. Were those photographs a startling memorial to irreversible loss and separation? Were those children victims of genocide, of the Holocaust? Once again, I was mournful; I felt the disturbing presence of death and was reminded of how unpredictable life is and how evanescent all that we cling to.

I moved to the next room. The silence grew heavier and more charged with the unrevealed. With the exception of the doorways, the four walls were covered with five rows of black shelves. These had telephone directories from all over the world leaning against each other. There were two rectangular tables with lamps and a ladder was propped against one of the bookshelves. I spotted one directory from Syria, a country where I had lived for three years. The date was 1995, written in Arabic. I was pleasantly surprised. Again, I was baffled. If I were to pick up one of them and glance through the list of names that meant nothing to me, how would that simple exercise affect me? What was I supposed to become more aware of, or whose presence was I supposed to acknowledge? I didn't know what to make of that room. All I felt was that my link with the world of mundane realities had momentarily snapped. That room with so many directories was a silent, unusual homage to all the people listed there—to humanity, perhaps.

We are just names or anonymous faces till someone takes a second look at us and gives a sign of recognition or acknowledgement. We exist for others when someone places us within a context, locates us in time and space and retrieves our history.

I quickly made my way across the large dark room with several large screens, which had short films and series of images being projected on them. I was uncomfortable sitting by myself to watch those films.

I felt very alone and wanted the security of the familiar. I longed to be with Ravi and Ananda. I was supposed to meet them for dinner around eight at the restaurant Dino on Chaussée de la Muette. It was only a quarter to six. I headed back to the apartment and was thrilled when Ananda walked in half an hour after me. I felt secure and he was a good companion on the metro ride to Passy.

Kancheepuram

In the second week of January 2007, we were back home in Hyderabad—back to concerns about my father's health, back to music concerts, back to visits to Chennai and back to journeys to temple towns.

Attending an Iyengar wedding in May was the ostensible reason for our visit to Chennai, which would be unbearably hot and humid at that time of the year. I did not fancy my clothes sticking to me like a second skin, nor did I fancy a perpetual sense of feeling unclean and unwashed but still decided to make that trip. The wedding and a change of place were just pretexts. Gradually and tactfully, I hoped to persuade Ravi to make a day trip to Kancheepuram. Resisting this journey in the peak of summer, he had been giving this non-committal response, 'We'll see.' I did not push him too hard for a decisive 'yes' because he wanted to play it by ear. In addition, an active campaign might invite an irreversible 'no'. Something in me said that we would go to Kancheepuram in spite of Ravi's tepid enthusiasm.

Why did I want to go to Kancheepuram so much? In my mind, it had always seemed inaccessible because I was in awe of the Math and the Paramacharya; Ravi had the good fortune of meeting him once.

I am going to deviate from the main story and give you Ravi's experience of the Kanchi Paramacharya in his own words:

> 'In 1974, I went to Kancheepuram with a friend. The Paramacharya was not at the Math but in some other place outside the town. After we reached, my friend met his father who was there at that time. The Paramacharya himself wasn't giving *darshan* at that time; disappointed, we got back to Chennai. I think I wasn't destined to see him on that visit. In 1977, I went a second time with my friends. This time we had to go to Kolavai. Although the Paramacharya was observing *mounam*, he was still giving *darshan*. He was sitting in a room which had a small window. We stood before the window for his *darshan*. I saw a small saffron-clad figure sitting against the wall at the far end of the room. (My *upanayanam* had been performed only a few months back.) I folded my hands and prayed to him through the bars of the window and retreated. Three of us were chatting in the courtyard when one of the attendants came and told me that the Paramacharya wanted me to come back. Full of trepidation, I immediately went back to the window again. He blessed me by giving some grapes as *prasadam*. Happy and deeply grateful, I ate the grapes, but didn't attach any unusual significance to the incident. Only later, when people spoke with open wonder about the incident, did I realise how fortunate and blessed I had been.'

Now coming back to my story, I felt that one had to be in a state of spiritual readiness to make the journey to the holy city of Kancheepuram. Of course, I must admit that my awe of the Math had diminished to some extent after a controversy that it had become embroiled in. What the Math stands for traditionally and the ideals of Hinduism that it represented in the time of the

Paramacharya, continued to impel me to make a visit. The truth is multi-layered and a lay person will never know the events and scheming that led to the temporary dimming of the Math's luminosity and spiritual significance.

After two days in Chennai, at the home of our hosts and dear friends, Venkat and Vidya, we rented a car for the day to take us to Kancheepuram. I was happy. Since early morning travel is just not Ravi's cup of tea, we left home at nine in the morning—rather late, according to Chandra. We had company on this journey—Chandra and Vidya. After a customary prayer from the car window at a roadside corner shrine of Vinayaka, we set off for Kancheepuram at a little after nine. Sitting in the air-conditioned car, the heat outside was something 'out there'; not for us to experience for the time being. I thanked god for small blessings.

We took the Sriperumbudur-Bengaluru National Highway. To our left, at the very beginning of that impressive road, a modern windmill cast its sovereign, unperturbed glance on the rush of vehicles. The wide divider in the road was planted with arali, which was practically flowerless. The impartial summer had not spared even the pretty, frail flowers. At a quarter past ten, we neared Sriperumbudur and caught a fleeting glimpse of the Adikesava Perumal Temple tower and the memorial to Rajiv Gandhi. It was a bit unsettling that in 1991, this had been the site of a human bomb, subsequent violent deaths and political chaos.

From Sriperumbudur began the industrial corridor. When we passed the Saint-Gobain factory, I remembered France. My mind needs the smallest trigger to take me back to Paris. Then a truck ahead of us brought me back home with a jolt. Thickly packed with people, it teetered along dangerously. Four or five young men had flung one leg over the hinged back door of the truck and were sitting astride it, unperturbed both by this uncomfortable mode of journey and the heat.

At three or four places along the road, young boys held out something for sale in plastic bags. I was curious about what they were offering. Chandra told me that they were selling nunge, a kind of fruit. He could not recall the English word for it.

'Have you never eaten it?' he asked.

'I wouldn't know till I see it.'

'You must have some now. It's excellent in this kind of heat.'

We stopped the car near the next vendor of nunge. I looked at the fruit and said, 'Oh, that's palm fruit. I have had it just once, in fact quite recently, in Hyderabad.' Its translucent succulent white flesh looks like two kidneys fused together. Moving closer to the vendor, I saw three such fruits entrenched in a shell that resembled the large coconut shell, except that it was shapelier, and the outer colour of the shell was brown. What was a discovery for me was a commonplace thing for the rest of them. My pleasure at discovering the palm fruit was amusing to them. It seemed like an exaggerated response to something very ordinary. Chandra selected two of the more juicy ones and gave them to me. Refreshing, they slaked my thirst. One had to peel off the thin creamy-brown skin covering the fruit before one could eat it. As I was throwing away the skin on the wild grass, I noticed a tiny single-petalled white flower, which looked like a miniature *deepam* with a wick. 'So unassuming, so inconspicuous and yet so pretty,' I exclaimed. Vidya turned around to look at it. 'That's tumba, one of the flowers offered to Vinayaka.' I had carelessly thrown palm fruit peels around it.

The sky was cloudy. On an embankment in the distance, palm trees skirted part of the horizon. At a little past a quarter to eleven, we left the highway and turned onto a side road lined with gulmohar. This road would take us to Kanchi, hailed as

Dakshina Kashi. Our first stop would be the Kamakshi Amman Temple and then we would see the Kailasanatha Temple and, if time permitted, the Ekambareshwara Temple. Vishnu Kanchi would have to wait for another trip.

My experience of the Kanchi Kailasanatha Temple that I am going to share now is from my second visit in February 2008. Five of us – Ravi and I, Chandra, my sister-in-law Subhadra, our niece Divya – drove from Chennai to Kancheepuram.

The rooms that we had requested for at the Circuit House, were dingy and full of stale air. Hence we were compelled to stay the night at a hotel attached to Saravana Bhavan. Barring some traces of mustiness and drab furnishings, the rooms were tolerable. The next morning I woke up early, around a quarter past six, to find baby cockroaches scuttling up and down the bathroom door of the hotel room. I turned off the air-conditioning, opened the windows to let in some fresh air and stood near the window overlooking the main street.

On the opposite side of the road were two exceptionally long rectangular billboards with Jayalalitha's face in all her various movie avatars splashed across them.

A skeletal bull pulled a long cart full of heavy sacks with painful slowness. Several trucks filled with construction material – sand, cement, bricks – went past. Two more bullock carts trundled down the road; the only pleasant thing about these overworked beasts of burden was their painted horns – bright red and green. So much heavy traffic and noise at seven in the morning for a temple town was disconcerting. Dressed in Kanchi silks, a group of women stood in front of the main door of the lodge across the road. Their rich colourful sarees, jasmine and kanakambaram in their hair, saved the morning from being burdened with the rush and clamour of an unappealing modern Indian town.

After a cup of coffee, as I sat on the bed reading the newspaper, I jumped out of my skin when Subhadra shouted in panic, 'Close the window Priti, quickly!' The urgency in her voice shook me out of my morning desultoriness.

'What's wrong?'

'Look, it's trying to come in!'

I looked up at the window which was partly covered by the air conditioner. A baby monkey, which had climbed onto the air conditioner and had almost thrust its head through the gap in the bars of the window, retreated momentarily. Subhadra kept up an unrelenting, threatening 'shoo, shoo' in its direction. It opened its small mouth in a silent angry snarl and slid off the air-conditioner, clinging to its edges with its forepaws while I shoved my hand through the bars to shut the two panes of the window. Frustrated in its attempt to enter the room, it gave me a dirty look and vanished. Generally, I find baby monkeys cute in a vulnerable sort of way but this one was ugly and saucy. Or, we had made him so.

This is how our day began—a petty scare and a surprise visit by an unwelcome dusty-brown guest. After breakfast, we headed straight for the Kailasanatha Temple. Made by Rajasimha Pallava and his son, Mahendra Pallava, in the eighth century AD, it is a very ancient temple. Away from the noise and bustle of the town, a world heritage site, it attracts foreign tourists and gives the impression of being more of a monument than a fully functioning temple.

Just outside the temple, two or three sellers of brass and bronze objects, like statuettes of deities, pots, lamps, bells, door handles, animal-shaped locks and other things, had set up makeshift stands and tables to display their goods. On one stand I spotted a *panchloha* seated Ganesha, who had managed to overpower a dragon and was on the point of boring his trident into the fiery creature's treacherously open mouth. As I hadn't seen Ganesha in this form, it was an unusual piece for me. However, the workmanship was poor. Hence I was not tempted to buy it. As most of the pieces there seemed to have come either from homes or were acquired by questionable means from various sources, the seller couldn't tell me anything much about the Ganesha slaying the dragon—how old or new it was and where he had got it from.

The previous time that I had been there, I had asked for an Ardhanareeswara. At first, in front of the temple entrance, the man who had been trying to entice me with commonplace, inconsequential pieces, said that he didn't have that particular piece. Then he looked around cautiously and asked me to wait. He dived into his shop, rummaged through a large basket full of brass and bronze artefacts and little statuettes of deities and fished out a seven-to-eight-inch tall *panchloha* Ardhnareeswara. One look and I knew that it was a remarkable piece. It was a beauty. The details of the face and form were well executed and the attributes of both Shiva and Shakti were clear. I asked the price. His eyes darted shiftily and he said in a low voice, 'Thirteen thousand.'

I was taken aback. 'That's too much,' I protested.

Clearly he didn't understand me. 'Costly. Big price.'

'You tell how much. Okay, give seven.'

'No, I can't give that much. Expensive.'

By that time Ravi's patience was wearing thin and the heat of mid-afternoon May was getting to him. 'Do you really want it? And how would you know its real worth?'

'Anyone can see that it is a well-crafted piece. As for its actual value, I can only go by my experience of bronzes at the Tamil Nadu cottage emporium in Delhi and Chennai, and Kalanjali and the Cauvery Arts Emporium in Hyderabad. I do have a fair idea of prices there, based on the size of a piece and the quality and intricacy of its workmanship.'

The man was eager to sell. He kept pushing the Ardhnareeswara towards me and said, 'You tell your price.'

'Three thousand,' I said, on an impulse.

'Take it,' he said, thrusting it into my hand.

Ravi was getting irked by this protracted, dubious transaction. He said firmly, 'Let's go, Priti. For all you know, it may be a stolen piece and I don't want to encourage this kind of a thing.'

I gave it back to the man, looked at the piece wistfully one last time and sat in the car. The man was foxed by my change of mood. The driver had barely started the engine when the man rushed to the lowered car window and said with persuasive urgency, 'Madam, one minute.' He thrust his arm through the window and flung the piece onto my lap. 'Take it. Give two thousand.'

This made Ravi even more wary of the entire deal. 'Priti, don't get tempted. Give it back to him. Let's move,' he said peremptorily.

On my second visit that February morning, the sight of the fresh green grass in the outer temple area and the hoary sage-like figure of Nandi at the eastern end uplifted our spirits. Lion pillars which once supported a mandapa, stood in regal composure in spite of having witnessed the vicissitudes of time. With a cursory glance at the eight small outer shrines, we entered the temple and met the priest, a thin man with a concave chest and scanty salt and pepper hair. He told us briefly about the Rajasimhesvara Temple, now known as the Kailasanatha Temple. Built in the first quarter of the eighth century AD by the remarkable Pallava king Rajasimha, its architectural splendour inspired the creation of the Chalukyan temple of Virupaksha at Pattadakal and the well known Kailasa temple of Ellora.

Chandra, who knew something about the temple, asked the priest if he knew an interesting story to do with the consecration of this temple. He did know it but seemed disinclined to narrate it at length. Later, Chandra narrated this heartwarming story:

> The day had been fixed for the kumbhabhishekam or consecration of the temple. One day, after visiting the temple to observe the progress towards its completion, the king, Rajasimhendravarman, went to bed, tired. That night he had a perplexing and curious dream. Lord Shiva appeared in his dream and told him that he wouldn't be able to make it to the consecration of the temple on the auspicious date that had been fixed. The reason was that he had to be present at the consecration of a temple built by his devotee Poosalaar of Thiruninravur. The king was surprised and intrigued. Wanting to know more about this Shiva bhakta and his temple, he set off with his queen and a retinue of ministers and other followers to see the shrine. On reaching Thiruninravur, he asked the people of the town about a new Shiva temple built by Poosalaar. No one knew anything. However, the people showed him the place where Poosalaar was meditating under the Iruppai tree. Seeing no signs of a temple anywhere, the king asked Poosalaar about it and also told him about his dream. Deeply moved by Shiva's love and grace, Poosalaar explained that he had been erecting the temple in his heart. He showed the king the image of this temple in his heart. This unique and beautiful devotion of Poosalaar motivated the king to build a temple here, called Manakkoil, according to Poosalaar's specific detailed vision of it. Lord Shiva is worshipped there as Hridayaleeswarar -- one who is enshrined in the hridayam.

As we climbed a short flight of steps to enter the front temple, the priest explained that it had been built by Mahendravarman III, Rajasimha's son. Inside, it was dark and suffocating. On the south wall of the narrow front hall, is an impressive image of Shiva as Bhikshatana, over eight feet high. On the north wall, Shiva performs *the samhara tandava,* the dance of destruction. In the centre of the sanctum, Shiva is enshrined as a fluted lingam with eight faces. On the back wall, a sculpture of Somaskanda is dimly visible.

As we stepped out of the front temple into the *prakaram* or the enclosure with cell shrines, the priest told us about the stones used in this temple. Granite was used in the foundation and some parts of the lower walls to give it strength but wasn't used elsewhere because, in the Megalithic period, it was conventionally used for funerary monuments. Hence it was not considered auspicious for temple sculptures. Instead sandstone was used. It also lends itself more easily to sculpting.

For the first half hour, we were the only visitors to the temple. I wanted to spend a lot of time looking at the sandstone sculptures in the fifty-eight smaller shrines or *devakulika*s along the outer ambulatory passage. Many of them have recessed seats for contemplation or meditation. All of them are supported by four pillars and most of them have squatting lions, with bared teeth and bulging eyes, at their bases. One can still see traces of the former frescoes on some of the walls of these shrines. The fragmentary traces of colour are pleasant and still beautiful.

The temple priest followed us as we tried to identify some of the sculptures. He gave the impression of knowing a lot about the temple but seemed reluctant to divulge information about it and only gave piecemeal fragmentary inputs about some of the sculptures. Before we went into the sanctum sanctorum, he pointed out some of the sculptures to us. Some of them are very dynamic, full of movement and a lively vigorous narrative. The sculpture of the Narasimha avatar with his muscular body and mouth open in a ferocious roar is fear-inspiring. About to destroy Hiranyakasyapu, he is full of demonic energy.

The priest pointed out Shiva, as the hunter Kirata, and Arjuna to us. It is a dramatic sculpture. We see them in readiness for combat, gearing up for a prolonged fight over a wild boar that both of them have killed at the same time. The wild boar can be seen behind Arjuna's left leg. With martial alertness, Arjuna is getting ready to shoot an arrow. Although both Shiva as Kirata and Arjuna face us, the way they stand in tense alertness for a duel and the way their arms reach out for their respective weapons, makes this panel very eloquent in its narrative.

In contrast to action-packed sculptures, there is one of Devi in *dhyanam* or Devi doing *tapasya*. Sculptures of Shiva with Parvati described as Umasahitamurti are images of calm and beautiful stillness. Somaskandamurti is one of happy domestic togetherness.

I looked at the sculptures erratically, flitting from one to the other, because I was concerned that the others would be in a hurry to move on to some other temple. Within a few minutes, the priest insisted that we go into the sanctum sanctorum. He said that he would tell us more about the sculptures and the temple after our *darshan* of Kailasanatha. The last time we had been there in the inner hall before the main shrine, there had been no electricity and I had seen the Shiva lingam in the light of the oil lamps which had heightened the numinous mystery of the ancient interior. In the flickering uncertain light of the lamps, the divine had seemed more palpably present, more tangibly enshrined.

On the wall behind the large black granite lingam, illuminated by the light of the brass oil lamps and the artificial light before the threshold of the *garbha griha*, I could see the stone sculpture of Shiva and Parvati. The priest spoke of a narrow ambulatory passage around the sanctum. He persuaded us to enter that passage, walk it and come out of it. Quoting from Adi Shankaracharya's composition *Bhaja Govindam,* traversing the passage had deep metaphysical significance, he explained. After reciting the opening stanza, *Bhaja Govindam, Bhaja Govindam mudhemate...,* he quoted the twenty-first stanza to explain the symbolic meaning of walking the enclosed passage around the *sannidhi*:

punarapi jananam punarapi maranam
punarapi janani jathre shayanam
iha samsare bahudustaare
krypaya pare pahi murare

We are trapped in the cycle of life and death: We are born again, die again, and once again we enter the mother's womb to be born yet another time. It is very hard to go across this ocean of samsara. Oh Murari, Oh Krishna, have mercy on me, save me.

Hence entering the narrow passage is like re-entering the mother's womb after having gone through death. Coming out of it successfully is like being born into new life—it stands for salvation from the repetitive cycle of endless births and deaths.

One had to enter the passage through a narrow aperture in the wall, crawl a little before one could place one's feet on the floor of the passage and stand. Fearful of getting stuck, Ravi was clear that he wasn't going to attempt it since he is tall and broad. He also hates confined spaces. The three of us went ahead: Subhadra, Divya and I. The passage was cool and dank and its narrowness didn't bother me. In less than fifteen seconds we were at the entry to the very short exit tunnel through which one had to crawl on one's belly to emerge. It could be suffocatingly small or confining if one panicked. I noticed another possibility for an exit, for those who could be squeamish at the last minute and feel claustrophobic at the mere thought of sliding or scrambling forward on one's stomach to get out. Three or four steps led up to a narrow ledge and then the same number of steps down and you would be at the threshold of the sanctum. Going through the passage was a fairly simple exercise. I wish the exit from the bondage of karma, or release from mortality, or deliverance from the cycle of birth and death, was equally simple.

The priest was waiting to give us the *prasadam*. Chandra and Subhadra placed some money in the *aarati* tray. Although they had left a handsome offering, he seemed disappointed. After coming out into the open ambulatory corridor along the sub-shrines, when we asked him to name some of the sculptures for us, he was unwilling and left us abruptly. A largish group of foreigners, who had walked in at that moment, claimed his attention. He mumbled something about making preparations for the midday puja and asked us to come back at one. I knew that was not going to be possible. We still had to see the Varadarajaswamy Temple and I didn't want to rush through its hundred-pillared *mandapam* with its unique wealth of exquisite carvings. We were now left to figure out the sculptures on our own.

Fortunately, Chandra was there to help us out wherever we faltered or were lost. There was a panel with seven female deities. I asked him who they were. 'They are the saptmatas or saptmatrikas.' He wasn't sure of the order but he told me the names: Brahmani, Vaishnavi, Indrani, Varahi, Kaumari, Maheshwari and Chamunda. There, the first and fifth ones were Brahmani and Varahi—easy to identify. Brahmani has four faces and three faces were visible to us. Varahi, with her boar face, was easy to place as well.

'What do they represent?' I asked Chandra.

'They represent the shakti aspect of Shiva, Indra and the other gods. These deities are destroyers of evil, terrible and fierce in aspect, but in sculptures, such as in this panel, we do not see that aspect of them.'

'Yes, they look benign and regal.'

We didn't have much time, so I couldn't figure out the remaining four. The last one was Chamunda, I assumed. Their faces, eroded by time, were either smoothed out, wiping out the features, or partially damaged. In spite of that, one could feel the life that the sculptor/s had breathed into this panel.

The saptmatrikas are not seated stiffly. With their arms and legs touching or moving into each other's space, their heads with their tall crowns (with the exception of Chamunda) inclining towards each other, their bodies in fluid interaction with each other, they tell a vivid story, impelling us to follow the narrative. They are as graceful and expressive as dancers. Interestingly, Brahmani has her left leg on Vaishnavi's lap. Chamunda's luxurious hair frames her face like a halo. She wears large earrings. In the picture I took, I see her *yajnopavita*. Is it made of skulls strung together, I cannot tell.

We spotted two sculptures that were identical except for minor variations and the difference in size. They showed an attractive mendicant with two small, barely visible fangs. The latter detail perplexed us. I quickly ran through the various forms of Shiva in my mind. 'Is it Bhikshatanamurti, Mr Chandra?' I burst out.

He thought for a bit and said, 'I think you are right. He is naked except for the ornaments around his waist and wears sandals.'

'Why does he have the two small side tusks? It takes away from his beautiful form and makes him look a little bit horrific if one looks too closely.'

'I think they have incorporated an aspect of Shiva as Bhairava into this sculpture.'

'Interesting. I wonder why.'

'I am puzzled too. I think you will have to read something about Shiva as Bhairava and Bhikshatana and the history of Shiva-related iconography to find out.'

The sculpture held our attention. Shiva, seen as a youthful mendicant, has a graceful strapping body with a wide chest and shapely buttocks. His left leg is bent at the knee and the raised sandalled left foot rests on the tip of the sandal to indicate movement, and wanderings of an ascetic. He wears large earrings and his untamed thick hair that looks like overlapping tubes of tightly coiled curls crowns his head and tumbles down to his waist with carefree abundance. With the index finger of his raised left hand he points to something in his hair. Or, is he pointing upwards? I wonder what it means. He carries his meagre belongings on a staff that rests across his right shoulder. Enchanted by his beauty, the rishipatnis who couldn't resist him and followed him, now kneel before him in prayerful adoration. In the upper left corner, a furious rishi raises his fist at the charming ascetic who has corrupted the pure and austere way of life of Darukavana and led the sages' wives astray. With all these elements, this Bhikshatana sculpture has a riveting narrative.

There were other sculptures that we could identify with ease and which claimed our attention. The ten-armed Durga brandishing many arms of destruction is an elegant, powerful warrior. With her left foot placed majestically on the prone vanquished figure of Mahisha, carved in low-relief in the flanks of her lion *vahana* with bared teeth, and her right hip jutting out attractively, she combines feminine grace with invincible energy. There was an impressive panel, which showed the diminutive Vamana avatar in one corner and Trivikrama in the centre, with his uplifted left leg pointing to the heavens, claiming them, and the right leg claiming the earth in one giant stride. This depiction is a magnificent display of divine power and supremacy made manifest in stone. The Urdhavatandavamurti is a joy to see. A beauteous smile on Shiva's face and Nandi's comic but unrestrained, enthusiastic participation in the *ananda tandava* makes this panel radiate with exuberant energy and vitality. The Lingodbhavamurti isn't very impressive there. Kartikeya as Shanmukha is a stand-alone piece in a niche, possibly in black granite.

I left the temple reasonably happy, yet for some time two regrets accompanied me. The first one was that I hadn't spent as much time there as I would have liked to. I also felt that if we had given the priest more *dakshina,* he may have obliged us with interesting details about the temple as he seemed knowledgeable about the temple's history, its architecture and iconography. The second regret went deeper and troubled me more: I had missed the image of Ardhanareeswara in the temple for the second time. It has Shiva seated on a bull while Shakti plays the veena. At this temple, I had neither been able to buy the *panchloha* statuette nor had I been able to see the same image enshrined in stone. *Prarabdha*?

Simhachalam

The Mahashivaratri of 2008, which fell on 6 March, found the three of us—Ravi, Chandra and I—in Vishakahpatnam.

We woke up to a glorious morning at the SAIL guest house. To experience the grass, trees, flowers, a quiet road and fresh air in the morning—what else could one ask for? One is supposed to fast on Shivaratri but we did not observe this rule. Chandra, who is our guide on all these matters, told us that during travel the religious fasting injunctions do not apply. Our meagre dinner on the train had left us famished and the three of us were looking forward to a good breakfast. The restaurant was playing Western pop when we entered. Fair enough. On a Shivaratri morning, Ravi and Chandra found it unacceptable. The waiters had a tough time fiddling and fumbling with World Space radio to get the Carnatic music channel. They had never had such a request before and looked confused and startled. Sruti, the Carnatic music channel, had a Shivaratri special and it was a treat, beginning with *Chandrasekhara* in Raga Sindu Bhairavi and Swami Dayanand Saraswati's composition, *Om Shambho, Shiva Shambho*. At this point the conversation moved to devotion and faith and how powerful a force bhakti is. Chandra told us a story connected with Muthuswamy Dikshitar's *kriti* in Raga Anandamritavarshini. A certain village suffered drought for two to three years, bringing great misery in its wake. The villagers were desperate for relief. Muthuswamy Dikshitar created a composition in this raga to pray for rain. All the villagers had gathered to hear this remarkable musical appeal but just one small boy among them carried an umbrella. Such was his spontaneous faith in the fervent plea and in God's grace.

The long thick curtains in the restaurant remained drawn across the large glass windows, blocking out daylight completely. Dimly-lit with concealed cold blue lights, the place looked dingy and felt enclosed on a bright, pleasant morning. I have never been able to understand this penchant for creating a claustrophobic and artificial atmosphere even in the midst of pleasing natural surroundings in the mistaken belief that people are creating romantic and private spaces. The first thing I did before sitting down was to draw the curtains aside and allow the room to take in the morning light. For the next six days there, I did this every morning because something in me felt sick and gloomy looking at that space, unhallowed by the sun. None of the other guests seemed to care or even notice. Ravi approved of my need for natural light and my need to enjoy the greenery while eating but also felt that I was over-sensitive to atmosphere in temporary spaces, where my stay was very transient.

The room resonated with Carnatic music. Sunlight settled into the room, touched the edge of the drab tablecloth, gilded the cutlery, burnished the glassware—after this I was ready for breakfast. I had asked for uttapam whereas Ravi and Chandra were going to have idlis and *upma*. The uttapam came and I looked at it doubtfully. It was way too thick and as large as the dinner plate. I nibbled at a bit of it with great difficulty and couldn't touch any more of it. It was underdone, dense, with the raw taste of unleavened batter. The sambhar tasted heavily of garlic. I pushed my plate away distastefully and wondered whether I was being chastised for craving for food on Shivaratri morning. Ravi looked at me quizzically, understood that I didn't like my dish and shared his steaming-hot freshly-made *upma* with me. I thought to myself with amusement, 'Since I have already transgressed by longing for food, might as well go the whole way and indulge my desire.'

The plan for the day was to go to Simhachalam, approximately fifteen kilometres from Vizag. The temple here, located 800 feet above sea level on a hill, is dedicated to Vishnu as Lord Narasimha. A guide would accompany us. He told us that the temple had been built in the ninth or tenth century. Major additions were made to it in the thirteenth century by King Narasimha I, the Eastern Ganga ruler of Kalinga. The temple's architecture is a combination of the Chalukya and Chola styles and is also reminiscent of Konarak's Sun temple.

We took National Highway 5 which goes towards Bhubaneshwar and Cuttack. Along the way, the guide told us the many names of Vishakhapatnam. He seemed to be good at information that any foreign tourist would love to have. It was bookish knowledge that he hadn't bothered to improve on through observation and personal experience. When we reached the foot of Simhachalam or Lion's Hill, he asked us to pray before the small shrine of Sri Varaha Lakshmi Narasimhaswamy before going up the hill. For those who wish to walk, they have to climb a thousand steps to get to the temple. In the early afternoon it was bright and hot. The idol here is painted blue and encased partly in thick transparent plastic. The entire protective covering gives the impression of a lingam. The small standing deity has the face of a boar, the torso and tail of a lion and the rest of the body is that of a man. It combines the two avatars of Vishnu, Varaha and Narasimha, boar and man-lion. I wondered why.

The place was full of flies and the floor sticky under the feet. A college student came in, took out her exam hall ticket from a small handbag, placed it near the flowers offered to the deity, prayed earnestly for a minute and then retrieved the exam entry ticket, which had apparently been blessed. Faith. Simple. Spontaneous. Submission. Unquestioning. Faith's different faces and expressions never cease to amaze me. Some instances of faith are charming and full of a wide-eyed innocence; others are desperate appeals for help; while others seem like persistence in folly and misplaced hope; there are some others which look like blatant uninhibited bargaining with the divine for grace and material goods.

I was curious about the *sthalapuranam* of the temple and wished to know the story before we saw the actual temple. I narrate the guide's story in my own words:

> The creation of the temple has to do with the story of Prahlada and Hiranyakashipu. Prahlada was a great bhakta of Narayana. This angered Hiranyakashipu, his father, because Narayana as Sri Varaha Swamy had killed his brother Hiranyaksha. He perceived his own son as his enemy when he saw his unfaltering love for Narayana. He decided to kill his son and made several futile attempts to do so with the help of his ruthless cohorts. Each time Prahlada was saved miraculously by the grace of Narayana. He threw his son to the ground from a hill and then placed the hill over his head to destroy him completely. On seeing his devotee's plight, Lord Vishnu went to his rescue, moved the hill a bit and created a safe path for him. It is said that the place where Sri Vishnu stood to protect his devotee, is the spot where Prahlada created and dedicated a shrine to Vishnu.

> In the form of Narasimha, Sri Vishnu killed Hiranyakashipu. After ridding the world of this asura, who was a cruel and jealous father, the Lord went and sat on Hiranyakashipu's throne. His angry form inspired fear in everyone. No one dared to go close to him, neither the devas, nor Brahma; not even Lakshmi. Long after the killing, Lord Narasimha's anger raged unchecked. This caused a great upheaval in the heavens, on earth, and in the nether world. The earth was traumatized by his wrath. The devas appealed to Lakshmi to appease his wrath but she feared to go near him when he was in that wrathful state. Seeing Lakshmi's helplessness, Brahma went to Prahlada and sought his help in calming the Lord's anger. He knew that if the Lord's fury did not subside, it would not augur well for the world and the heavens. Prahalada went near Narasimha and fell at his beloved Lord's feet. As Lord Narasimha placed his hand on his young bhakta's head, Prahalada's entire being was filled with great joy and the glory of the Lord was revealed to him. He began to sing his praises. He begged him to renounce his anger and asked for this boon, that his form should reside in his heart forever. Pleased with his bhakta's steadfast devotion and tender appeal, Narasimha became a shantamurti. Encouraged by this transformation of the Lord's terrible form into a peaceful and benign one, everyone ventured near and sang his praises. Lakshmi came and sat by his side and he became Lakshmi-Narasimha.

'It is a beautiful story with a beautiful assurance—God is moved by bhakti.'

Prahlada worshipped Narasimha at the spot where the Lord had rescued him from under the hill. He expressed a wish that he should see both the Varaha and Narasimha avatars of Narayana in one single form. The Lord granted his wish. Prahlada created a shrine and worshipped his Lord as Sri Varaha Lakshmi-Narasimhaswamy. That is why the deity has the face of a boar, the torso and tail of a lion, and the form of a man waist downwards.

In the ages that followed, this temple gradually lost its original significance and fell into a state of neglect and disrepair. A second story associated with the temple shows how the temple was re-discovered and re-instated as a powerful place of worship.

In the Chandra Vamsa, there was a handsome and noble king called Pururavas. He fell in love with the divine dancer Uravashi and married her. After spending several blissful years in heavenly gardens and on Mount Kailasha, Pururavas and Uravashi moved south in his Pushpaka vimana or aerial chariot. They landed on the Simhadri hill, verdant and beautiful. Here, Uravashi recalled that she had been to this hill earlier when Lord Vishnu had taken the form of Narasimha to save Prahalada. She felt that the temple which was no longer visible must be hidden somewhere and they should make an attempt to discover the shrine. Pururavas decided to do *tapasya* or penance in order to be blessed with a vision of the Lord. The Lord appeared to him in his dream and told him that the idol was buried under an ant hill in front of him. While he was removing the earth that had covered the idol, he heard a voice from the heavens which told him to cover the discovered idol with sandal paste as it was too *ugra* (fierce) to be exposed without a soothing, cooling covering. Henceforth the Lord would be worshipped only in this form. Only once a year, on the third day of Visakha, the devotees could have *darshan* of the original form of the deity.

The hill road to the temple was lovely, with lots of vegetation. The cashew and champa trees were in full bloom. On the way we got off the car to look at the sacred bathing tank, *Pushkarini*, which is some distance from the foot of the hill. Skirted by palms and other trees, it looked untainted and lovely from that height and distance. We picked up a tulasi garland, a coconut and a small strand of peach orange champa blossoms to offer to the deity. It was the first time I had seen orange champa flowers and it made my day. The orange of the champa was delicate and charming and the flowers left a gentle lingering perfume on my hands.

After climbing a steep flight of steps that lead to the northern gateway of the temple, we headed first for the *kalyana mandapam* with its ninety-six pillars. Each pillar was unique in its decorations, motifs and bas-reliefs. The variety of ornamentation on these pillars was a rich feast for the eyes. One of them had a ring of elephants in a frontal view with elegantly curving trunks. Another had several animals like a horse, peacock, a lion and others, as a decorative motif. Pearls, ornate leaves and vines also adorned the pillars. There were musicians with different instruments, like the mridangam, trumpet, flute, forming a circular band around another pillar. There were lions with stiff raised tails at the corners of one pillar—two bodies with a single head. One pillar had a rolypoly four-armed Nritya Ganapati with *shankha* and chakra in his two hands at the back. One hand held the tip of his trunk; the other was in the *varada mudra*. There was a staff behind him with a snake coiled around it.

We came out of the sanctum sanctorum to find a crowd around one of the pillars in the *mukhamandapam*. It is called the *kappastambham*. The guide told us that if a childless couple embraced that pillar they would be blessed with a child. He added, 'Other wishes will also be fulfilled. Do you want to embrace it?' He looked earnest when he said this but Ravi and I were both wary of that suggestion. The idea didn't appeal to us. The couple embracing the pillar at that moment looked rather comical and I was instantly ashamed of my irreverence. The pillar was draped in silk saris, purple, orange, peacock blue, tied in such a way that they billowed out like long skirts; it was decorated with tulasi garlands and artificial kanakambaram ones. While this dressing up of the pillar splashed some colour on the pale grey stone, it also made it look ludicrous.

The outer walls and the *vimana* or tower of the main temple are rich in sculptures, bas-reliefs, and mythic stories depicted in great detail in stone. At the base of the *vimana,* and just above the prodigally ornate eaves of the main temple roof, stories from the life of Krishna are depicted in meticulous detail in stone. These miniature sculpted stories are located just below the wide fanged mouth of a rakshasa-like lion's face. With their hideous tongues, round popping-out eyes and angry flaring nostrils, these demonic lion faces provide a lively and conspicuous contrast to the life of Krishna illustrated below them. With my glasses meant only for reading, I had a tough time peering at the sculpted narration to identify the stories. The stories I could make out were: Vasudeva braves the waters of the swollen Yamuna to save Krishna from Kamsa's wrath and takes him to Gokula; Krishna sucks the life-force out of Putana, the dreadful asura woman; Krishna as a baby on a banyan leaf; Krishna as the adorable unrepentant butter-thief; Krishna tied to a mortar as punishment by Yashoda, crawls out and drags the mortar, encircles the two Arjuna trees with the rope and brings them down with a resounding crash, thus releasing the two sons of Kubera trapped there; Krishna subdues Kaliya, the four-headed serpent; Krishna as the enchanting flutist; Krishna holds the Govardhana hill in hand like an umbrella to shield the people and cows and calves of Brindavan from torrential rain, the result of Indra's anger; Krishna answers Rukmini's prayer; Rukmini *kalyanam*; the Jambavan story; Satyabhama's arrogance and the *tulabharam*.

The *ashtadikkapalakas* or the guardian-deities of the eight directions are also represented here on the tower at another level.

Since I had no idea which deity guards which direction and what their attributes and mounts are, it was a mini lesson in mythology for me. That Yama is associated with the south was all that I knew.

There is an impressive niche sculpture of a standing Lord Narasimha on one of the outer walls of the sanctum sanctorum. A figure with four arms, he is fear-inspiring. His lion's head is framed by a handsome halo-like mane. Out of a mouth opened in a blood-curdling roar, his tongue hangs out ominously. In the two upper arms he holds a conch and a *ghatyam*. On his raised left thigh rests the body of Hiranyakashipu who seems very small, weak and helpless, compared to mighty Narasimha, with a large chest and a slender waist. The asura's legs and head dangle helplessly on either side of Narasimha's left thigh like an inverted limp U. The towering figure of Narasimha, fierce and focused, digs his deadly nails into the abdomen of the asura. They tear open his flesh and dig into the entrails. It is ghastly and terrifying, and would have made me feel fearful if I didn't know that this is Sri Vishnu himself in his *ugra* form. Just below this panel are three seated figures, praying to the Lord. One of the supplicating figures could be that of Prahalada.

Just above this sculpture of Narasimha is the figure of Krishna as Kaliyanartana.

On either side of Narasimha, lions squatting on elephants were depicted on pillars. Their shapely plump behinds rest on the heads of the elephants, which dig their forepaws into the wall and grip it tenaciously. In a spectacular acrobatic-yogic feat, the lions throw their heads back over their shoulders, arching down halfway to look angrily at the overpowered elephants below. This motif of the lion overcoming the elephant is repeated elsewhere on the temple pillars with slight variations. Our guide told us that the lion represents Hinduism and the elephant represents Buddhism, which was suppressed by the more strident Hinduism. He added that this motif could also signify the suppression or overcoming of the ego by the higher consciousness. Whatever it meant, visually it had a dramatic impact.

We went back to the *kalyana mandapam*. A lot more people had gathered there, seeking respite from the afternoon heat. They were eating the *prasadam*, chatting, sprawling, reclining, resting, enjoying a mini picnic or sharing some family gossip or concerns. Many of them were breaking the second half of the coconuts they had received as *prasadam*, so the floor was sticky and full of coconut shell pieces and splinters. I frowned at this messing up of the temple premises. The *mandapam* had begun to look like a choultry.

At the other end of the *kalyana mandapam*, a hollow wooden lion stood upright on its hind legs. It was tied to a pillar for support. A dusty pink body, a fierce black mane, a valiant moustache, large popping out eyes, made it look comically fearsome. On each of its exposed pointed teeth, people had written their names and, on its body, someone had inscribed 'Shiva'. It was amusing and curious to see people's need to put their personal stamp on such an unlikely spot as a lion's fangs. This lion which looked more like a demon had mutely accepted its defacement. With this funny image in my mind to add to other impressions of this temple, we walked out to look for a snack somewhere.

Pithapuram

The next day when we were heading towards Kakinada for lunch, Ravi suddenly suggested that we should see the Kukkuteswara Swamy temple in Pithapuram. This temple is also one of the eighteen shakti peethas. Here, shakti is known as Puruhutika Devi. The previous year, in January, before catching the train from Kakinada for Hyderabad, we had stopped by there very briefly. Even though the *darshan* of the deities, Shiva as Kukkuteswaraswamy, Sri Dattatreya and Puruhutika Devi, had been easy and unhindered, the visit had left me dissatisfied. For no good reason at all, there was a sense of an incomplete and hurried visit. Hence I was glad to have an unexpected second chance.

Off the highway, towards Kakinada, it was pleasant to see the different colours of green—the dark sober green of the casuarina groves, the fresh green of the young sugarcane and (after the village of Varkalapudi) the alive, surging-with-new-life green of the field after field of paddy.

Before we reached Pithapuram, Chandra told us the story of Mukkur Lakshmi Narasimhacharya of Kakinada. A recollection of our previous day's visit to Simhachalam led to this. Chandra narrated:

> He was an orthodox Iyengar Brahmin from Chennai and a great Narasimhaswamy upasaka or devotee. He had performed 107 Narasimhaswamy yagnas. As he felt that he did not have the divine permission to perform the 108th one, he began to perform a series of yagnas under the penultimate one: 107 (a), 107 (b) and so on. As a result of his passionate and unswerving devotion, towards the end of his life, he himself had begun to look like the deity he invoked and worshipped—very red-faced, with two protruding teeth on either side. He went to live in Kakinada on the request of a rich man who had a daughter who was supposedly possessed by a spirit. The rich man sought the help of the orthodox Brahmin to free his daughter from the spell of that disagreeable spirit. During one of the *homams* for that purpose, Narasimhacharya managed to rid her of that obstinate spirit. While he was trying to do that, under the influence of the powerful spirit, the young woman lifted him and tried to hurl him to the ground. He managed to overwhelm the beastly spirit inside her and cast it out of her.

The narration of this unusual story made me feel a bit uneasy and I said that I preferred the benign forms of the gods to their fierce ones. At this point Chandra mentioned totally out of the blue that Lord Narasimha's *nakshatra* or star was Swati.

'That's my star,' I exclaimed, not too pleased. Chandra laughed.

'I am going to think of Yoga Narasimha whenever I think of him. I prefer his deeply meditative state although poor Prahalada couldn't have been saved if he hadn't appeared in the fear-inspiring half-man half-lion form that he did. I think there is a shrine dedicated to Yoga Narasimha in the Varadarajaswamy temple.'

Chandra asked, 'Do you know how Lord Narasimha became a shantamurti after his *ugra* or terrible and fierce form?'

'I know the sandalwood paste bit after our Simhachalam visit.'

We entered Pithapuram around one, and lost our way in the narrow streets because we were misdirected. The clogged open drains and the wandering muck-coated fat pigs left a very unpleasant impression of that town. We had forgotten the way to the temple although we had visited it a year back. Finally, we stopped near some ashram gate to ask the way from a bunch of scraggy-looking rickshaw pullers. Ravi explained in Telugu that he was looking for a Shiva kshetram, a dattapeetham, an *ammavaru gudi* or a Devi temple with a large temple *koneru* or tank. They consulted each other, looked lost, gave contradictory confusing directions and tapped on the window glass churlishly when we refused to trust their information. 'They are completely drunk, Ravi, don't you see? No point in asking them,' I said. Their bloodshot bleary eyes, tired and encrusted, their unfocused slurred responses, their teetering footsteps were ample proof but Ravi hadn't registered.

Finding our way back to the main road, we managed to get long-winded directions to the temple. It was the day of the weekly market and the half-kuccha half-pukka road to the temple was lined on either side with temporary little shops, handcarts or a plastic sheet spread on the earth with a variety of goods. The fluorescent colours of the plastic toys dazzled you in that heat. A lot of sweets were displayed uncovered. The flies had a field day on the *khaja* and the huge pile of sticky dates. Their raid would go on uninterrupted.

Outside the temple wall, lay a pile of discarded damp dirty clothes. A religious ceremony was coming to an end inside the temple and the loudspeaker was blaring out the chanting of the mantras in a choppy head-splicing manner. The loud sound had begun to hammer my head and I could feel a headache building up. After ten minutes, when the loudspeaker fell silent, I breathed a sigh of relief. We looked for someone who would help us with the *darshanam* and tell us more about the temple's significance although Ravi and Chandra were already familiar with the *sthalapuranam*.

The lingam inside the sanctum sanctorum was covered with protective silver plates, ornaments, and had a silver face mask. The shrine room had a smooth dark floor and speckled deep brown granite walls. The tube light facing us was off but the other two on the side walls were lit. A spotlight high up above the doorway of the *ardha mandapam*, where we stood, fell on the lingam. A moving ceiling fan sliced the light as it turned, creating a distraction. The mounting heat, the well-lit sanctum, the effect of the ceiling fan interrupting the steady flow of light was not the best physical environment for even a short prayer. Glossy granite walls, smooth floor, tube lights—in an attempt to modernize things, cut costs, and facilitate convenience, I felt that a traditional atmosphere was being thoughtlessly sacrificed.

The uncompromising need to create and maintain a sense of the sacred while renovating and preserving an old temple has either become weak or non-existent. In some cases the renovation work is done by those who believe either in cutting corners or choose to be illiterate in the time-honoured ways of creating temples and shrines. Apart from dedicated research, all this needs a deep comprehension of sacred spaces and the architectural and metaphysical doctrines that dictate the way it should be done. I was thinking of all this while the priest narrated the Gayasura rakshasa story. My thoughts preoccupied me and there were gaps in my understanding of that story. I felt the need to look up the Vishnu Purana to get the details right. The priest raced through the story:

> There was a demon called Gayasura who had become very powerful because of his rigorous *tapasya*. The gods and the demi-gods feared him and the powers he had acquired. They went to Vishnu for help. Vishnu appeared before Gayasura and expressed a desire to perform a yagna on his body since the gods and rishis were looking for a spot that would not be subject to tremors like the earth is. He agreed but asked for three boons in return. The first one was that the places where his body rested would become *teerthas* or places of pilgrimage. Vishnu agreed. Brahma, Vishnu and Shiva, in the form of rishis, started the yagna on his prostrate body. So massive was Gayasura's form that his head was in Gaya in Bihar and his legs reached Pithapuram. Hence the lake or the temple tank where his feet reached is called Padagaya. The sacrifice would take seven days and seven nights. In order to curb the power of Gayasura, Shiva played a trick on him. Before the dawn of the seventh day, he took the form of a cock and crowed. Thinking that it was daybreak, Gayasura rose, breaking the continuity of the religious sacrifice and ceremony. As Shiva took the form of a cock, he is worshipped as Kukkuteswaraswamy (*kukkuta* means cock in Telugu) in Pithapuram. The lingam is a swayambhu lingam (self-manifest) and it is shaped like the back of a cock.

As we neared the Dattatreya shrine, the priest told us that Pithapuram was the birthplace of Sripada Sri Vallabhaswami, an incarnation of Dattatreya. The shrine has brown granite walls and a small tower which is painted orange. The use of shiny granite and the orange colour outside undermined the sense of sacred mystery. It was redeemed by the black stone three-faced *murti* of Dattatreya inside. The attimaram (medi chettu) or the fig tree here has three large trunks merging into a single tree. The number three is significant because Dattatreya has three faces; he incorporates in himself the attributes of Brahma, Vishnu and Shiva. (I didn't know this as I didn't know the story of Dattatreya.) The tree is called the audumbura or wish-fulfilling tree since it grants the prayers and sincere wishes of the devotees. Women with menstrual or gynecological problems go there to seek help for their suffering.

The priest gave me a flower called nagamalli, mallikarjuna or the Shivalinga flower to offer at the feet of Sri Dattatreya. He lifted the central part of the flower a little bit to show me something that looked like a miniature Shivalingam. As I placed the flower on the divine feet, the priest said in Telugu, '*Ee puvvu Swami ki chala preeti*'. This flower is dear to Sri Dattatreya. The word that he used to say that Swami was fond of the flower was '*preeti*'. I took it as a sign that my offering had been accepted.

Before we moved on to see the shrine of Puruhutika Devi, I asked Ravi to tell me the story of Dattatreya.

The little enclosure which has the shrine of Puruhutika Devi was under renovation. The earlier floor tiles had been peeled off completely. As we entered the enclosure the priest accompanying us chanted the shlokas by Adi Shankaracharya which mention the eighteen Shakti peethas:

Lankayan Shankari devi, Kamakshi Kanchika pure
Pradyumne Shrinkhala devi, Chamunda Krouncha pattane...

Puruhutika Devi was gorgeously adorned in ornaments and beautiful silks. She is a radiantly beautiful deity with a sword, a shield, madiphala and *amrita kalasam* in her hands. This idol was installed by the present Kanchi Shankaracharya some years back.

We sat on the steps of the shrine while Ravi told me the story of how the Shakti peethas came into existence. I knew the first half but not the second half:

> 'Daksha Prajapati, the father of Sati, made preparations for a yagna to which neither his daughter Sati nor his son-in-law Shiva were invited. Sati insisted on attending this religious ceremony because daughters don't need formal invitations to visit their father and participate in events such as that one. When she got there she was not welcomed. She soon realized that her father had deliberately excluded Shiva from the yagna. Feeling insulted and angry, she jumped into the sacred fire to pollute it and prevent the completion of the ritual. The fire god Agni refused to harm her. So great was Sati's fury and sense of humiliation that she used the fire within to burn herself. (I knew the story till this point.) When Shiva heard of Sati's death, he created a fearsome warrior called Virabhadra and sent him along with his ghastly army to destroy Daksha's sacrifice and create bloody havoc in that sacred space. After that gruesome episode of death and destruction, Shiva picked up the burnt body of Sati and wandered around the world consumed by grief. Looking at Shiva's agony and suffering which knew no bounds, Vishnu feared that the order of the world would soon be affected adversely. He used his *sudarshan chakra* or the serrated discus at that point to restore Shiva's balance and composure. When he flung it, it cut Sati's body into eighteen pieces. With the body gone, Shiva regained his balance and serenity. Each spot, at which a certain part of Sati's body fell, has become a Shakti peetha.'

Along the outer face of the wall of the shrine of Puruhutika Devi were pictures of the goddess in the remaining seventeen Shakti peethas. It started with Shankari Devi in Sri Lanka and ended with Saraswati Devi in Kashmir. I looked at Jogulambadevi at Alampur in Andhra Pradesh (my state) and decided that I was not going to see that terrifying aspect of the goddess. While I was noting down the names of the Shakti peethas, I smelt something foul in the air. Just as I was wondering what it could be, Chandra walked up to me and said, 'Don't you smell cooking gas in the air?' 'Yes, that's what it is. Do you think there is a gas leak somewhere?' We stepped out of the enclosure and Chandra quickly approached two people and asked them to check if there was a gas leak from the house or office adjoining the temple. They rushed in to check and told us that one of the temple cooks had forgotten to turn off one switch of the gas stove. A major mishap had been averted. I was horrified at the callous neglect of basic safety precautions in a public place where people congregate in large numbers, especially on a day of festivities and large religious ceremonies.

My headache had become worse. Afraid of the onset of a vicious migraine, I was ready to go.

On our way out, we stopped by the temple tank where a young man was scrubbing his feet vigorously against the stone steps and then soaking his feet in the water to wash off the dirt. At that moment Ravi asked me if I had sprinkled the holy water on my head. I did not respond but winced distastefully at the suggestion. My faith faltered. I took a picture of the tank and was just about to walk out through the main entrance when a poor boy in his teens rushed up to me and gestured excitedly that he wanted his picture taken. He posed before the shrine by the temple tank. His old baggy trousers were gathered at the waist and his dirty discoloured shirt was rolled up at the cuffs showing his thin sun-burnt forearms. The top button of his shirt was open, revealing his slender neck and collar bones. He pushed the open collar back from his neck, stylishly adjusted the thin handloom towel over his shoulders like a scarf, clasped his hands in front of him, smiled a carefree bright smile and posed unselfconsciously, jauntily, for a picture. It was all over in less than half a minute and then he was gone after giving me a quick charming smile. He looked thrilled. I was puzzled. What did that moment mean to him? I would never be able to give him his photograph. He would never know how he looked there. Then why was he keen to have his picture taken? Was the moment's pleasure enough for him? In his own eyes he was perhaps a minor celebrity for that passing moment. If I had taken his address (assuming there was a postal address) and offered to mail the photograph to him, the mystery and delight of that moment would have been diluted by that practical consideration. I look at his picture now and find him good looking because of his smile and his spontaneous pleasure of the moment. I find him attractive...I see him—warm brown smooth skin, round ears jutting out, a well-shaped nose and coal black hair hugging his scalp. A stranger. A picture. A smile. A moment captured. A moment that came and went. A brightness that remains. I wish him well.

Draksharama

After a late lunch in Kakinada we moved towards Draksharama, which is about twenty-eight kilometres from the busy port. It is believed that sage Vyasa installed the Shivalingam there. I had visited this temple town in the year 2000 along with Ravi, Ananda and my father-in-law. At that time, the old temple had been in a sad state of neglect and disrepair. Abandoned by the affluent devotees, it had looked impoverished. I was curious to see the change that had taken place since I had last visited it. Ravi had been there the previous year. Since it had been taken over by the Archeological Survey of India, he felt that it was in much better condition.

About fourteen kilometres away from the temple town, there were paddy fields and more paddy fields. The fresh green carpet of paddy was broken only by border plants, trees, and palms. On the upper reaches of the palm trees, black pots had been tied to collect palm juice that would later be fermented to make toddy, the local alcoholic beverage. While I was looking at the palm trees, Chandra mentioned that cross-pollination is done manually for date palms. This led him to recall a story about the Shaivite saint Tirugnanasambandar, who is associated with the town of Acharapakkam, which is about hundred kilometres from Chennai.

The story goes that the saint came to this town and changed a male date palm to a female date palm.

It was early evening by the time we reached Draksharama. We missed the main entrance or the south entrance to the temple and went through the west entrance with its five or seven-tiered *gopuram*. At the entrance sat a shriveled old beggar with long bony legs, wearing a plastic bag as underwear, the two ends of it held up at the front and back with the help of a cord around the waist. He looked like an unwanted, discarded thing, decrepit and useless. A grievous image of neglect.

As soon as we entered the temple precincts, I was agreeably surprised. There was grass, lots of flowers and plants. However, some of these green areas were inaccessible to the public—wire fencing was in place. It looked reasonably clean and pleasant unlike the previous time when I had gone away feeling miserable that such an old temple was uncared for. We looked around for a priest who would be able to tell us the *sthalapurana* and the significance of the temple. We found someone who was in a major hurry and wanted to breathlessly hurtle through the stories and rush us through the visit. We had to slow him down.

He began in Telugu and this is what I gathered:

> The eastern Chalukyan king of Vengi built the temple during very turbulent times in the ninth and tenth centuries. Draksharama has come from the two words 'Daksha' and '*arama*', or the garden of Dakshaprajapati. According to legend, Daksha had performed his yagna in this place. In this temple, Lord Shiva is worshipped in Lingakara. The limestone lingam is a cylindrical pillar, 20 or 25 feet high. It is believed that it is part of an original lingam that broke into five pieces and fell at five different places or *aramas*—Bheemarama or Bheemavaram in Kakinada, Ksheerarama or Palakollu in West Godavari, Amararama or Amaravati in Guntur, Kurmarama or Kotipalli in East Godavari and Draksharama.

The lingam, which broke into five pieces, was put in place by the Sun God and worshipped by the seven rishis, who are present as the seven branches of the Godavari as it flows towards the sea.

Lord Shiva as Bhimeshwara Swami, manifested himself as a lingam in the Saptgodavari. On seeing Lord Shiva, the sapt rishis went to the Godavari to bring its waters to perform *abhishekam* to the lord before sunrise. On their way back to Draksharama, Tulya Maharishi who was performing a yagna, stopped them. He was afraid that the waters of the Godavari would wash away his ashram and the sacrificial spot. The sapt ṛishis and Tulya Maharishi began to argue with each other about their respective needs. Since they couldn't resolve their quarrel, Vyasa stepped in and told them that the waters of the Saptgodavari would flow under the earth as *antar vahini* to Draksharama, emerging as the *Saptgodavari Pushkarini Teertha*. The water from this *teertha* could be used for Lord Shiva's *abhishekam*. The sun rose before the rishis could arrive at Draksharama, hence the Sun God himself came and performed the first *archana* to Lord Bhimeshwara.

After listening to the *sthalapurana*, we walked along the outer *prakaram*. The loudspeaker, which was giving out light devotional music at full blast, was an irritant in the peaceful surroundings. It rent the air, overwhelming and drowning the serenity of the place. '*Ma tandri Sreenivasa, ma tandri Venkatesa*' failed to evoke any feeling of bhakti in us. Ravi asked me to ignore the shallow music. Stopping at the Kalabhairava shrine, which faced south, I noticed that there were eight lingams there with the offering of kumkum, one of them with a broken *avudaiyar*.

The peepul tree was massive. Its leaves, dusty and punched with holes, looked weary. On the large stone around the tree, there were several entwined naga bas-reliefs on stone. Several piles of small flat stones surrounded the tree. Chandra told me that these stood for people's wishes for a house. The tree was a shrine – a small idol of Vishnu, a lingam with the Nandi facing it, a *dwarapalaka* and a yogi completed the hallowed spot. The tree itself was Brahma. The divine trinity resided there, still and solemn, moment after moment of each passing year, to give a willing ear to the devotees' prayers. So many soulful prayers and so many earnest wishes had found a home there—a home that could house countless prayers and countless wishes. The tree shrine faced the *Saptgodavari teertha* in the east. Little boys dressed only in shorts played with gleeful abandon in the water.

The priest took us to the south entrance of the temple. At first we stopped before a large sculpture of Ganesha called Boja Ganapati. To the right of the walkway leading to the doorway was a niche sculpture of Nritya Ganapati or Tandava Ganapati—more appealing to me because it had a certain joyous energy and grace. He stood under the boon tree and his hands held the single tusk, the elephant goad, the axe (*parashu*) or the hatchet (*kuthara*). I have no clear memory of this.

As soon as we entered the inner *prakaram*, we first paid our obeisance to Sri Lakshmi Narayanaswamy, the *kshetrapalaka* of the temple. The two-tiered pillared corridor that runs along the four sides of the inner *prakaram* has little shrines, idols and stone sculptures of various deities: Sri Virupaksha Swamy and Rajarajeshwari, Nataraja, Saptmatrikas, Subramanya Swamy, Bala Bhimeshwara Swamy, the ashtabhuja Mahishasuramardini and others that we would see later. In the southwest corner of the inner courtyard, a miniature stone model of the temple had some white powder sprinkled around it. It didn't smell good. We asked the priest what is was. He said it was bleaching powder. It was being used to remove the oil stains. The temple funds' endowments officer was coming the next day to inspect the premises. Hence a large-scale, vigorous cleaning operation was in progress with water pipes, buckets, brooms everywhere and a generous use of detergent and other cleaning agents. There was water everywhere—little shallow puddles and very wet stone floors. We stepped gingerly. While the place was beginning to have a freshly-cleaned look, all the water and all the scrubbing had also washed away the auspicious smells associated with a temple—a unique blend of incense, camphor, oil lamps, the fragrance of flowers and coconut water. Instead, I was taking in something nondescript, with a liberal hint of chemicals in it.

The two-storey sanctum has two flights of steps leading to the upper level. Bhimeshwara is enshrined in the form of a ten-foot-high Shivalingam. We walked around the sanctum at the lower level. There are two ambulatories. The outer one was wet and slippery and dark except for one dim light. As soon as we entered, on the left wall, I discerned protuberances that looked like obstinate eruptions. The priest told us that those spots on the wall had earlier been studded with diamonds. Some invaders and raiders had tried to remove them. When they had tried to yank them out, they turned into stone, and the spots where they once were, now looked like uneven round stony swellings. He wasn't sure who had attacked the temple. He mentioned Mohammed Ghazni, Gauri, the kings of Golconda, all in the same breath. As we walked around, we had to squeeze through the narrow space between the wall and a pillar. This passage is called the *moksha dwara* or the doorway to salvation and the pillar or *stambha* has a guardian called the *stambha purusha*. Here it is Subramanya. The well-built priest with a large belly could go through the narrow passage but Ravi was apprehensive about attempting it. No amount of gentle persuasion or encouragement would make him do it. Chandra laughed, 'This passage is giving us a health message. Keep your body in good form. Then you won't be afraid of getting stuck.'

Ravi ignored this good-humoured chiding and chose the simpler option. He walked through the more spacious passage and stepped out for a breath of fresh air.

As we climbed the stairs to the actual shrine, I wondered whether the pillar was the *axis mundi,* a pole connecting to heaven, and made a mental note to check with Ravi. Before we worshipped Shiva as Bhimeshwara, we were asked by the priest to worship Kailasha Ganapati standing opposite the shrine. The consort of Bhimeshwara is Manikyambika and she has a separate shrine at the ground level. However, there is an idol of Dakshayani in the main sanctum. The priest explained why it is so in a long-winded way, 'No one is supposed to come between or walk between two Brahmins, a man and his wife, the lingam and the Nandi, or cut through a herd of goats. Similarly, since no one is supposed to step between Ishwara and his consort Shakti, which is Manikyamba below, another deity was installed here to prevent this from happening. She is Dakshayani or Dakshaprajapati's daughter.'

After praying at the Navagraha shrine and the shrine of the *ashtadikkapalakas* or the guardians of the eight directions, we walked along the two-level corridor and saw the remaining shrines: Sri Veerabhadraswamy, Sri Vatuka Bhairava, Sri Lakshmi Ganapati and Sri Nalakuleswarudu. I was writing down the names of the deities in my notebook and overlooked one shrine. An old woman nudged me and said in Telugu, 'You didn't see this one. Write down this one also.' I was surprised since I didn't want to miss even a single shrine. All the stone idols there had a grave, unadorned beauty. I had skipped Sri Chaturmukha Brahma. All three of the divine trinity were present there once again, just as at the peepul tree shrine opposite the Saptgodavari. To have missed Brahma's *darshan* would've amounted to an incomplete visit.

Sri Kurmam

The next day was set aside for Arasavalli and Sri Kurmam. After Arasavalli, we headed for Sri Kurmam, the only major temple dedicated to the Kurma avatar of Vishnu. It was nearly a quarter to six when we reached the temple. Among the total of six temples we had visited, this was the only temple that had a row of saffron-robed sadhus at the entrance begging for alms. Soon after we entered through the outermost gateway, the first impression was that the temple was poor, neglected and falling apart. The *mandapam* outside the main temple had a gathering of scruffy, travel-weary devotees with their bundles of clothes, small cooking pots, and thermos flasks for tea or coffee. Very close to this *mandapam* was a flight of steep steps leading to the temple tank called *Swetapushkarini*.

We entered the main temple through a pillared passage to discover that there was no electricity. The priest rushed to get a hurricane lamp to light our way to the main sanctum. Apart from the three of us, there were just two others waiting for a *darshan* of the deity. As we crossed the threshold and moved deeper towards the sanctum, a strong smell of rancid coconut water mixed with trapped hot air made me feel slightly claustrophobic.

At the same time, the absence of electricity made me feel as if I was about to enter a womb-like space, mysterious yet reassuring. I was surprised when the priest led us right into the sanctum. Apart from the light from two large oil lamps, the room was dark, mildly damp and far removed from the world of day-to-day reality. I can't say if I felt a sense of the sacred there, but I felt the presence of silence—deep, very deep, lofty and enduring. The idol, which is in the shape of a large tortoise, has not been sculpted by human hands. The *shaligramam* or sacred stone, that forms the central piece of the main shrine or deity (*moolamurti*), is very large. While I joined my hands in prayer, I found it difficult to relate to this deity, which is not anthropomorphic. It is said that Adi Shankaracharya placed the *Sudarshana shaligramam* as the tail of Sri Kurmam.

As soon as we came out of the sanctum, the electricity came back. We sat in one of the pillared corridors surrounding the outer *prakaram*, waiting for some priest to tell us the *sthalapuranam* and other interesting details about the temple. A sumo wrestler-sized priest trundled into view and sat in *padmasana* with surprising ease. A prominent *naamam* on an ample forehead, thick arms like huge mounds of flesh, hefty legs, large gapped teeth, long greasy hair brushed back—he was impressively outstanding. All of us looked puny and insubstantial beside that man-mountain. He was a good storyteller and well versed in the scriptures. His Telugu was scholarly. I had to ask Ravi to fill in the gaps for me in the story of the temple's significance.

It is believed that the temple originally had a lingam. Sri Ramanujacharya changed it into a Vaishnavite shrine. In ancient times, a couple from the Bhil tribe lived in the region that is now Srikurmam. One day, after finishing her work in the fields, the Bhil woman felt hungry and thirsty. She drank water from the *pushkarini* and took a dip in it. Feeling beautifully re-energised, she spoke of her experience to her husband, who also took a dip in the *pushkarini*. At that moment Sri Kurmanatha appeared before him with *shankha*, chakra, *gada* and *padmam*. The Lord asked the Bhil man to have a temple erected there. The Bhil told the then ruler of the region of his singular experience and the lord's wish. The ruler gladly made the temple, dedicating it to Sri Kurmanatha.

The lord asked the Bhil to go to the Sadangmuni Ashram and lead an austere life in order to attain moksha.

The priest told us another story—of Naraharitirtha, who established the shrine of Yoga Narasimha in this temple and set up the images of Rama, Sita and Lakshmana in Saka 1215.

Naraharitirtha's guru, Purnaprajna, asked him to go to the capital of the Gajapati king and rule that country. Perplexed by this strange command, Naraharitirtha asked his guru why he should do so. His teacher explained that in the Gajapati kingdom there were images of Rama and Sita that he must try to get, so that he may worship them. Obeying his guru, he ruled the country for twelve years in the time of the local king, who was a minor. When the prince was old enough to rule, Naraharitirtha handed him back his kingdom and, as recompense for his help in ruling the kingdom, requested the king for the images of Rama and Sita that were in safekeeping in the royal treasury. Returning to Srikurmam, he gave the *vigrahams* to his master, who later on bequeathed them to his worthy disciple.

Interesting stories.

It grew dark rather suddenly and I had no time to look at the murals on the walls of the two-pillared corridors. I couldn't see the niche sculptures clearly either. Disappointed, I left the temple with a sense of an incomplete journey but with the blessing of the *archaka* echoing reassuringly in my mind—*punarapi darshanam prapti rastu*.

Two years later, in March 2010, we went back to Sri Kurmam. It was totally unplanned and unexpected. Ravi's aunt, who had been quite ill in Mumbai, had passed away and the tenth, eleventh and twelfth day of her last rites were performed in Rajahmundry. After the *antim samskaras* were over, we proceeded to Vizag since Ravi had some work there. I suggested hesitantly to him that I wanted to see Sri Kurmam again. He vetoed it immediately. I did not insist but messaged him mentally that I really wished to see the temple again. The next morning he asked me, 'You really want to see Sri Kurmam?' I nodded vigorously, pleasure writ large on my face.

We set out around one in the afternoon and had a two-hour drive ahead of us. We drove to Gara, the *mandal* headquarters first, to pick up a local government official from his office. His assistance would be valuable in getting a knowledgeable priest to explain the temple's significance to us. As we neared Gara, the countryside seemed drier than the one we had passed. However, there was palm, coconut, teak; there were cashew and mango groves and harvested paddy fields that looked a thirsty dry brown. On the way to Sri Kurmam, which was less than ten kilometres from Gara, I spotted paddy in the middle of the road at two spots. I wondered why the vehicles were being allowed to run over it.

Ravi told me, 'Easy way to dehusk, separate grain from chaff.'

'Won't the grains break or get damaged?'

'I guess not.'

The priest was waiting for us. I noticed his deep-set penetrating eyes, salt and pepper hair brushed back from his forehead and tied in a small knot at the nape of his neck and a bushy handle bar moustache merging into his beard. His legs looked slender in comparison with his thick, chunky torso. What was really impressive about him was his voice—deep and reverberating. As he led us to the temple tank, he began his narration of the temple's significance in English and I was thrilled. No more frustration and feeling helpless while straining to catch each bit of a narration in Telugu.

As we descended the steps to the *pushkarini*, the priest told us that we had come on a very auspicious day—*shani tryodashi*. A bath in the *Swetapushkarini* gives respite from *pitrudosha*. That is why it is called the *pitruaashirvadateertham*. All the *asthikas* immersed here change into stone. The religious call it a miracle. The scientists call it a chemical reaction. On our previous visit, the hefty priest had told us that the bones of the deceased change into *kurmas* or tortoises.

An idol of *ugra* Narasimha stands in the centre of the tank and the fierceness of this deity is balanced by the meditative calm of yoga Narasimha inside the temple. The shrine of Yogananda Narasimha is attributed to Naraharitirtha.

We bathed our feet in the temple tank, sprinkled some of the holy water on our heads and then climbed up the steps to make our way to the temple. The priest pointed out that the temple has two *dhwajastambhams*. Sri Ramanujacharya, who, as mentioned earlier, converted this shrine from a Shaivite to a Vaishnavite place of worship, erected the second one. Passing under the Gajalakshmi *toranam*, we entered the main temple. Entering the *garbha griha* was a wonderful experience. To be so close to the deity in a shrine where only the flickering light from the oil lamps lit up the sacred space and enhanced the divine mystery was an experience that one could call to mind in days of dimming faith in life. I looked at the tail of Sri Kurmanatha and felt as if I saw an eye there—its gaze sober, yet direct and potent. Very likely, I was imagining it all. Nevertheless a connection was forged. And I prayed, 'Give me only that which is best for me.'

Once out of the sanctum, the priest led us to the Thiruchettu Mandapam with its seventy-two granite pillars, each divided into three parts, and each unique. Some of the pillars have inscriptions and others are replete with carved images of deities, animals, birds (for instance, a *hamsa* inside the *naamam*), ordinary human beings, dancing girls, floral designs and other decorative motifs.

The priest paused before one of the pillars and said something about Sri Maha Pratyangira Devi. Was she depicted there, I couldn't figure out. He spoke of her as powerful and ferocious, iconographically depicted as half-lion and half-human. The lion head is that of a male and the body is that of a female. Together, it represents the union of Shiva and Shakti. Also known as Narasimhika, she is said to have destroyed Sarabheswara's arrogance. Sarabheswara is the *ugra* form of Shiva. I recall visiting a temple with Shiva as Sarabheswara. He has a form that combines the mouth of a crocodile, the tail of a serpent, a pointed nose and the long wings of a bird. Was Shiva as Sarabheswara carved on one of the pillars?

On one of the pillars I saw a woman churning curd for butter. And a small figure stood facing her, holding a long stick. Was she Yashoda and was he the child Krishna? The face was slightly damaged and kumkum was smeared everywhere.

The *mandapam* also has a *kappastambham*. The belief is that if a childless couple embraces it, they are blessed with a child. The priest explained further, 'The figures in the *stambham* are supposed to stimulate the libido. That is why this belief.' The figures are that of Veenapani, Nritya Ganapati, Yoni and the dancing girls.

We took another tour of the *mandapam* to look at the murals. These were damaged and faded in places; however, one could still discern the theme of some of the paintings. Their clay brown, brick red, fawn, muddy yellow and black pigments were still appealing and pleasing to the eye. The priest pointed out the paintings: Dasavatar; Gopikavastraharanam—the gopikas waist-deep in the Yamuna are shyly and smilingly pleading with Krishna for their clothes—the women have been drawn with carefree and luscious sumptuousness; *Kaliyamardanam*—this painting is fairly intact and the beautiful details with mermaids and water flowers is very pleasing—Kaliya looks like an innocuous snail; Govardhana Giridhari—Krishna stands like a dancer, poised and self-immersed, playing his enticing flute with the Govardhana Mountain resting on his little finger, whereas the people mistakenly believe they are the ones propping up the hill with their sticks and poles; Lord Vishnu as Kamalanabha—Lakshmi is doing *padaseva* while Garuda stands guard, sentry-like. From any angle that you see, Lord Vishnu's eyes seem to follow you, look at you. Half-reclining, he looks bright and alert. The other paintings were: Lord Krishna's birth; Putana *vadha*—the killing of Putana; Makarasura *vadha*; Bakasura *vadha*; Lord Krishna and Balaram with their parents; Kamsa.

The priest deliberately skipped one particular mural—women with sensuously pleasing breasts and alluring figures and in intimate companionship, are enjoying themselves with charming abandon. The effect is sensual.

After doing our namaskarams at the corner shrine of the Ashtabhuja Vaishnavi Durga, we stepped into the *prakaram* where the priest pointed to the south-facing *vimana* Narasimha. On the east of the *vimana* is Hanuman or Kapeesa and in the west is Vishnu or Dandivaktra. Hayagreeva guards the north.

After this I went around looking at the niche sculptures on the outside wall of the main temple. Kaala or Yama is seated on his buffalo, with kumkum and *chandan* liberally smeared on his forehead, and speckling his nose and lips. Wide-eyed, he looks youthful, chubby and harmless. His *vahana*, the buffalo, looks equally plump and benevolent. The next niche sculpture is that of Rama and Lakshmana. Richly adorned in princely attire, they are amiable and smiling. The kumkum falling untidily on their faces hides the clarity of their kindly features. Parsurama wielding his dreaded axe is a figure of effeminate grace. Vishnu seated in *padmasana* with *shankha* and chakra in the two upper hands is a picture of divine splendour and serenity. Simhavahini, with her wide smile, is a maternal figure with a broad face verging on the masculine. Her wide jawline and big chin adds to that impression.

As I took in the niche sculptures leisurely in that Vaishnavite shrine, it was heartwarming to come across a niche figure of Shiva with his trident, *damaru* and begging bowl.

While I was taking pictures of the pillars in the Tiruchettu Mandapam, a child rushed past me urgently, lowered his shorts and peed into the *prakaram* unselfconsciously. Chiding him mildly after the job was done, I looked around hastily to see if anyone else had noticed and was relieved that no one had.

Stepping out of this *prakaram*, we walked to the enclosure where the tortoises, so many kurma avatars, huddled closely next to the twisted wire fence. How aware were they of their privileged status?

Our final visit was to the cows in the cow shed. Feeding them grass and green stalks of some grain, I couldn't help but notice their ribs jutting through the desiccated flesh. I wanted to leave some money for their feed but couldn't. In a hurry to get to Salihundam, a Buddhist ruin site, before nightfall, Ravi rushed me out of the temple. Anyway, I wondered if the money would've really been spent on fodder for the cows.

Salihundam

Salihundam was nowhere in the picture when we planned a visit to Sri Kurmam. I hadn't even heard this name. Earlier on in the evening, when we had reached Gara, the *mandal* headquarters in the Srikakulam district, the official accompanying us had suggested that after Sri Kurmam, we should also see Salihundam, an ancient Buddhist site.

The setting sun was a mellow orange-red fruit when we took the narrow curving road up to Salihundam. The small museum at the base of the hill rested its grateful glance on the many beds of pretty flowers that scampered down the shallow slope. From there, we drove a little further up to another base point of the hill. As I got off the car, I was totally unprepared for the view before me. An uneven stone-paved ramp-like pathway, flanked by low brick walls, led to the remains of a Buddhist monastery or vihara on either side of it and up the gentle hill. We were transported back to the second century BC when the place would've been teeming with the presence of monks in chaitya-viharas. With each step forward, we left the mundane world of shops, offices, stores, malls, roads crammed with noisy vehicles behind us. But, not quite. The sound of hurtling vehicles from the road below came up with insistent unhindered clarity. However, it remained a non-bothersome background noise.

The light was fading. A bluish softness moved in. We walked up the stone-paved sloping walkway, carefully making our way up to the summit of the hill. The stones were worn smooth by treading feet and the inscriptions on these had become less and less noticeable. Only the bases of different kinds of stupas remained on either side of the kuccha pathway. The top of the hill had the remains of an interesting structure—two concentric brick-laid plinths, with low ridges radiating from the top one. On three sides one had a magnificent view of the surrounding terrain. I walked up to the brink of the summit of the hill and looked around with heartwarming gladness. Resting my arms on the protective metal railing, I took in the view. The Vamsadhara river to the right was a wide meandering fawn-sandy path with islands of silvery-grey water in places. The name Vamsadhara means a stream of water that originates in the *bamsa* (Hindi—*baans*), that is bamboo groves. An apt mellifluous name. The hill in front was a dark mysterious form. One of the men accompanying us said, 'There is a Venugopalaswamy temple on the top of that hill. On *Bhishma ekadasi* every year, there is a big festival that attracts thousands of devotees who first bathe in the river, ritually cleanse themselves and then climb the hill.'

The sound of moving traffic, the heavy rumble of trucks, the honking of horns came up from my left, interspersed with delightful squeals of children. The village of Salihundam perked up its white structures in the midst of the different greens of cashew trees, mango groves, palms, coconut trees, fields of paddy, bajra (pearl millet), green gram, horse gram and green chillies. Soon, all would merge into the descending dark.

Resting against the low wall of the circular plinth, I let the fresh air and the solitude fill me with calm. Away from the dredge and drumming of the routine, it would've been a singular experience to stay there for a while. I wished I could spend a few hours there just reading, resting and musing about nothing in particular. If one could get this gift of a few hours of solitude there, visualise the scenario: No talk, no companion and yet plenty to keep one company. All forms of regular connection with the world dissolve. All anxieties melt away. All grievances dissipate. All worldly aspirations slip away. Breezily, thoughts drift in and out of the mind, which latches onto nothing to cause disquiet or discomfort. A book that one may or may not read. A piece of embroidery that one may or may not do. Each moment affirming that an experience of the extraordinary is available and possible in the midst of the ordinary. Be open to receiving it. I could visualise the experience—the palms sway somnolently in the light breeze and send up messages that shush thought; the fields display their verdure to make you forget all that wilts and shrivels up with time; the hills raise their grave heads to make you renounce thoughts of weary submission; the river, though summer-shrunk, surviving as a rivulet reminds you it will flow and churn with life once again. The perennial underlying all transience reveals itself at such moments.

The light was fading fast. Darkness descended in a trice. We groped our way in the dark with our feet feeling gingerly for footholds in between the smooth, irregular stones. The strong light used to light up the summit of the hill blinded us and did not light up our descent. It was quite exciting to fumble our way down this way. I enjoyed it. Ravi didn't.

We reached the small museum, almost decided that we would give the museum a miss. It was nearly seven and we had a long drive back to Vizag. If Ravi and I had been alone, I could've persuaded him to linger in that unique peaceful place. We were about to leave when the caretakers of the small museum said, 'Won't you take a look at the *murtis* inside?'

'Shall we, Priti?'

I was delighted that he was inclined to spend some more time there. It was cool and haven-like inside; at the same time one felt a bit strange, as if one had entered a forbidden, hallowed space. While we did not speak in low voices, the place seemed to admonish us gently to speak only in hushed whispers. The inward-turned dhyana Buddha and the Bodhisattva Manjusri remained unperturbed by our intrusive presence.

In the centre, right opposite the door of the museum, was the figure of the goddess Ashtabhuja Marichi, with three heads and eight hands. Three of them were missing and one was half broken. Her anklets were large and ornate. What were her weapons, her attributes? I couldn't tell. Her front face, speckled with brown spots was smooth and featureless—the effacing hand of time. A youthful figure, she exuded power and vitality. Her posture was that of one in readiness for battle—militant and valiant. A female deity sat beneath her and below her were seven horses. Who was she? Chhaya Devi, said the caretaker promptly.

For the caretaker, Marichi was the goddess Durga, the destroyer of Mahishasura, the buffalo demon. He told me a story. A small-made thin man, he was eager to please. While it was difficult to check the veracity of the tale, it was nevertheless interesting. He spoke excitedly and his Telugu was hard to follow: 'My father used to tell this story. The statue was found in the village of Salihundam. It lay prone on the earth, so heavy that no one could make it stand straight. In my father's time, there was a raja who noticed that many people had been unsuccessful in moving it. He took up the challenge. Strong and determined was that raja. Single-handedly he managed to haul up the statue to make it stand properly. Depleted of all strength, completely drained by this massive task, he went back home, lay down, and never got up again. His body snapped under the strain.'

'Pompous and foolhardy,' said Ravi.

The caretaker waited for the import of his tale to sink in and then said, 'I sleep here at night. And I sleep soundly, without fear. No bad dreams.'

Suddenly he lowered his voice to a confidential whisper, 'She walks here on some nights. No fixed time. Keeps vigil. Guards her territory.'

'Who?' I asked, perplexed.

'The goddess.'

'You have seen her?'

'Yes, and I feel safe.'

Was he fabricating? Had he been hallucinating? Who knows? Best not to judge. There are many things in the world beyond our limited comprehension and outside the confines of rational explanation. True, or not, if the belief in the goddess' presence made the caretaker feel good and secure at night, I saw no harm in that innocuous calming belief. After all, he was not marketing the belief for personal profit.

Right through the narration of the story, Ravi was distracted by the talk of the other two people accompanying us and was disinclined to ask the guardian anything about his nocturnal experience there. My Telugu faltered while asking specific questions. Hence there were bound to be gaps in communication and my understanding. In addition, someone was pushing the visitors' book into Ravi's hands for his comments. This too ruined the possibility of getting a more coherent story from the caretaker.

With the experiences at Sri Kurmam and Salihundam for company, we drove back to Vizag in congenial silence.

My Nameless Tree

I am going to move ahead by a few weeks to the fourth week of April 2008 and speak of a different journey, a different quest.

Sometimes it takes very long to find an answer to very simple things, to clarify simple doubts. In my case, I think, it was not for want of strong desire or effort, although the effort may not have been concerted or consistent.

In the year 2004, when I had visited Hyderabad from Paris, I had noticed a tree in my neighbour's garden. It wasn't a very high tree and because it was right next to the boundary wall, its branches arched out above the dirt sidewalk sprinkling the dry-leaf-draped soil with fragrant white flowers. The leaves of this flowering tree were large and deep green and its white flowers growing in small clusters crowning a leaf cluster. presented a delectable contrast. The tree's form, the colour and shape of its leaves, made it stand out from the rest. I picked up its white flowers and took in the delicate fragrance. It wasn't as if the tree or the flowers were entirely unfamiliar; it was as if I had no distinct memory of noticing them right through my stay in, or visits to, Hyderabad. It was as if I was looking at the tree with new or fresh eyes and wondering at the beauty of something that was always part of my environment but which had remained veiled from my regard. It was as if someone had removed a blindfold and guided me to this tree. The pleasure upon seeing it was unrestrained. As I walked further into my colony that wonder-filled morning, I found this tree in several places and with each discovery my pleasure in seeing it grew. Anxious to know its name and the name of its flowers, I asked several people. Many of them called the flowers champa or tella ganneru (white ganneru) or pedda ganneru (big ganneru) in Telugu. For four years, I mistakenly assumed that it was the champa till I visited the botanical garden in Araku valley in March 2008 and saw a plaque naming the champa tree. It was different from the tree I had assumed to be champa. My quest to name my tree began all over again. Before I visited Araku valley I had visited the temple at Annavaram in the East Godavari district of Andhra Pradesh. I had seen a tree similar to the tree of my quest. It had clusters of white flowers at the end of the branches but I couldn't spot even a single leaf, which would help me recognize and confirm that it was my tree. A pilgrim told me that it was the temple tree. I was thoroughly confused.

For the purpose of avoiding confusion, I will call my tree, the nameless one. There is a young nameless tree in my father's garden. That year it had two small clusters of beautiful white flowers.

Towards the end of April 2008, I went to the plant nursery close to home and pointed to my tree and said that I wanted the champa. The man looked at me uncomprehendingly. Then I addressed him in Telugu and asked him the name of my flowering tree. He called its flower deva ganneru. I asked him if he had a champa sapling also. He showed the champa and I realised that its leaves and stem were different from the leaves of my nameless tree. I bought the pink variety of deva ganneru and the champa. (The pink variety is perhaps called muddu ganneru or cute ganneru).

After coming home, I began an impatient and frantic search on the Internet for my nameless tree. Deva ganneru was translated as divine oleander. After an intense search of nearly half an hour, I stumbled upon a site showing the forest flora of Andhra Pradesh in the form of a classification table, giving the botanical and common name of a tree and its equivalent name in five Indian languages. I also discovered that my tree belongs to the Apocynaceae or the dogbane family, which includes over 400 genus and 1,500 species. My tree belonged to the genus Plumeria; it was the Plumeria alba or the deva ganneru or the temple tree, also known as the pagoda tree or the West Indian jasmine tree or the white frangipani.

The Plumeria rubra has different colours of flowers, white, yellow, orange, pink and red. Its red or deep pink variety is referred to as lal champa in common parlance. Hence I imagine, the confusion in my mind with the champak (champa, champaka, sampige in Kannada). The botanical name of champak is Michelia champaca and it belongs to the Magnolia (Magnoliaceae) family.

My nameless tree, the tree that went unnamed for four years, now has a name, frangipani or the temple tree. In April 2008, the young temple tree in my garden had very few branches and two clusters of white flowers at the edge of those branches. The leaves were eight to ten inches long. Oval shaped, they tapered nicely to a fine point. Greyish green in colour, the leaves had a deep midrib or mid-vein. The upper surface of the leaf had a dull sheen. I ran my finger along the prominent ridge or spine of the mid-vein on the underside and the subsidiary veins branching off from the centre. The leaf was very pliable like soft linen fabric. I snipped it off the branch and a sticky white substance oozed out. It felt as if the leaf had suffered an injury. The greyish green branches had small basket-shaped impressions or shallow stabs on them. The white flowers in half-bloom were funnel-shaped with five, overlapping waxy petals. The inner half of the petals was a bright yellow deepening to amber inside the tube. The flowers had a delicate fragrance—inviting and evanescent.

There were three frangipani trees across the road from our house. They were much older than mine, with spreading branches and a handsome head of dense leaves. The leaves were slightly different from the leaves of the tree in my garden. They were longer, narrower and oblong, with a more rounded front tip. Their colour was deeper, darker, a glossy bottle green. The underside of these leaves was leathery. They were also thicker and firmer than the leaves on my temple tree, hence when they fanned out from the edges of branches, they look liked flamboyant verdant flowers. Their white flowers had long individual white petals with small sunny yellow centres. I walked to a different part of my colony to see the deep pink frangipani. I had forgotten my camera at home. I saw a few flowers on the earth. They had wilted. They looked limp and listless on the ground. On the tree they looked like vibrant exuberant clusters of lasting beauty. I picked up one flower from the ground. It still retained it fragrance—heavy, fruity, slightly cloying. The flower had three different colours. The wine red or burgundy moved into the mustard yellow, streaked with a pastel pink that blushed an even lovelier pink closer to the centre. It was ravishing in spite of being heat-weary and life-sap-bereft.

I was thrilled to know my tree and call it by a name or several names, each more evocative than the other. My pleasure was heightened when I further discovered on the Internet that the Plumeria or my frangipani was so named to commemorate the work and significant contribution of the seventeenth century French botanist, Charles Plumier, who travelled to the New World and documented many plant and animal species. In the summer of 2004, I came from France to India to fall in love with my tree in my home city and I discovered four years later to my pleasurable surprise that it was named for a French botanist. My tenuous connection with that foreign land which I had grown to love and call home was now strengthened.

Postscript: At a wedding that I attended the same evening of my beautiful quest, I discovered that the frangipani or the temple tree flower is also called nidra ganneru ('nidra' as in sleep) in Telugu. At the same wedding, someone gave me a very pale orange champa. It had a heady perfume. For two whole days I had been thinking of nothing else but the frangipani and the champa. I had found what I had looked for, passionately, single-mindedly. Deep gratitude was my response.

A Healer

Concerned about my hyperacidity and migraines, Chandra had suggested that I see a siddha vaidya or physician he knew. This was sometime in March. Chandra's wife had benefitted considerably from his treatment and Chandra was confident that the vaidya would be able to help me also. I was getting weary of the uneasy feeling of food stuck in my throat and of the fire in my stomach which would die down for a few days only to rekindle itself again, if there was a change in my diet either because of travel or some social engagement which involved not eating at home.

Siddha medicine is a very ancient form of treatment and cure developed and perfected by eighteen important siddhars in ancient times. It uses a variety of herbal preparations and minerals to treat people holistically.

It was blazing hot and sultry that afternoon; all the same, we decided to see the siddha doctor. Around two o'clock, Chandra took us to his home cum clinic in Triplicane. If I failed to keep this appointment, I would have to wait till our next trip to Chennai, which was iffy in the near future.

Ravi told me about Triplicane, 'It used to be middle class economically, but upper class intellectually. Dr Chandrashekhar and Subramanya Bharati are from Triplicane. It used to be a Brahmin stronghold. Now it has an interesting mix of Hindus, Muslims and Christians. It used to be called Thiru-veli-keni or Thiru-alli-keni. If it is the first one, it means, "god's fence".' This wasn't correct, I discovered. It was called Thiru-alli-keni which means 'sacred lily pond'.

Once in Triplicane, we got off the car while Chandra looked for a parking spot. Different kinds of smells, pleasant and disagreeable, assaulted our nostrils—fresh popcorn and freshly roasted coffee mixed with the nauseating odour of rotting garbage disinterred from the rain water drain. 'This place stinks!' I exclaimed.

'Ignore it,' said Ravi. 'Please remember that we are going to visit a healer and healers come in different, often unlikely, forms and are found in unexpected places. Let me tell you a story as we walk to the doctor's place.' We walked past a school and then entered a long narrow lane where teenagers were playing cricket. It was chock-full of houses that shared common walls, with no breathing spaces between them. Shaded and relatively traffic free, it made a constrained cricket playfield for the teenagers who were least concerned about the ball making frequent flying forays into the open windows and doors of houses on either side.

Ravi began his story, 'In 1994, when I was in Tiruvannamalai, a man at the Ramana Maharishi Ashram told me about a healer. This healer's story happened more than a hundred years ago. A man who lived in Tiruvannamalai was suffering from some chronic stomach problem. He was in great distress. One night, Lord Nataraja appeared to him in a dream and asked him to visit a healer in some part of Tamil Nadu. I forget if it was Chidambaram. The lord showed him the way to the healers's home, the locality and the street in which he lived. The suffering man trusted his vision and set off on his journey with great hopes. When he arrived in the town, he located the healer's street which was narrow and dirty. In a shabby, one-room house, he found the man who would supposedly cure him of his stomach problem. Cranky and belligerent, the wild unkempt-looking man was as unlike a healer as a crow is unlike a peacock. Upon seeing his fearful, reluctant patient, the healer exclaimed in Tamil, "I know that lame man has sent you here to me!" His reference was to the dancing Lord Nataraja. Then he picked up a fistful of dirty soil from outside and ordered with churlish insistence, "Eat this." The sick man had no choice but to obey. He was cured of his chronic stomach problem.'

'Amazing!'

We were at the main gate of the siddha doctor's house. Cutting across a small stretch of barren land where a shiny red four-wheel drive was parked, we entered a greener patch with plants, trees, some flowers and an inconsequential patch of ragged grass. In one corner was a pile of dried leaves, blackened palm fronds, vegetable trash and some plastic wrappers. Beside the wall on the opposite side, there were large bags filled with empty plastic bottles of different sizes. There were heaps of discarded newspapers and the narrow verandah behind the staircase leading to the doctor's clinic was a dust-layered mini junkyard. The panes of the closed windows reflected our curious uncertain faces. The place had a deserted look. I was momentarily dubious about the wisdom of our afternoon venture although I had been sufficiently warned to ignore my surroundings.

My passing doubts were laid to rest when I met the siddha vaidya. I shall tell you more about him based on my second visit to him on 17 September 2008.

I had stayed back in Chennai for two extra days to be able to see him. The memory of my first visit was so vivid that once I was near the Parthasarathy temple in Triplicane, I found his home without any problem. I had been told that the chakkara pongal (sweet pongal) in that temple was superb but it was nearly one and the temple would be closed. I was also running late for my appointment. I pushed the divine taste of the chakkara pongal out of my mind.

Sun-dazed, the two streets that led up to the healer's house slept languidly. My friend Vidya and I entered the rectangular plot of land that leads to the front yard of the house with its relaxed, wayward, yet benign juxtaposition of various things. On the extreme ends of the rectangular patch were creepers of *dosakaya* and snake gourd that sprawled comfortably on the earth and reigned undisturbed, away from curious passing feet. A young neem spread its ample branches over the corrugated tin sheet that roofed the makeshift shed for the car. As it swayed softly in the slow afternoon breeze, the freshly washed look of its leaves soothed the eyes. We crossed a threshold to enter the front yard, which looked more organised than before, and walked briskly along the short walkway. It was quiet, very quiet—tranquil. There was no sign or flicker of life in the ground floor rooms. Leaving our slippers at the foot of the yellowing marble staircase, we went up as soundlessly as possible. The two of us entered the waiting room that only had a handful of patients. I was relieved that the wait wouldn't be long. It was so restful there that it didn't feel like a doctor's clinic. It was a very functional ordinary room verging on the shabby, yet the air there felt pure. The sunlight filtering in through the trees was mellow and gentle.

I gave my name to the doctor's attendant and we sat down on grey plastic chairs. The doctor's closed door had this printed message on an old partly-torn browning sheet of paper, 'This is a sacred place. All patients are equal'. I looked at the discoloured walls that pleaded for a fresh coat of paint. It was strange that although the creamy yellow of the walls had dirt streaks and imprints left by the passage of time and the people who had waited and continued to wait patiently for their turn to see the siddha doctor, they didn't look disagreeably unclean. The walls had posters of Western babies, each with a nice terse message or a homily (irksome for those who don't fancy pat sermons or clichéd sayings). One of them with a pretty young child in a peach dress reassured: 'God keeps His promises'. I responded within myself, 'For Him to keep His promises, there are loads that we have to keep to ourselves and to each other.' There was another one with a happy child clasping its hands, chirping out this encouragement, 'Say that you can and you will'.

Facing me, at the L-shaped left corner, was the dispensary behind translucent-brown stained glass windows. Behind me was a large window with a black metal grille in an austere square pattern. It overlooked the playground of a school, swept clean and empty. Then I noticed a woman framed in the doorway of a room at one corner of the playground. She wore a drab sari. Her face looked as crumpled and worn out as her sari. She dragged a large covered cooking utensil forward and waited. Suddenly there was the scrape and scuffle of several feet—children in blue uniforms streamed out of a small gate into the playground. Most of them had examination clipboards in their hands. Some of them were in rubber slippers. They made a beeline for that room. Each was given a large steel *thali* which he promptly proceeded to wash at the long narrow basin with its row of taps at the beginning of the field. Each boy then took his *thali* to the woman who gave each child a modest helping of salt pongal and one boiled egg. On the large *thali*, that food looked meagre. The famished kids wolfed down that food and washed it down with a drink of water. With their clipboards tucked under their arms uncomfortably, most of the kids struggled to eat. One smart kid clipped his board to his shirt collar. With both hands free to hold his large plate, he proceeded to enjoy his insubstantial but welcome meal.

Six or seven kids still waited to be fed. Scrupulously scraping the bottom of the pot, the woman gathered the remaining pongal into small balls and placed one each in the open right palms of the kids. They did not protest that virtually nothing was left for them. Relishing the balls of pongal like a tasty savoury or *boondi laddoo*s, they licked their fingers clean, gulped down a large drink of water and went away quietly. Vidya looked at me with tears in her eyes and said, '*Aiyo, paapam*—poor little things.' We had eaten a substantial lunch before coming—steaming hot rice with a vegetable curry, *kootu* and rasam and we were miserable that some children had gone hungry.

It was my turn to see the doctor. Sitting behind his L-shaped glass-covered table, he smiled a greeting. Under the glass top of the table were innumerable pictures of gods, goddesses and saints, vying with each other for space. A short man, he sat on a large easy chair draped with a towel. His blue-grey cotton bush shirt with a geometrical motif in dull mustard was trendy in comparison with the rest of his appearance. A balding man with a large forehead smeared with *vibhuti,* he looked traditional and avuncular. From behind his thick glasses, his eyes were balmy and smiling. He exuded reassurance and quiet confidence.

I sat down on a high stool to his right. He asked me how I was feeling while he lightly touched my wrist with his fingertips to feel the *nadi*. I told him that my acidity problem was much better but my headaches were still there though not as severe as before.

'My eyes hurt a lot sometimes and the eyelids are heavy and painful.'

'Do you work?'

'No, but I write on my laptop and do a bit of dictionary work from home.'

'You are a writer!' He beamed with pleasure.

I was embarrassed. 'Yes, my first book will be published by Penguin but...I write for myself...'

'You must try for the Booker,' he said very casually as if he were encouraging me to win a high school essay or story competition.

I murmured, 'To see my book in print is like a dream. At the moment even that seems so unreal. It's more than enough if I see my novel in a bookstore.'

He did not pay attention to my sluggish hope. Smiling encouragingly he asked me if I was sleeping better.

'I still dream a lot and most of my dreams are very vivid. I also remember some of them in the mornings.'

'Do you dream of death?'

'No.'

'I have a patient who dreams of the death of someone and then that person passes away,' he said matter-of-factly.

I shuddered. 'I am glad I do not have that strange gift,' I said, in an undertone. 'I dream of climbing heights, of water, the sea, among other things.'

'Have you read Freud's *Interpretation of Dreams*?'

'I have read about it.' I asked boldly, 'Have you read it?'

With childlike annoyance came the prompt response, 'Then what for am I telling you about it? I have a big library with one lakh books.'

I nodded appreciatively in wide-eyed surprise.

'Dreaming of water, of oceans is good. It means you will have more and more compassion with time.'

There was no time to have a conversation with him. His time was precious. I wanted to ask him how he had arrived at that conclusion because I hadn't narrated any of my dreams to him. Also, it was important to know the following with respect to the ocean or the sea: Is it calm or choppy and stormy? What is the colour of the water? Is it fresh and clear or is the water thick, oily, turbid? Am I sitting on the beach or on a sea-washed jagged rock with the waves crashing against it? Am I contemplating the sea from a distance? Do I enjoy the experience or do I feel troubled by the waters? Does the sea retreat from the land or does it threaten to overtake the land and submerge it? What are the other accompanying images that make the sea dream and what is my predominant emotion in each of these?

While I was running through these questions in my mind, he wrote down the herbal preparations in my medical history booklet and on a slip of paper for his assistant. I looked around his dusty and topsy-turvy room which was cluttered in an agreeable sort of way. However, the air was clean and benign; the windows framed shade-giving trees which subdued the harshness of the afternoon sun. The sunlight came in gently and soft shadows dabbled in idle play among the myriad corners created by clutter. There were books everywhere—in piles tied together with thin rope, in collapsing heaps, in precarious bundles on the ledge above the door, in stacks against the wall that separated the balcony. I read some of the titles—there were books on yoga, metaphysics, on Hindu samskaras, on rishis, modern sages, thinkers, on gods and goddesses, on Shirdi Sai Baba, on mystics and prophets from other religions, on Hindu philosophy, on Ayurvedic medicine and nature cure, etc. As I wondered how many of those he had read, he turned to me and said, 'There is a small shrine of an east and west facing Vinayaka, that is Shiva Shakti Vinayaka, in my garden. Please have *darshan* and go. The idol belonged to some women from Coimbatore who couldn't take care of it. They were happy to give it to me and I have installed it here. It is a very powerful deity.'

Thanking him, I went into the waiting room to wait for my medicines. I wished I could've spent more time that afternoon getting to know more about that unassuming healer. A man of few words, he was tranquil and confident. His childlike innocent smile endeared him.

Vidya and I went down to the front yard with its potted plants and saw the shrine that we had missed. It rested under a peepul tree and a plantain tree arched its long-leafed branches over it sedately. The peach-pink shrine had an octagonal tower shaped like a finely tapering cone. Along with incense and pink roses, a banana had been offered to Vinayaka who sat in deep eternal repose. Inward-looking, his face had the gravity and stillness of a sage. Awed by that solemn deity, I did a namaskar, said a hushed prayer and turned to look at a tall hexagonal cage opposite with a low conical roof that looked like a wide-brimmed hat. Curious, I peeped through the metal grid to see small birds. I was perplexed. Why would a compassionate man such as the siddha vaidya place birds in a cage? Did they belong to him? Puzzling over that question my eyes took in the details of the semicircular green enclosure with its spiked iron posts that fenced off that area from the marble-tiled footpath. There were quite a few planters and flower pots but none of them had a healthy plant. Some were clogged with twigs and rotting leaves and the others were either filled with dark damp earth or a weak sapling. Only one planter had a young, healthy aloe vera plant.

Uneasy about the birds in the cage in such a restful place, I stepped onto the walkway and then turned around to take one last look at the Vinayaka shrine. Startled, I saw something that I had failed to register earlier. The blinders were suddenly gone and I saw a young neem tree near the shrine. With absorbed focus I traced its form with my eyes. It had one upright branch and three that undulated sideways, hindered from growing upwards by the wall of the staircase and the first floor. Its interesting artistic form took me back with an instantaneous jolt to the tree in the Jardin du Lux which had a very similar form—except that the neem tree was vibrant and surging with fresh sap whereas the other had looked old, winter-blasted, with a stoically tenacious hold on life all the same.

Holding on to these contrasting impressions of two similarly sculpted trees, I walked out of the siddha doctor's place hastily before nostalgia for Paris could overwhelm my awareness of the present and weaken the will to stay there.

Now I am going to share the following story, which may seem far-fetched to you as a reader, but which is inextricably connected in my mind with healers and healing in a larger sense.

The Razor's Edge was either the first or the second novel I read when I was in class nine or ten. Way back in 1974 or '75, during one of the short school holidays, when I was desultorily rummaging through cupboards for some interesting find, I discovered it quite by chance in one of the rarely opened cupboards in my grandmother's house in Delhi. It was hardbound, with brittle yellow pages, and had my father's signature inside. Since I had nothing better to do I started reading it and soon found myself deep in it.

The book left a profound impression on me but, over the years, the details of the story faded. Only this remained—that the main character is called Larry and he travels to India where he meets a Maharishi. I began to associate the book with faith, the healing touch, and a spiritual journey. I forgot everything else, including the fact that most of the story takes place in France. This impression of a quest and the healing touch (although to be accurate, the latter should be modified to include healing through suggestions or positive input) has lingered with me like a soothing fragrance. Larry heals his childhood friend, Gray, of vicious headaches and draws helpless souls to himself and spontaneously gives what each person needs without attaching any importance to the giving. I think as he matured spiritually he would have been a powerful healing presence.

I had added my father's copy of *The Razor's Edge* to my book collection in Hyderabad but for the past several years it had disappeared from sight. Hoping that it would miraculously resurface someday, I never bought myself another copy. However, sometime in September, when I spotted it among a nice range of Maugham books at a bookstore, I couldn't resist the temptation of buying it. I started reading it and once again I was grateful for the experience it offered – of sharply observed characters and a story of a 'rare' wanderer, an engaging 'loafer' (Larry), whose quest for true knowledge leads him to connect meaningfully with others, including a whore, and benefit them as only a charmingly selfless and compassionate human being can.

On a different note, I have often felt sad as I reflected on the transience and impermanence of things in life and the inevitable change that takes place constantly in everything around us and in human relationships. I found useful reflections on it in the novel. Larry lives in the ashram of Shri Ganesha in Tamil Nadu for two years. Shri Ganesha is none other than Ramana Maharishi whom Maugham had met during his travels in India. Larry reflects on what the sage had told him, that 'the satisfactions of the world are transitory and...only the Infinite gives enduring happiness' and tells Maugham, the narrator, 'nothing in the world is permanent, and we're foolish when we ask anything to last, but surely we're still more foolish not to take delight in it while we have it. If change is of the essence of existence one would have thought it only sensible to make it the premise of our philosophy. We can none of us step into the same river twice, but the river flows on and the other river we step in is cool and refreshing too.' The last sentence is lovely and one must remember that Larry is not putting forth an argument for hedonism or irresponsible loose behaviour. I think what he is saying is—the present moment, the immediate now is all that matters. Make the most of it. Other 'chosen' moments that follow cannot and will not replicate the present one but they are as precious or as pleasurable. Our perspective changes everything.

Larry himself was like the flowing river and those who stepped into it were refreshed.

When Larry had been living in Shri Ganesha's ashram for two years, he had gone to his forest retreat to be alone for his birthday. There he had experienced moments of supreme happiness and rapture. He tells Maugham in the context of the Aryans coming down into India and their subsequent experiences, 'If in those moments of ecstasy I had indeed been one with the Absolute, then, if what they had said was true, nothing could touch me and when I had worked out the karma of my present life I should return no more. The thought filled me with dismay. I wanted to live again and again. I was willing to accept every sort of life, no matter what its pain and sorrow; I felt that only life after life, life after life could satisfy my eagerness, my vigour and my curiosity.'

Initially I was dismayed with his dismay and could not for the life of me figure out why a person who has experienced moments of union with the Divine should wish to be born again and again into a world that is as sordid as it is noble, that is as full of suffering as it is of respite from it, that is as repulsive as it is attractive, that is as enervating as it is rejuvenating—in short, it is full of contraries. I was perplexed by his desire to return again and again to this world. After a few hours I realised that Larry is very young and energetic. His intellectual curiosity is still very strong and the zest for life flows with bounding energy. Hence he speaks of wanting to experience many births. Then Ravi added this acute observation, 'At the stage of spiritual evolution where he is now, that is how he can or will speak. Give him time to evolve and he will speak differently.' It made perfect sense.

I have shared my reflections on *The Razor's Edge* here because, in my mind, through all these long years, the book has been associated with faith in something higher than oneself and with the wonderous power of the healing touch. It fits in with my continued interest in healers.

Lamps

Dear reader, the inclusion of the following story about lamps in a book of journeys might seem strange to you but as you read on you will discover its relevance to the larger framework of sacred journeys, pleasure trips and journeys of discovery of the beauty of seemingly ordinary people.

As you are well aware, lamps signify the journey from darkness to light—*tamaso ma jyotir gamaya*. And I leave it you to decode my dreams about lamps.

Sometime in August, I went to Kalanjali, the handicrafts and handloom articles emporium. I have always loved traditional brass and bronze oil lamps and have this desire to fill my future home with different kinds of lamps: Free-standing ones, lamps that hang from doorways, pyramidal ones with five individual *deepams* at each tier, peacock lamps, bird lamps, Gajalakshmi lamps, lamp with a seated Ganesha or Lakshmi at its pinnacle, *aarati* lamps, Kerala style Malabar lamps and so on.

At Kalanjali, a lamp with an antique finish caught my eye. It must have been a little over nine inches tall. It had a single large circular *deepam* which one would have had to fill with oil and place wicks in, at even intervals. It looked more like a medium-sized *uruli* (a shallow circular vessel with an open mouth used on festive occasions...it can be partially filled with water to hold floating flowers or small *deepams*) to me. This circular *deepam* was supported by three or four kneeling female figures, with one knee resting on the floor. They were crudely made. The short central stem or spine of the lamp, surmounted by a large graceful *hamsa*, was very ornate and elaborately carved. While the *hamsa* enhanced the beauty of the lamp, the crudely-made half-kneeling women figures took away from it. I wouldn't have minded clumsy-looking elephant figures. The antique look of the lamp made me debate for a long time whether I should pick it up. The elegant *hamsa* was an eye-catching ostentatious beauty. I gave the lamp a miss because of the unappealing base and found another interesting brass piece of which I had already bought one of a pair a few months back—a brass nandi, with a delicately engraved *kalasam* on its back. This whole piece was suspended from triple chains joined at the top. The Nandi's hind legs were folded and tucked in and its head, with a slightly open mouth, faced downwards. It was a small replica of the larger one used for Shiva linga *abhishekam*.

Then I went around looking at other lamps but all of them looked new and common and shone like burnished gold. I was looking for something that evoked the sacred mystery of the sanctum sanctorum and nothing there fit the bill, nothing came close to the deeply etched image in my mind of the much-used oil-dripping burning-wick-darkened lamps framing the doorway of the innermost shrine. These lamps both deepen and enhance the sacred mystery of the *garbha griha* and in turn slowly assimilate it into their moulded metal forms, making them glow with a divine inner beauty.

The same night I had a strange dream related to lamps: I am inside a large cottage emporium located far away from the city in very pleasant natural surroundings. Its ground floor is fully stacked with brass and bronze statuettes of gods and goddesses and a wide variety of lamps that shine so brilliantly that they fill the room with dazzling effulgence. Everything looks very new and shiny but I am looking for something sober—something that has aged beautifully, something that evokes memories of a sanctum sanctorum seen in the flickering light of suspended oil lamps that have seen centuries of devotion and ardent offerings to the enshrined deity. I want a lamp that has both given the shrine a sense of the sacred and absorbed it—a lamp that has soaked in, bit by bit, every little drop of faith, inhaled the incense of each prayer, absorbed each little chant of adoration of the divine and then shines forth with a never-to-be-dimmed inner glory and sacred mystery.

I move away from this room with its blinding luminosity and make my way to one on a higher floor. But there is nothing like a higher floor. I find myself on the summit of a gently sloping hill. In the distance I spot a sole oil lamp resting very close to the edge of the hill. Walking up to it, I know at a glance that it is very old and precious. Otherwise, there is nothing remarkable about it. It is ordinary with a circular base that one can fill with oil and a *deepam* on the top, where one can place five wicks. I look at it again and I discover that it has one imperfection—a slight unevenness on the topmost *deepam*. I am sad. I wonder why the hilltop has only one lamp and where the cottage emporium has vanished. I am perplexed. While I am still debating whether I should take the oil lamp, I suddenly hear and then see something strange and fearful. A sound of ever so many spades crashing and digging into the earth! In the far distance, three giants loom up from nowhere. Rooted to my spot, I can see them very clearly in spite of the distance. They are practically bald with three or four thinning tufts of hair spiking up sharply from their scalps. Heavy-jowled, with fleshy faces and leering ravenous eyes, they are digging away at a part of the hillside with great ferocity and belligerent energy. They look like vicious plunderers. I begin to fear for myself. They look in my direction but I am pretty sure they haven't seen me. My legs feel like soft boneless flesh. I am petrified as escape seems impossible. I wake up with a voiceless scream trapped in my throat. I am relieved to find myself on my bed with Ravi sleeping soundly next to me.

I sit up in bed, take a few deep breaths and then recall the brief prayer that my grandmother-in-law, Ammama as I called her, used to say before switching on any light in the evening and before lighting the evening lamp: *Sayantram jyoti parabrahmam; sayantram jyoti namostute!*

I am going to leap forward by a year to the first week of October 2009 and share another lamp dream.

I had been feeling weak and drained for over a fortnight. I guess anxiety about my father's health had added to the sense of fatigue. Generally, I don't like to sleep in the afternoons or even take a nap because I feel miserable and disoriented after it. But one October afternoon I did, and dreamt this: I am with two people and a playful young girl. Do I know them in real life? Can't place them. It is dusk. Soon the sky darkens pretty quickly and is smudged with smoky grey clouds. We are standing at the head of a flight of steps that resemble ghat steps, leading to the bank of a river or a riverside. The stone steps are narrow and dirty. There must have been thirty or more of them. I am about to descend the steps, which are old, as if they have been around for decades and decades, when the woman who is with me warns, 'Step carefully!' Down their centre, the first few of them are wet with dog urine. I skirt the dirty patch gingerly and walk down the steps and find myself on a stone-tiled embankment. Then I turn left at the foot of the steps and reach the head of a sandy beach with a steep gradient. The sand is a pale walnut-brown. Suddenly the man who is with us points to something in the sand excitedly. There are small patches of beautiful white sand—pristine white and as fine as icing sugar. I bend down, take a fistful, hold it tight to form a ball and then release the pure white dust slowly through my fingers. It leaves my fingers clean—not a speck clings to them. Fascinated, the young girl streaks down the sharply sloping sand bank. She squeals with pleasure even as I am fearful for her safety. I marvel at her speed and her bold run down an almost vertical precipice-like slope, a good 10 feet below. Soon, I see something floating in the dark water, queued up against the pier—lamps. They have a curious shape and appearance. A creamy white flat base on which rest fixed lamp shades, which are made of egg-shell-like material—brittle and translucent—both of a grainy grooved texture and a glossy pearl-like texture. Or, they look like the *prasad batashe* in terms of the feel. As shallowly hollow as two palms pressed together in prayer or appeal, they are illumined by a mellow golden light. Their uneven edges are fringed by a golden lining. Are they really floating on water or on a dark emptiness, I cannot tell. No, they are not floating, actually resting, because they are still, very still—almost fixed to their spots. There is something very dainty about these lamps and the sight of so many softly illuminated ones gives me hope. I remember telling myself during the dream that I must save this image for my waking moments.

Connections in Unlikely Places

We were in Chennai for Deepavali of 2008 and I pestered Ravi into going back to the Dubba Chetty shop which I had seen in 2004. We have visited Chennai several times since our return to Hyderabad in 2006 and have gone past this shop several times too. But each time I told Ravi that I wanted to go back to the shop, he didn't take my desire seriously and indulged me with a reassuring, 'Next time, for sure.'

The Dubba Chetty shop is small and narrow but has a wide range of Ayurvedic herbs, oils, *lehyams* and other medicinal preparations. It is quaint, has an old world charm to it in its every nook and cranny. It has been in the same family for three generations and I am sure it is fighting hard to keep its place in a world of neatly and conveniently packaged Ayurvedic herbs produced by reputed companies such as Himalaya, Dabur and Baidyanath. The place has nostalgic value for Ravi who lived not far from it as a child and visited it with his grandparents, Ammama and Tatagaru, primarily to buy shikakai, amla and soap nuts. The first time, I visited the shop for his sake as he sauntered down memory lane in Chennai one unhurried afternoon;

I also saw it for the sake of Vaidehi, a dear friend, who loves Chennai and always wanted to take me to her favourite spots there and 'show off' her city to me.

In 2004, when I had visited Dubba Chetty (one can't enter the shop; one has to stand on the road and ask for things), a man who worked there listened to my requests patiently for different herbs and powdered herbal mixtures for common ailments like cough, cold and fever. Of course my requests were made in Hindi with the Sanskrit names of the herbs and Ravi had to translate that into Tamil. The man was affectionately amused by my requests and queries in Hindi. I must have spent over fifteen minutes at the shop asking about many herbs and herbal preparations curiously and not even for a single moment did that man show any impatience even while he had other customers to serve. Smilingly, he showed me samples of various herbs and even offered oils for hair growth and migraines. He was patient with my endless queries, kind and eager to help. Throughout the time that I was at the shop he smiled at me as if he were indulging a demanding child. I had a strange feeling then, as if something in him knew me from elsewhere but I brushed it aside as a silly and wayward fancy.

When we were in Chennai for Deepavali, my friend's mother had made a herbal preparation that is called *Deepavali maranda*—basically a digestive to be taken during the Deepavali season as people tend to overeat or gorge on sweets. Apart from its medicinal value, the *lehyam* is also very tasty, especially if one has an uncommon taste for *kashayams*, *lehyams* and *ghritams* as I do. I was curious about the ingredients that went into this *Deepavali maranda* so when we chanced to pass by the Dubba Chetty shop, I insisted that we stop there for a brief while. It was way past lunch time and others in the car were awfully hungry but I begged for a few minutes of grace. Earlier, whenever we had whizzed past the shop I had wondered about the nice man, the gracious shop assistant. As we crossed the road to the shop I wondered whether he still worked there and if I would get to see him. In the first fifteen seconds at the shop I didn't see him. Something in me sank with disappointment. Then I saw him emerge from a storeroom in the back. He came to the front of the shop to weigh something for a customer and spotted me. He gave me a beauteous engaging smile of instant recognition. I read an awareness of me in his eyes, in the radiant smile that lit his entire face. It was almost as if he knew that I would be there. There was no surprise on his face. Then he turned away and went in to look for something else. After that, the few moments that I was there, I saw him bustling around in that constrained space of the shop at the back but he made no attempt to look at me again. I was glad he didn't try to reconnect with me. The previous moment had been so candid and heartwarming that nothing would replicate it. Later, a serious-looking woman gave me the herbs I wanted.

I looked around. After a lapse of four years, the shop was an interesting blend of the old and the modern. While herbs were still kept in rows of horizontally placed tin canisters with open mouths, there were other cosmetic items, beauty products and herbal preparations in their contemporary glossy outfits.

I was puzzled by the shop assistant. I was delighted by his spontaneous recognition of me after four and a half years when he must have served customers and customers and customers in between. Some of you will say that I am reading too much into it. A sceptic will say that I wish to read too much into it because this makes me feel good. Just another self-deluding exercise... sentimental drivel etc. Whatever be the verdict of others, this incident has given additional fillip to my interest in past life regression.

What did that worker at the shop look like? I won't be able to tell because I just have a sketchy impression of him before my mind's eye, although a very pleasing one. How old was he? Difficult to say. In his late fifties or early sixties? He looked lower middle class, if not poor. Bony, with salt and pepper hair, high cheekbones and deep-set dark eyes in a burnished brown face, there was nothing spectacular about his appearance. It was his smile, an open inclusive smile that made him attractive. It was the kind of smile you would wish a dear friend or family member to have—a smile that you would wish to begin and end all days with because its lingering after-glow would keep all blues at bay. Strangely, I remembered his shirt and lungi better—a subdued bluish-green full-sleeved shirt with a matching checked lungi—a very dignified colour.

I am going to take this story forward by a year as I feel impelled to share something more about that gracious Dubba Chetty shop assistant. Although we had been visiting Chennai every two months, I didn't get a chance to visit the Dubba Chetty shop for a year. From the train station to Venkat and Vidya's place in Mylapore, we would take the beach road and then take the right turn onto Kutchery road where that small unpretentious *kadai* is located. However, since we always went past that shop around six in the morning, its shutters were down as expected. Ravi was very amused each time I got excited seeing that shop and mentioned the helper there. He found my fascination for that shop a bit exaggerated although his own fondness for it was deeply entrenched too.

I visited the shop on 30 September 2009, on the day of our departure for Hyderabad. I saw him again, my helper friend. Not immediately though. My eyes searched for him quickly. He wasn't around. Two women were serving the customers, one of them unsmiling and matter-of-fact. I asked for these herbs—pipali, sundakka, haritaki and the fragrant incense *sambhrani*. Had he stopped working here, I wondered. But something told me I would see him. He emerged from an inner storeroom, framed in the dark doorway for a split second and soon busied himself with packing herbs into newspaper packages tied with string. Standing right opposite me in the unhindered direction of my direct gaze, he kept his eyes lowered as he worked. 'Please look up,' I urged silently. 'I want to see whether you know me.' He looked up, met my gaze for a split second, lowered his head and smiled a shy tentative smile. It vanished as quickly as it had come. It barely reached his eyes. From the corner of his eye, he darted a hasty look vaguely in my direction. A smile hovered uncertainly on his face again and then it was gone. To me, it seemed that as he occupied himself in the shop for the next three-four minutes that I was there, he rigorously avoided meeting my gaze again. He kept his eyes lowered and scrupulously averted. Was I imagining all this?

I noticed him—a white and grey checked shirt with full sleeves flapping at the cuffs, a white veshti folded up above his knees and secured at the waist. His face looked older and thinner. More creased. The cheeks looked more sunken, with two deep grooves running from the nose to the edge of the lips. His dry dishevelled salt and pepper hair had an air of neglect. In general he looked bonier, frailer, with shoulders that had stooped in one year.

My connection with him had lost its flashy charm. Time had altered it, lent it a perplexing sobriety. Or, was everything just a product of my desperate imagination? Of dubious value?

Moments come and go. Connections come and go—form, dissolve, reform, disappear. Gratitude for a precious moment, a precious tenuous connection is everything.

Chikamagalur

There were visits to small temple towns and other journeys in the time between October 2008 and May 2009 but nothing stands out as worth sharing. Or, the truth is that I was lax and did not make detailed notes to give form and substance to hazy impressions. What I am going to share now is a journal entry on 9 May 2009, from a visit to a resort in Chikamagalur in Karnataka.

> I wish I knew trees and flowers better. It is a wet morning after four days of bright sunshine and warm days. Drizzle, drizzle, drizzle for about two hours. After a late and lazy breakfast, I take a walk on my own, leaving my sister-in-law and friend Vidya behind in the swimming pool. They are like kids delighted to splash about in the water. I feel the need to be on my own, with trees and plants as my only companions and partners in solitude.
>
> It is a quarter past eleven and the rain has stopped. The sun is out and it feels mild. As I walk the path away from our room, I recall what I had written about trees a few years ago and know that I feel the same even now:
>
> *I want to feel the height of each tree, vicariously experience its shade; feel each branch, its stretch, its curve, its reach; I want*

to feel the peculiar nature of its wood, its strength, its inner resistance to nature's changing moods and vagaries. I want to outline the shape of each leaf, run my fingers along its surface and experience its texture. I want to know the different kinds of leaves—thin and papery; thick, smooth and glossy; young and tender; tough and coarse; long and slender; large and wide; like needles but silky soft; velvety; furry; stiff; pliable as fine muslin; satiny; sandpapery; deep-veined; fine-veined; with serrated edges; with curling edges...

The air is refreshing, cool. And the earth is wet, wet, wet. It is thickly covered with pale greyish-brown soggy banyan leaves, twigs and broken branches. In some places the chocolate-brown earth flaunts its rich fertile hue.

I hear several birds I do not see. My eyes strain to look through the plants, peer into the foliage of the trees but these feathered creatures remain tantalisingly concealed.

The path I take is lined with banyan trees, hoary guardians of perennial wisdom and profound mysteries. Their shade is deep and widespread. The coffee plants grow under them. The younger leaves of the plant are glossy green with curvy edges. Smooth and pliable. When the leaves hang down from the branches of the coffee plants, they look like so many open palms lowered in an offering. Or, is it the bhumisparsha mudra? On one plant I see a new leaf at the edge of a stem. Upright and eager, it takes in the light and fresh air. My eyes linger on the tiny coffee beans—closely clustered green beads or a secret clique sitting bunched together to formulate strategies. A close-knit community—a rarity! Whatever it may be, I gladly take in their fresh green colour, their small round firmness and rejoice in nature's pleasing variety.

The third row is formed by the silver oaks—tall and robust with the pepper creepers moving valiantly up their trunks. The paan-shaped leaves are a dull bottle green—firm, rather stiff.

I trace their prominent longitudinal veins with my finger and marvel at the fine network of smaller veins.

I see a banyan tree so huge that its trunk looks like several elephants' legs fused together. Then, there are two trees growing from the same base, very unlike each other and going their separate ways. The healthier one has leaves which are a bigger version of tamarind leaves and white flowers with fine thread-like petals. The second one's trunk is scooped out as if eaten away by some inner rot or disease. A part of it is just a sad shell and yet it has the will to survive, with its two feet planted firmly on the earth. I salute it.

I see two trees—inseparable, embracing. Or, if you, my reader, like a less pleasing description—an unflattering one—a tree with a greenish-white trunk forces itself onto the other one with the brownish-black trunk, which is coarse and scaly. It clamps its heavy form onto it. Long-lasting happy union or an unalterable undesirable close connection—reader, choose whatever suits your passing fancy or deeper proclivity. The tree with the paler smoother trunk has sprightly green leaves that taper to a fine point. The darker one has ovate leaves with a rounded front; the leaves are duller and thicker than the ones of its fairer companion or adversary.

Walking further, my gaze rests on a robust jackfruit tree. On the earth squats an oversized jackfruit—weary and slouchy. A huge unseemly thing, unable to manage its own weight.

Retracing my steps part of the way, I turn left into an uneven side path where the touch-me-nots creep undisturbed on the ground. For the first time in my life, I know what a touch-me-not or chui-mui looks like and really experience the shyness of this sensitive plant. My finger gently touches the tiny fern-like leaves with purplish edges and they fold up, shrinking from my intrusive touch. The touch-me-not has been touched by rain and it accepts this graciously.

A pleasant surprise awaits me further down the path. There are clusters and clusters of the *tummichettu,* or *tumbe guda* (in Kannada), or Leucas aspera, one of the plants dear to Ganesha. With its grass-blade leaves and tiny white flowers with a jutting-out petal-tongue, it is a beautiful miniature plant. I am thrilled as I have never seen so many of them. In fact, I began to know of it only after our return to India in 2006. And on the occasion of the previous Ganesha Chaturthi, my vendor of leafy greens had generously handed me a small bunch for the puja.

I look at the young Halvan and orange trees that shield the coffee plants and move on. As I walk back to our room, I recall chopped off trees—their lifeless forms, stripped off branches and leaves. I saw these on our way to Sravanabelagola from Bengaluru. The road was being widened in several places, hence the trees that were in the way of this 'impressive' and 'public-serving' project had to be cut. These long-standing glorious forms looked like hapless mammoths. Like defeated Titans, they cut a sorry figure. Here, I was glad to be surrounded by living breathing ones.

Thiruvalangadu

Vijayadashami of 2009 found us once again in Chennai at Venkat and Vidya's place. Our friends had played host to us many, many times during our six-year stay in India. Our Chennai visits wouldn't have been so pleasurable and enriching if it hadn't been for their generous hospitality.

After Saraswati puja and a sumptuous lunch, we visited our friend Chandra's place to see the *gollu*. He has a fine collection of dolls, collected from various places during his journeys over the years. Among them was a Vinayaka made from yak bone and a baby Vinayaka reposing on a cushiony shiny silvery mattress. This cute, huggable toddler lay on his stomach, with his folded legs and chubby feet resting on either side of his plump bottom encased in a yellow diaper. He was an enviable picture of blissful rest.

We spent some time with Chandra's family and then left for Thiruvalangadu. I knew we would be seeing a few temples in and around Chennai on this trip, but I had no idea that we would be visiting the temple of Thiruvalangadu where Shiva is the Ratnasabhapati and where Nataraja is in the form of the Urdhavatandavamurty. I was thrilled.

Thiruvalangadu is about an hour and a half away from Chennai. We took National Highway 205 and for more than half the way it was a bad bumpy ride on a road eroded and damaged in several places. After Kakkalur the road improved, thankfully. I noticed a moped with a huge bundle wrapped in a green plastic sheet tied to the back seat. The bundle was bulky but light, with plastic mugs peeping out like dazed puppy heads. It had so overwhelmed the driver that I felt it was being transported on a self-impelled vehicle. The wiry driver in a hibiscus-red shirt and dark hair tied in a stern knot looked diminutive in comparison with his burden. Soon we passed three people walking barefoot—two in yellow veshtis and the third one in a pair of black shorts, a vest and a yellow angavastram. I knew that they were pilgrims but I wondered where they were headed. Chandra told me they were going to Tirupati, walking all the way from Chennai and would also walk up the holy Tirumala Hill. I was humbled by their faith. I was ashamed that I had been whining about the rough drive.

Towards the last leg of the drive, we left the main road and turned left. In patches of clearing of hardened earth, interspersed with thorny bushes and clumps of wild grass, some boys were playing cricket with gusto and élan, sans proper bat, stumps and a suitable ball. I saluted them.

The parking area in front of the temple was empty. Business at the nearby stalls was desultory. As soon as we got off the car, a boy rushed to us with a parking ticket of twenty rupees, higher than what it is back home in a crowded area. Who had printed the tickets, on what basis, and who was benefitting from the collection? All this was very hazy. Seeing us question the tongue-tied boy, a man walked up to support him. Presumably, it would go towards the upkeep of the temple environs. Who was there to verify or ensure that?

Thiruvalangadu is where the extraordinary and tough dance competition between Shiva and Kali took place. The story goes that after vanquishing the rakshasas Sumba and Nisumba, Kali's rage blazed unchecked and the earth was in danger of being annihilated. Hence Narada appealed to Shiva to intervene and control Kali's fierce rage. To do this, Shiva agreed to a dance competition with Kali and defeated her by performing a clever feat. He raised his left leg to replace his earring which had fallen during the contest. This is the Urdhavatandava – a skilful dance move executed with stunning balance. To imitate this would have been indecorous for Kali; she admitted defeat.

Nataraja dances in Thiruvalangadu in the *Ratna Sabha*, a hall studded with precious gems and is therefore, called the Ratnasabhapati. However, in reality, the hall is bare. I forgot to ask the priest what had happened to the precious stones. Vandalised, no doubt. The other four *sabhas* or halls where one can witness the dance of Shiva are: *Kanaka Sabha* in Chidambaram, *Rajat Sabha* in Madurai, *Tamra Sabha* in Tirunelveli and *Chitra Sabha* in Kuttralam. Above the doorway and eaves of one of the *prakarams*, are five ornate niches, each a *sabha*, where the stucco figure of Nataraja dances. At the centre is the Ratnasabhapati of Thiruvalangadu. The arches of these niches are surmounted by fanged demonic heads and the prominent colours in the five *sabhas* are blue and red.

Above the doorway leading to the inner *prakaram*, a story is depicted in technicolour stucco. Chandra told me that it was the story of Karaikkal Ammaiyar, one of the sixty-three Nayanmars, the Shaivite saints. I looked curiously at her marriage scene and then saw an old woman doing a handstand near Shiva and Parvati, who are seated on the summit of a disproportionately small, mound-like Mount Kailasha. For me Karaikkal Ammaiyar was just a name and her story unfamiliar till a priest inside the temple offered to narrate it.

We entered the temple and stood before the *Ratna Sabha* (a bare rectangular shrine) with its three images in bronze. At the centre is the Ashtabhuja Nataraja as the Urdhavatandavamurty, dancing on the request of the rishis, Munjikeshwarar and Karakotagar, who desired to witness this cosmic dancer. His left leg is raised upright to replace his left earring, in a spectacular skilful dance move. He holds the retrieved earring or *kundalam*, fire, snake, trishul and *damaru* in his hands. One of the hands in the *natya mudra* keeps the beat and the other points to the demon *apasmara* which represents ignorance. Draped in a red veshti with a green and gold border, wearing an imitation ruby, emerald and diamond necklace that shines splendidly, he is the embodiment of perfect absorption in the moment; he is pure blissful entranced movement – moving yet unmoved, full of beautiful movement yet serenely still. Against the rich backdrop of a green and cream yellow silk curtain, Shiva performs his singular dance. To his left is Samiseenambikai, his consort, and to his right is his devotee, Karaikkal Ammaiyar.

I looked at Ammaiyar's bronze statue. With her prominent cheekbones and sunken cheeks, she looks old but not a hag. In fact, her appearance is quite pleasing. Her streaking hair forms a halo. (The priest pushed back the muted maroon sari from her arm to reveal how emaciated she was. It seemed like a casual gesture but I found it unnecessary, if not intrusive.) She is playing the cymbals for her lord, who had promised that as long as she played the cymbals he would dance for her pleasure. So she still sits beside the dancing feet of her lord, an eternally enraptured witness of his eternal cosmic dance.

After reaching home, I searched the Internet and found a picture of a bronze statue of Karaikkal Ammaiyar. It belongs to the Nelson-Atkins Museum of Fine Arts. A wasted seated figure, Ammaiyar's rib cage is visible. Large ears with long lobes, a narrow shrunken body frame, a fleshless throat, an unpleasing mouth, a narrow shrivelled chin, a small forehead, prominent nose, arched eyebrows, a look of surprised wonder in her eyes – this is Karaikkal Ammaiyar, Shiva's unflinching devotee.

We asked a priest in the temple to tell us the story of Karaikkal Ammaiyar. He wore a dreary white veshti and a sacred thread. No angavastram. Of medium height and thinning oiled hair pushed back from his forehead, there was nothing distinctive about his features or appearance. And yet, as he told the story, his eyes lit up, his voice was choked with emotion and his mild-featured sweaty face was radiant with admiration for Shiva's devotee. The narration was in a mixture of Telugu and Tamil as he understood that I could follow the former reasonably well. I report his narration in my own words:

> She was born in the sixth century in the Chola town of Karaikkal to a wealthy merchant. Named Punithavathy, she was a charming young girl completely absorbed in the worship of Shiva from her early age. When she grew up, her father gave her hand in marriage to Parmadathan, an enterprising merchant. Even after marriage she continued her devotion to Shiva with the same steady fervour and continued to serve his bhaktas with the same appealing devotion. When Punithavathy performed a mango-related miracle, her husband realised that she was no ordinary mortal. She was worthy of worship and hence he could no longer live with her in a conjugal relationship. He left her on the pretext of business, moved to a town in the Pandyan kingdom and remarried. After hearing of this, she prayed to Shiva to take away her beauty and femininity so that it would not prove a hindrance in her worship of Him. Shiva granted her wish and she became old and shrivelled. (In some depictions she looks quite unpleasing…in fact, ghastly.) A venerable figure, she came to be known as Karaikkal Ammaiyar, the mother of Karaikkal.

Ammaiyar went on a pilgrimage to Mount Kailasha. Considering it a sacrilege to place her feet on the sacred ground, she covered the last part of the journey on her hands. This astonished Parvati. Then Shiva explained Ammaiyar's greatness to her and welcomed his devotee with joy. When asked to seek a boon, she prayed for this: Never to be born again. Pure devotion to him—to sit at His feet singing hymns of praise wherever He danced. Lord Shiva granted her this boon and asked her to go to Thiruvalangadu to witness His dance.

Ammaiyar began her journey to Thiruvalangkadu. When she was a kilometre or so away from the place, it grew dark. She sought refuge in a temple, perplexed about the right way to her final destination. Seeing his devotee's predicament, the lingam in a Shiva shrine close by turned around, facing an opposite direction now to show her the way. As she started walking, each stone seemed like a lingam to her. Placing her feet on them was unthinkable. She traversed the path on her head. On the way, she had to go through a cremation ground where skeletal ghouls with dark hollows for eyes pranced gleefully, feeding on half-burned corpses. There, in that forest, teeming with brooding dangers, she saw the beautiful lord dancing, 'holding the fire in his hand'—a splendid spectacle.

While Karaikkal Ammaiyar was moving towards the temple, the Pallava ruler of that time received a message from Shiva in a vision—his bhakta was arriving there and would merge with Him. The king should get his workers to create an enclosure around the spot where this would happen. And the king obeyed the Lord's wish.

Behind the constrained rectangular corridor-like space of the *Ratna Sabha* is a solid stone wall concealing the sacred space where Karaikkal Ammaiyar became one with her Lord. Out of intransigent, vulgar curiosity, two people in the recent past had tried to invade this holy space by drilling a hole in the wall. The consequence—they had heard news of illness in the family or of some other calamity.

A major part of the *Ratna Sabha* has since been sealed off.

After the beauteous form, splendid balance, grace and energy of the Nataraja as the Urdhvatandavamurty in Thiruvalangadu, I experienced a radically different Nataraja. This was at Cholamandala, the artists' village in Chennai, in December. We had gone with Chandra and his daughter to meet with the Paris-based painter Vishwa and stopped by to look at the art galleries. Chandra drew my attention to a painting of the Nataraja figure (Acrylic on paper, 2006). I was puzzled, intrigued and jolted by the artist's take on Nataraja.

The background of the painting is a smudgy sea-green blue. Against this Shiva dances—a muddy ochre brown figure with a lifeless slack body. The head looks bandaged. His streaking hair has no wild joyous energy. Part of the tired hair falls in skimpy strands. Contrast the sumptuous locks of Nataraja whirling joyously. The oval face looks dull; in fact, shocked or stoned. Half-formed nose, half-formed lips leave you wondering about the intention of the artist. And Nataraja has only three arms. Why was the fourth one left out? In the archetypal depiction, the second right hand is in the *abhaya mudra*—'do not fear' gesture. How does one interpret this? This effete image cannot offer freedom from fear or even a small semblance of release. The *thiruvasi*, the fiery arch fringed with flame, is an inert loop. The snake wound around his arm is a shabby grey nonentity. Quite dead. A dirty grey loincloth encircles the waist. Impoverished image. No jewels, no adornments. The limbs are limp—totally wanting in vitality. The *apasmara* crushed (if lassitude can crush) under Nataraja's foot looks like an unhappy child—too skeletal to cry out in protest. The dance here is sans meaning. Represents nothing—no *srishti,* no *sthiti,* no *samhara,* no *tirobhava,* and no *anugraha.* Has no connection with Karaikkal Ammaiyar's Lord Shiva.

A *shithil* form. Tired, faded. All ananda has been leached out of this Nataraja's form. I tried to keep the image of the Chidambaram Nataraja gloriously intact and untarnished in my heart. Celestial dance, eternal, in the sacred tillai within the heart of the devotee. Freeing the seeker from *punarapi jananam, punarapi maranam,* from samsara.

Images of Death

Three days before my teacher Meenakshi Mukherjee passed away on 16 September, I was preoccupied with death, obsessed with stories and images of death. A friend had posted a black and white picture on her Facebook profile page and that had led me to various reflections on death and my immersion in its images. The picture shows a grotesque carnival procession of masked faces, with the light falling on some of them with eerie luminosity. The other faces lurk uneasily in the shadows. What are they enacting? Mimicking? In the forefront, a skeleton with its set of grim leering teeth drapes its arms around two women's shoulders in bleak bonhomie. The painted face masks with fixed smiles, the women have donned, seem to be a part of some fantastic theatre. A fanged snarling figure lunges forward. You draw back from the dark caverns of its eyes. A hooded figure rests its shadow-eclipsed head on the shoulder of a grubby-looking tramp-like man, whose face is all nose. Another masked woman with dark painted lips looks away haughtily into the distance. Where are they off to? Deathwards?

Various images of death moved before me in a starkly silent procession:

I see the Dance of Death from Bergman's *The Seventh Seal*: Death with a sickle in its hand leads a group of dark figures holding hands. Walking along the dark crest of a hill, silhouetted against the dawn sky, Death leads his captives, his booty, to his realm from where no one returns to describe its landscapes, its histories.

The image of Death as the Grim Reaper holds no fascination for me. I see it—a hooded skeleton in a flowing robe with choppy edges. Dark pits for eyes. A bony finger stretched eerily. A curved scythe with a threatening blade. This picture of the dreaded equaliser is very alien to me. However, the mention of Yama tugs at certain memories of stories heard in childhood.

I see Yama. He appears differently to the virtuous and the wicked. Riding a fierce-looking black buffalo, this is how he appears to the good—a dark complexion, four arms or two arms wielding a mace and a noose, lotus-shaped eyes and a resplendent smile.

I see Savitri, beautiful and intelligent. Four more days remain for Satyavan to live. Fearful of his hour of death, she fasts day and night for three days hoping to ward it off by doing this penance.

She follows him to the woods on the last day when he goes to chop firewood for the sacrificial fire. He complains of a headache, feels faint, rests his painful head in her lap—the appointed time of his death is here. Savitri beholds the terrible Yama with a noose in his hand—dark red eyes, flaring nostrils, hair like monstrous reeds. The Lord of Death casts his noose and draws out the life-force from Satyavan's breast and starts moving south, back to his realm. Savitri follows the effortless traveller through difficult terrain, unwilling to let go of her husband. Admiring her loyalty and steadfastness, he grants her two boons but she persists till he blesses her with a hundred sons. Then she puts forward this plea, this faultless argument—how can this be fulfilled without the gift of her husband's life, without 'union with her husband'. Yama is charmingly outwitted. He gives her back Satyavan, his health and a promise of prosperity. This image of the Lord of Death, considerate and merciful towards a woman of blemishless virtue, a pativrata, appealed to me greatly as a child.

I see the youthful Nachiketas waiting sincerely for three days for Yama's return from his journey. Impressed by his patient wait, Yama asks his unexpected and unusual guest to ask three boons of him. Nachiketas rejects kingship, wealth, lands, a hundred sons, fairest singers of Indra's heaven. Instead, he seeks knowledge of 'the great mystery of what comes after death'; he seeks that sacred wisdom which leads beyond grief and delusion, frees the soul from the cycle of birth and death and leads to the ever-present awareness of the Supreme Self that resides within every creature's heart. Death here is a great teacher, a sage, a mentor, a benign path-shower—how different from the dark and macabre images of death that I had come across in Western literature and painting.

I see Markandeya, think of his encounter with Yama, and reflect on Markandeya's saviour, Shiva, as the Kalasamharamurti. I recall the sculpture that I saw on my third visit to the Kanchi Kailasanatha temple and I share the poem I had been inspired to write:

Kalasamharamurti

I adore Shiva as Mrityunjaya,
As Kalasamharamurti.
A strapping body.
From the top knot
The unleashed magnificence
Of wild flowing hair.

Arched eyebrows,
Full lips, strong shoulders.
The fire in the eyes now quiet,
The gaze veils, unveils, the divine mystery.
Difficult to read what the face
Eroded by time says.

The left leg bent at the knee
Valiantly placed on a low pedestal,
The right leg like a slanting pillar
Planted firmly on the earth.
The thrust of the trident
Like the clap of a million thunders.

Not crushed under Shiva's left foot,
Where is Yama or Kala,
Helpless as a rag doll,
Puny as a toy bear?
Where is the lingam
With the mark of Kala's noose?

Where is Death,
The impotent one?
Is this after Yama's release
From under the foot of Shiva?
For Death's work must go on!

Markandeya, Yama's victim,
Shiva's youthful devotee,
With huge relief I see
A half-kneeling figure with folded hands,

Below the dread prongs of Shiva's trident,
Adores Shiva's graceful soaring form.

I stand before the murti and pray:
I fear not my own death,
But the death of those dear to me.
Release me from this fear
And fear of fear,
O Shiva, O Mrityunjaya.

Remove the mark of Kala's noose
From my days, thought-scarred,
O Shiva, O Mrityunjaya.

Starting 4 January, 2010, I was once again shadowed by thoughts of death while I was reviewing this chapter. There was no respite from this even in sleep. On the morning of 6 January, I heard that the veena vidwan Trivandrum Venkataraman was no more. He died along with his daughter in a car accident. He was driving to Tiruchy to perform his wife's *maasikam*. She had passed away less than a month ago. Terribly shaken by the sad news, when Chandra called us, both Ravi and I were terribly shocked too. We had met the maestro and his proud family on 1 January at the Music Academy, after the *sadas*, where he had been honoured with the title of Sangeet Kala Acharya, an honour that meant so much to him and his fans.

It was a beautiful and memorable moment for all. Guru Venkataraman spoke to us after the event in the lobby of the Music Academy. He asked us to visit him at home soon. We promised to see him on our next visit to Chennai. He repeatedly told me not to give up the veena and said that he wanted to hear me play it.

I told him, 'Not in this janma. I haven't made any progress. I will play it for you in my next lifetime.' Tragic. I wouldn't even see him again in this lifetime or hear him play again.

Images of death that had circled inside my head, in each instance for three days, before my teacher's passing away in September 2009 and the veena vidwan's passing away in January 2010, were laid to rest with their deaths. Unsettling...disturbing, this connection, this premonition.

In March we visited Vizag again and took the beach road to Bhimunipatinam or Bheemli and, from there, drove to Vizianagaram to see the fort and the Pydithalliammavaru Temple. In 2008, around the same time of the year, when we had visited Vizag, I hadn't been able to go inside the Dutch cemetery.

At a half past two in the afternoon, the black wrought-iron gate was locked. The driver said in Hindi, '*Aisa lagta hai kuchh dinon se kisi ne taala khola he nahin.*' That was the last thing I wanted to hear. I was sorely disappointed but Ravi was secretly glad not to be able to enter it. The people at the tea and refreshments shop, right outside the gate, told us that it would open at a half past four. We proceeded to Vizianagaram. On our way back, I asked Ravi if we could stop there briefly to see if the gates were open. He conceded reluctantly. I was in luck—they were open and the caretaker was showing three visitors around.

Bheemli was a major Dutch settlement and a flourishing port in the seventeenth century. It was ransacked by the Marathas in 1754 and destroyed twice during the Anglo-Dutch wars in 1781 and 1795.

Before entering the cemetery, I read a brief description of it on the display board: 'There are 52 tombs spread over two locations, viz. Kummaripalem and the Beach...A pyramid-shaped grave of Frederick Kesselrus, who died on 8 October 1861, is considered to be the earliest known Christian grave in this part of the country. Most of the graves are intact and the inscriptions visible even today.'

The boundary wall of the cemetery was black in parts with old moss and dampness. It hollered for a fresh coat of paint, or a whitewash. We walked down a stone-paved central pathway. Windblown leaves gathered along the sides seemed to crackle after the day's heat. Pink and white nandivardanam plants brought respite in small pockets of colour to that grave place. A young palm and a young mango tree vied with each other for the title, 'I am mature though young'. To my right, in one corner, a tree spread its slender branches and sprawled on the earth. Later, the caretaker told me that it was the drumstick tree. Ravi prevented me from going and taking a closer look. At the end of the walkway and directly opposite the gates, was an arch which reminded one of Arc d' Triomphe in Paris. Sparsely decorated, a curving vine with a single blade of grass at regular intervals was carved on it. The pyramid structure of a Dutch grave rose above it.

The caretaker of the cemetery greeted us enthusiastically. A genial smile lit up his bleary eyes and brightened his sun-burnt skin. He had a grey moustache and a scruffy beard. He told me that he had been busy working on some Buddhist excavation site on Pavuralukonda and had come to open the cemetery after five or six days. We were in luck. He knew each of the graves intimately—he couldn't read very well, but could tell you whose grave it was, when and how they died and how old some of them were when death took them away. It was a sobering moment. I felt as if the present time had fallen away from me and I had moved into different periods of time simultaneously. The connection with the present became tenuous as I visualised the bold adventurers and the mariners who had braved the uncharted seas to come here in search of intriguing newness and fortune or treasure houses.

One of the taller pyramid-like graves had the names of the buried dead engraved on black granite in Dutch: *Onder deese... rusten*—under this rest the following people—a list of people followed. A stork with a fish in its mouth was carved above the names. Blackened with age and corroded by sea air, the pinkish-red colour of the pyramid looked jaded.

On one side of one of the tombstones there was a jagged opening in the wall. Beneath, a deep hollow space was visible. The caretaker told us that some miscreants had tried to break into the grave in the hope of unearthing some hidden treasure. I shuddered. He showed us different graves and pointed out the description on the tombstones, inviting us to be attentive to the concise, often poignant stories, written there:

William RH Young of Liverpool, Chief Officer
SS Clan Murray, twenty-nine years, fell into the ship's hold.
Died 22 November 1891.

A family grave of Helene Steur.
Ici repose son mari, son enfant et sa mere.
(A French family—Helene rests here with her husband,
her child and her mother.)

David Mackie, born December 1835. Died June 1878,
of heat apoplexy in Bobbili. His wife Emma Therese's grave
was next to his. Born 1839. Married 10 December 1862. Died 8
October 1863. (Their marriage lasted barely ten months and
then death intervened.)

The caretaker paused pensively before the graves of two siblings and pointed out—Phillips Brooks Morse survived only for five days. Born 23 June 1892 and died on 28 June 1892. His sister Frances RH Morse was only four months and eight days old when she died in 1899. I wondered about the parents, their grief, and if they had had any more children. I didn't recall seeing their graves.

The light was fading and Ravi was getting uncomfortable with my excessive interest, or what he would have liked to call, my unhealthy curiosity, in the dead. I could see that he was restive and wanted to be back in a place throbbing with life. The caretaker seemed to be in no rush. Perhaps he expected payment for his expert guide services. When I gave him some money, he took it gratefully.

The sight of wind-ruffled palms greeted us as we stepped outside. The sculptural composition with the dark forms of fishermen in a boat in the centre of the road was a stark reminder of the hard labour, grit and dignity of man, even as he braves stormy seas or life's tumultuous challenges. Ravi took deep breaths of the fresh sea breeze. I said goodbye to all gloomy thoughts of death and its different forms. Contemplation of a good drive back along the sea road, a good bath, and a good dinner revived me. Life asserted its presence.

A Postscript

I am going to fast forward this narrative to January 2013 and share something that is connected to the last chapter, 'Images of Death'. I have been in Vancouver for nearly six months now. Two weeks ago, I visited my sister, who lives in Boston, and got a chance to see the Boston Museum of Fine Arts. Among the paintings and sculptures that appealed to me, there was one sculpture that left a very deep impression—Käthe Kollwitz's *The Lovers*. I had never heard of Käthe Kollwitz (1867-1945), a German painter, sculptor and printmaker, whose work offers a very moving, austere and jolting depiction of the poor, the wretched and the war-harrowed. In the mid-1930s, she completed her last major cycle of lithographs on the theme of death, which had fascinated her for a long time.

A descriptive note on the sculpture, *The Lovers*, shared this insight about the art piece on display: 'There has been much speculation about the subject and title of this sculpture—*The Lovers, Mother and Girl, Pièta.* Recent researches show that it may be related to Kollwitz's later lithographs, *Death Holds a Girl in His Lap…*' If the sculpture is reminiscent of Death with a girl in his lap, then it is the most poignant, tender and singular depiction of Death, himself in mourning, that I have seen.

The sculpture shows a man with a woman in his lap. The man's face burrows into the woman's right cheek. His hair frames his face like a tight skull cap. Both his hands clasp her head tightly, sorrowfully, unwilling to let go of her. Limp, the woman sits hunched in his lap like a child. Her legs dangle down on the side. Her left arm hangs down listless against his left leg. The curved ridge of her spinal column and the delicate curve of her throat make her seem vulnerable, frail. With her head thrown back, chin raised, lips parted, either she is a picture of an inert body in Death's embrace or a woman overwhelmed by love so complete and so consuming that she has no choice but to die to live again.

Is it love or loss? I am not qualified to say. However, one knows that the connection between eros and death is a significant one in literature and art. If the man in this sculpture stands for Death, his sorrow is very palpable; his sense of loss is deeply moving. The girl-like woman, with a gaunt face and high cheekbones, who is held in a tight embrace by her lover, Death, who shields her and grieves for her, even as he deprives her of life, is one of the most evocative art works that I have seen on such a theme. Restrained in its expression yet stark in its effect, it will stay with me for a long, long time.

I would like to end my journey through my own book, as I review and revise it, with my sentimental poem:

Death-Dish

Death-dish comes
in many flavours —
if I may,
I would like to choose one
that is quiet

on my loved ones' tongues
when I am gone.
That is
if I am missed
at all.
(That is
if my life-flavour
is missed
at all.)

Glossary

Aarati: It is a Hindu ritual of worship, a part of puja in which light from ghee lamps or camphor is offered to a deity or deities. It includes a devotional song sung during the ritual.

Abhaya: Fearlessness.

Abhaya hasta: A deity's hand in *abhaya hasta mudra* offers freedom from fear and protection.

Abhaya mudra: In abhaya mudra, the right hand is raised to shoulder height, arm bent, palm facing outward. This gesture symbolises protection, peace, and the dispelling of fear.

Abhishekam: It is an important part of idol worship. As part of *abhishekam*, the idols are bathed with different things, for example, milk, curds, honey, turmeric etc.

Abhishekapriya: Shiva is referred to as *abhishekapriya*—one who loves worship.

Acharya: Teacher.

Adisesha: Vishnu's snake.

Alankaram: Ornaments, embellishments.

Alankarapriya: Vishnu is referred to as *alankarapriya*—one who loves to be adorned with jewels. He is depicted with flowers, pearls, precious stones, jewelry, and other embellishments.

Aksharabhyasam: A ceremonious ritual by which a child is initiated into the world of reading and writing.

Ammavaru gudi: A temple dedicated to the mother goddess.

Amla: Indian gooseberry.

Amrita kalasam: A pot which holds the divine nectar or the elixir of life.

Ananda Tandava: Shiva's dance of bliss.

Annadaata sukhi bhava: Among all forms of charity, the giving of food is considered very high in the order of things. Hence the blessing, 'May the giver of food be happy.'

Antim samskaras: The last rites or the funeral rites performed after the death of a person.

Anantshayana: A name for Vishnu in reclining position.

Anugraha: Grace.

Apasmara: The dwarf on which Shiva as Nataraja dances. He symbolises ignorance.

Archaka: A temple priest.

Archana: During worship, 'offering of praises' to the deity, for example, chanting the 108 names of a god.

Archana Samagri: The implements and ingredients of worship.

Ardha mandapam: The intermediary space between the temple exterior and the sanctum sanctorum.

Aradhana: Worship.

Arudra darshan: It celebrates and commemorates the occasion when Shiva manifested himself to his devotees as Nataraja, the cosmic dancer.

Asthikas: Bones that remain after the cremation of a body.

Asura: Demon.

Ashtabhuja Nataraja: The Nataraja with eight arms.

Ashtadikkapalakas: In a shrine, guardian-deities of the eight directions.

Atmasamarpanam: Total submission.

Attimaram: Cluster fig. In Telugu *atti* or *medi*. In Hindi, it is *gular*.

Avadoota: A saint or an ascetic who has renounced all worldly-things and attachments.

Avudaiyar: The pedestal or base (circular or square) of the Shiva lingam. It faces north and regulates the outflow of *teertha*, that is water, or milk.

Axis mundi: The cosmic axis or the world pillar. In religion or mythology, it connects Heaven and Earth.

Bael: Aegle Marmelos. The *bilva* fruit, also known as the Bengal quince.

Bali: Ritual sacrifice.

Baans, bamsa: Bamboo.

Bilva: Bengal quince, stone apple or wood apple.

Bhelpuri: A snack. It is a mixture of different savoury things—puffed rice, sev, potatoes, finely chopped cucumber and tomatoes, tamarind and mint chutneys tossed together.

Bhumisparsha mudra: Earth-touching *mudra* or gesture. It is the most common way in which the Buddha is depicted in iconography. This gesture symbolizes the Buddha's victory over Mara, the demon who stands for all the doubt, temptation and impulses that obstruct spiritual practice.

Brahmachari: A student. Traditionally, he goes to live in the ashram of a spiritual teacher, under whom he lives a life of strict celibacy and morality, dedicated to learning.

Brahman: The Supreme Consciousness.

Bhagavathar: A scholar well-versed in the scriptures. One who gives religious discourses.

Bhishma Ekadasi: An auspicious day which marks the birth of the Vishnu Sahasranama Stotram, a hymn in praise of Vishnu.

Bhoomi: Earth.

Chakras: Energy centres in the body.

Chakkara pongal: Sweet *pongal*. A traditional sweet usually made for the festival of *Pongal* or *Sankranti* that falls in mid-January. It is made with newly harvested rice, de-husked green gram dal, jaggery, ghee, cashew nuts, cardamom, edible camphor and cloves.

Chapas/Chatais: Traditional floor mats.

Chandan: Sandalwood.

Charu annam: Rasam (a South Indian lentil soup) and rice.

Chin mudra: Called the 'gesture of understanding', it is a gesture that denotes spiritual awareness.

Chui-mui: Touch-me-not. Botanical name—Mimosa Pudica. It is a sensitive plant; its leaves fold inside when touched. They shrink and droop for a brief while.

Daddojanam: Andhra style curd rice with flavour-enhancing seasoning.

Dakshina: Traditionally, after a Vedic sacrifice ceremony, the recompense paid by the sacrificer to the priest for the ceremony. A more general meaning, 'a gift expressing thanks'.

Dakshinamurthy: The south-facing form of Shiva. In this form, Shiva is the Supreme Teacher who imparts jnana or wisdom in silence.

Dal: Lentils.

Damaru: An hour-glass shaped drum; it is associated with Shiva.

Darshanam: Vision of a deity or a saint or a holy person.

Dhatura: Thorn apple. It has trumpet-shaped flowers, long and prickly fruits and narcotic properties.

Devas: Celestial beings.

Devakulikas: Subsidiary shrines.

Deepam: A lamp.

Deepavali maranda: A digestive to be taken during the Deepavali season to alleviate the effects of over-indulgence in sweets.

Dhyanam: Meditation.

Dikshitars: Brahmin servitor community from Chidambaram in Tamil Nadu.

Dosham: A flaw in one's horoscope because of certain planetary positions at the time of one's birth.

Dwarapalaka: Guardian or gatekeeper on either side of the entrance of a shrine.

Dhwajastambham: Symbolic flagpole in a temple. It is the medium by which the earth is connected to the heavens. Hence, by inference, it connects us 'earthlings' with the Divine.

Drishti: The evil eye.

Elaichi: Cardamom.

Gaali marra: Casuarina equestifolia L.

Gada: Mace, the weapon.

Ganas: The fearsome attendants of Shiva.

Ghat: A broad flight of steps leading down to the bank of a river.

Grihastha: Householder. It is the second phase of an individual's life according to the Hindu ashram system—marriage and a family-centred life.

Ghatyam: A percussion instrument used in Carnatic Music.

Ganesha Chaturthi: A festival that is celebrated as the birthday of Lord Ganesha.

Ghritam: In Ayurvedic medicine, medicated ghee.

Gollu: Dolls. Bommala Koluvu or Bommai Kolu—an arrangement of dolls during the time of Navaratri and Dussehra in Tamil Nadu, Andhra Pradesh, Karnataka, and among certain communities in Kerala.

Gopuram: A tower, usually ornate, at the entrance of any temple, especially in South India. *Gopurams* serve as gateways into a temple.

Gotram: Broadly speaking, family lineage.

Halahala: Or, *Kalakootam*. It is the name of the poison created from the ocean when the Devas (Gods) and Asuras (Demons) churned it to obtain Amrita (the nectar of immortality).

Hamsa: Or, Hansa bird; a swan—*vahana* (vehicle) of Goddess Saraswati. Also used as a decorative motif in temples.

Haritaki: Terminalia Chebula in Latin and Chebulic Myrobalan in English. Its fruit is sweet, sour and astringent in taste, as well as slightly bitter and pungent. It strengthens immunity while exerting a mild laxative effect. In Ayurvedic medicine, it is part of Triphala, the well-known three-fruit formula.

Homam: Also known as *homa* or *havan*. It refers to an elaborate ritual in which offerings are made to a consecrated fire, amid the recitation of prescribed prayers and chants or mantras.

Hridayam: Heart.

Janma: Birth, lifetime.

Jhumkas: Dangling earrings.

Jiva: A living being or a living entity. Or, more specifically, the immortal essence of a living being which endures beyond physical death.

Jholas: Bags.

Kajal-lined eyes: Kohl-lined eyes.

Kaala: It is used as one of the names of Yama, the God of Death.

Kalasamharamurti: One of the forms of Shiva, the destroyer of Yama or Death; or, one who liberates from the fear of death.

Kaala paasa: God of Death's noose on the lingam.

Kalyana Utsavam: A ritualistic ceremony that replicates the divine marriage.

Kalasam, Kalasa, Kalasha: A rounded metal (brass, copper, etc) pot with a base and a mouth large enough to hold a coconut. For certain pujas or rites, it may be filled with water, and topped with a circle of mango leaves and a coconut.

Kamandalam: A water pitcher or pot, usually with a handle and sometimes with a spout. It could be made of a gourd, a coconut shell, wood, clay or metal.

Kamalam: Lotus.

Kama: The God of Love. He is depicted as a handsome youth who shoots love-producing flower-arrows.

Kamasamharamurti: Shiva as the destroyer of Kama. Encouraged by the gods to arouse Shiva's passion for Parvati, Kama disturbed Shiva's meditation. Enraged, Shiva burned him to ashes with the power of his third eye. After the entreaties of Kama's wife, Rati, Shiva relented and restored him to life. This story has a deeper significance.

Kanakambaram: Firecracker flower. An orange flower, often strung together with jasmine to adorn the hair of women. Also used in garlands.

Kancham: A plate.

Kanaka Sabha: The Golden Hall in the temple of Chidambaram, where most of the daily rituals of worship for Nataraja are performed. Its roof is made of copper, though.

Kanjira: A South Indian frame drum. Of the tambourine family, it is used in Carnatic (South Indian classical) music concerts.

Kappastambham: A monolithic pillar in the temple of Simhachalam. The devotees believe that their wishes can be fulfilled by embracing this pillar.

Kashayam: A medicinal drink prepared from herbs and some spices.

Kartik masam or Karthika masam: It is the eighth month in the Hindu lunar calendar.

Karma: It is a complex concept. Very simply put, it is the totality of our actions (in our previous lives and this life) and the attendant consequences and reactions in this life, all of which shape and determine our future.

Khaja: A sweet made from refined wheat flour, Bengal gram flour, sugar or jaggery, ghee and oil.

Koil: Temple.

Kolam: A decorative design drawn using a grid pattern of dots. Traditionally, coarse rice flour is used to make designs outside the main entrance of a home. The rice flour also serves as food for birds and ants.

Koneru: Tank (temple tank).

Kootu: A dish made from vegetables and lentils. There are different regional variations of it.

Kriti: A musical composition typical to Carnatic music.

Ksheerasagara: In Hindu cosmology, the ocean of milk. The devas (gods) and the asuras (demons) churned the cosmic ocean to obtain amrita (the nectar of immortal life).

Kshetram: A sacred place where a temple or collection of temples exists along with the temple tank. Punyakshetram is a holy place, a pilgrimage centre.

Kshetrapalaka: The guardian-deity of a temple.

Kukkuta: A cock.

Kundalam: Earring.

Kumkum: A red powder worn by Hindu women in the form of a red dot on the forehead. It is also used during worship, pujas and ritual prayers.

Kumkum archana: A puja ritual in which kumkum or vermilion is offered to a female deity while invoking and reciting her various names.

Kundalini: An indwelling spiritual energy that needs to be awakened in order to attain self-realisation and bliss. It is described as a coiled sleeping serpent at the base of the spine. The kundalini can be awakened with the help of spiritual practices such as yoga and meditation. A guru can initiate and guide one on this path.

Kutcheri: A Carnatic music concert.

Kumbhabhishekam: A religious ceremony to sacralise and sanctify a newly constructed temple.

Kurma: Tortoise.

Kurma avatar: Vishnu's second incarnation as half-man and half-tortoise.

Kuthara: Axe.

Lehyam: In Ayurveda, a herbal preparation that has the consistency of a jam; it is used to treat health problems, such as digestive, respiratory, and others.

Laddoo: A ball-shaped sweet.

Madiphala: Citron; a fragrant citrus fruit.

Madisar: It is the way in which the sari, nine or ten yards long, is worn by the womenfolk of the Brahmin community in Tamil Nadu.

Mahisha: The buffalo-headed demon vanquished by Goddess Durga.

Mangalsutra: This word is derived from two words—'mangal', which means auspicious, and 'sutra', which means thread. It is the sacred necklace which the groom ties around the bride's neck on the day of the Hindu wedding during the ceremony called 'mangalya dharanam'.

Maranda: Medicine.

Masikam: The monthly *shraadh* ceremony.

Medi chettu: Cluster fig tree.

Moksha: Liberation from the cycle of birth and death.

Moolamurti: Embodiment of a god, deity, in a temple, usually made of either clay, wood, stone or a combination of metals.

Moksha dwara: Doorway in a temple that is believed to lead devotees towards salvation.

Moolasthanam or *garbha griha*: It is the sacred centre of the temple where the main idol is placed and sanctified.

Mukhamandapam: Front pavilion or pillared hall in a temple.

Muhurtham: An auspicious time for performing a significant event, such as a marriage or a sacred thread ceremony.

Muni: Sage.

Muyalaka: Or, *apasmara*. The dwarf who represents ignorance.

Mrityunjaya: Shiva, the Lord of Immortality.

Naamam: Worshippers of Vishnu wear the naamam or tilak at the ajna chakra (the space between two eyebrows). Sandalwood paste and vermilion are used to form the naamam.

Nada Brahmam: The cosmic sound associated with the creation and sustenance of the universe.

Nadaswaram: A wind instrument considered very auspicious. It is played in South India at weddings and at religious ceremonies in a temple.

Naivedyam: Food offered to a deity as part of the worship ritual. It could include any other offering also.

Nakshatram: Birth star.

Naradapakai or Narthangai: Citron.

Natya mudra: A dance posture. Natya mudras are the gestures and postures used in a South Indian Classical dance style.

Nunge: Palm fruit, translucent pale white. Called munjalu in Telugu.

Nayanmars: The 63 Tamil Shaivite saint-poets.

Nritya: Dance.

Neelakantha: The blue-throated Shiva.

Padmam: Lotus.

Padmasana: Lotus position in yoga.

Panchloha idol: Found in many Hindu temples, especially in South India. The idol has gold, silver, brass, copper and iron.

Pandal: A temporary structure set up for a puja or a religious ceremony.

Pappu annam: Lentils and rice.

Pancharatna kritis: A set of five songs in Carnatic music, composed by Tyagaraja, the 18th century saint-composer.

Paan: Betel leaf.

Pasi: Hunger.

Parashu: Axe.

Pariharam: A kind of ritual penance. The negative effect of a certain planet or the consequences of certain karmas accumulated over past lifetimes can be countered or alleviated by offering special prayers or participating in a specific religious ceremony.

Paris tu me manque: 'I miss you, Paris.'

Pativrata: A chaste, devoted and loyal wife.

Papa-bhakshana: Shiva as Kaala Bhairava; one who devours the accumulated sins of devotees.

Papa-vimochana: One who liberates from all sins and consequences of sins.

Payasam: A creamy pudding that has many variations. It can be made with rice, milk and sugar or jaggery. One can substitute broken wheat, or vermicelli, or sago, or green gram lentil, for rice and use a combination of milk and coconut milk.

Pipali: Indian long pepper, used as a spice in certain food preparations, for example, rasam (South Indian lentil soup). Since it aids digestion and has rejuvenating properties, it is used in Ayurvedic preparations.

Pinaka: Shiva's divine bow.

Pitrudosha: It is present in the horoscope of a person when his/her forefathers or ancestors have committed some mistakes or have been guilty of some sin/s. Hence the person with the *pitrudosha* has to pay the karmic debt by doing good deeds or offering special prayers.

Pradakshina: 'In Hinduism and Buddhism, the rite of circumambulating in a clockwise direction an image, relic, shrine, or other sacred object.' (Encyclopaedia Britannica.)

Prakaram: In a temple, the *prakaram* is the temple compound or the circumambulatory passage around the sanctum. Depending on the size of a temple, there may be several *prakarams* with each smaller *prakaram* enclosed within a larger *prakaram*.

Prarabdha: Simplictically put, destiny.

Presque bon: 'Almost good' or 'quite good'.

Puli: Tiger.

Pulihora: A sour spicy rice preparation, common in the four Southern states of India. In Andhra Pradesh, it is called *Pulihora*. It can be made with tamarind, lemon, or raw mango.

Punarapi darshanam prapti rastu: A blessing which means, 'May you revisit the temple and enjoy the good fortune of another *darshan* of the deity.'

Punarapi jananam, punarapi maranam: The repetitive cycle of birth and death until one is liberated from it.

Pungai: Indian Beech tree.

Rasam: A South Indian soup, traditionally prepared using tamarind juice as base, to which tomatoes and cooked lentils are added. Chilli pepper, pepper, cumin, coriander, mustard, asafoetida, are some of the spices used in the preparation. There are several varieties of rasam.

Rasam-saadam: Rasam and rice.

Rasi or *rashi*: Star-sign.

Rasika: In Carnatic music concerts, the people in the audience are called *rasikas*.

Ratham: Chariot; in the book, the temple chariot.

Sabhas: Literally, halls. In the book, the reference is to the five halls in five specific Shiva temples—Chidambaram, Madurai, Thiruvalangadu, Tirunelveli and Kuttralam. Each one has a unique *sabha* or hall where Shiva danced to delight and bless his devotees. For example, the *Kanaka Sabha* (golden hall) in Chidambaram; the *Rajat Sabha* (silver hall) in Madurai; the *Tamra Sabha* (copper hall) in Tirunelveli; the *Ratna Sabha* (hall of precious stones) in Thiruvalngadu; the *Chitra Sabha* (hall of mural paintings) in Kuttralam.

Sadhana: In the case of religious sadhana, a discipline undertaken for the purpose of reaching a spiritual goal.

Samadhi: A state of consciousness in which the mind becomes still, when the person concerned reaches a state of equilibrium.

Sambhrani: Benzoin resin or styrax resin obtained from the bark of special species of trees in the genus Styrax. In India it is burned on charcoal as an incense.

Samskaras: 'Any of the personal sacraments traditionally observed at every stage of a Hindu's life, from the moment of conception to the final scattering of his/her funeral ashes...' (Encyclopaedia Britannica.) There are sixteen traditional samskaras.

Samhara: Destruction or dissolution (of the universe).

Samsara: The material universe.

Sanjeevani thailam: In the Ayurvedic system of medicine, a medicated oil used in the treatment of certain health problems.

Sankalpam: A deliberate, intentional act, performed with a motive and determination. Through the performance of a ritual puja, the motive is to propitiate a particular deity for a particular desired result, such as prosperity, health, welfare of the family, and so on.

Sannidhi: *Garbha griha*; sanctum sanctorum.

Saptmatrika: A group of seven mother-goddesses, each of whom is the Shakti, or the female counterpart, of a god.

Sapt rishis: The seven great sages in Indian Mythology. They had attained great yogic powers as a result of years of meditation and rigorous penance. In the sky, they figure as the constellation Ursa Major (Big dipper).

Sapt swaras: In the Indian Classical system of music, the seven notes.

Sashtanga namaskar: It means namaskar or prostration before a deity, a sage, or an elder, wherein eight specific parts of the body touch the floor.

Satvic: Or, Sattvic. Pure. In terms of food, that which is fresh, clean, nutritious, doesn't disturb the equilibrium of the mind, doesn't debilitate or weaken the mind and body in any way.

Sev: A popular snack food in the form of crispy noodles made from chickpea flour paste.

Shikakai: Acacia concinna. Its fruit known as shikakai is used traditionally for hair care in India, for washing the hair.

Shaligramam: A sacred black stone found only in the Gandaki river in the Himalayas. It has the *sudarshan chakra* (Vishnu's discus) symbol engraved on it. Apparently, such impressions or engravings are made by river worms.

Shankha: The conch shell which is of religious importance. One of Vishnu's attributes.

Shantamurti: God as an Embodiment of Peace.

Shani Tryodashi: The thirteenth day of the lunar calendar is tryodashi. When tryodashi falls on a Saturday, it is called Shani Tryodashi.

Shloka: A verse of two lines, a hymn of praise of a god or goddess. Chanting of shlokas forms an integral part of a ritual prayer or a religious ceremony.

Shraadh: The Hindu ritual of paying respectful homage to one's deceased ancestors. It is performed every year on the anniversary of death of the person/relative as per the Panchang. It is believed that after the performance of this ritual, the soul of the relative finds peace and attains moksha (liberation).

Siddha: One who has certain siddhis (supernatural powers). In the book, one who has achieved spiritual realisation.

Siddha vaidya: A practitioner of the ancient Siddha system of medicine.

Skanda Purana: It is the largest of the eighteen Puranas, Hindu religious texts. It is devoted mainly to the birth, life, deeds and legends of Skanda (Kartikeya), the younger son of Shiva and Parvati.

Srishti: Creation (of the universe).

Stambha: Pillar or column.

Stambha purusha: The guardian deity of an important pillar in a temple.

Sthala vrksha: The temple tree which is considered holy. The banyan tree is the sthala vrksha in the temple of Thiruvalangadu.

Sthiti: Preservation (of the universe).

Stuti: A prayer sung in praise of a god or goddess.

Sukshama sharira: The energy body or the subtle body. Yoga speaks of three bodies—the sthula sharira (the gross or physical body), the Sukshama sharira (the energy body) and the karana sharira (the causal body). All these bodies should act in harmony to have a sense of well-being.

Sundakka: Solanum torvum (Turkey Berry)—a bushy, erect and spiny perennial plant. Its fruit is a berry. In Tamil Nadu, it is used in some food preparations like sundakka pulikozhambu. It is also used in Siddha medicine.

Sudarshan kriya: Created by the Art of Living guru, Sri Sri Ravi Shankar, it is a simple, yet effective, rhythmic breathing technique that re-energizes the body and calms the mind.

Swarupa: Form.

Swayambhu lingam: A lingam that is not man-made or created by man; it manifests itself on its own. It is believed to have appeared miraculously and mysteriously, without any human effort.

Sweta: White.

Tapasya: Spiritual discipline or practice of austerities, undertaken to achieve goals.

Tyaga Brahmam: Sri Tyagarajaswamy, one of the greatest composers of Carnatic music, or South Indian Classical music.

Tea-*kadai*: A tea shop.

Teertham: A temple tank.

Thali: A largish plate, generally in steel. It could be in other metals like copper, brass and silver too.

Thevarams: The devotional songs written by the three Tamil Shaivite saint-poets—Appar, Sambandar and Sundarar.

Tika or tilak or *tilakam*: In Hinduism, a mark worn on the forehead. *Vibhuti* (sacred ash), *kumkum* (vermilion), and *chandan* (sandalwood) paste may be used for the tika or tilak.

Tirobhava: Veiling, embodiment, illusion—one of the five activities of Shiva as Nataraja, the Lord of Dance.

Tiruvasi: The Nataraja stands on a lotus pedestal from which rises tiruvasi, an encircling glory, fringed with flame. It is touched on the inside by hands holding drum and fire.

Toranam: A sacred gateway. It may also refer to a decorative door hanging decorated with marigolds and mango leaves.

Trishul: Shiva's trident.

Tummichettu: Leucas aspera, commonly known as 'thumbai', is found throughout India. In Sanskrit, it is called dronapushpi.

Ugra: Fierce.

Udukkai: Or, *damaru*. The hour-glass shaped drum in Shiva's hand.

Undralu: Rice rava (semolina) and Bengal gram balls eaten with sesame oil and coconut chutney.

Unchavritti: Sadhus and saint-composers like Tyagarajaswamy would walk the streets of a village/town singing bhajans and receive offerings of food and grain from the householders. Unchavritti Sampradaya is the practice of a high way of living.

Upanayanam: It is the Samskara or the ceremonial rite of passage by which a young boy is invested with the sacred thread, given the instruction of the Gayatri mantra (a sacred chant), and initiated into student life.

Upma: A savoury breakfast dish made from roasted semolina. It is made as a thick porridge, with or without vegetables, and seasoned with ginger, green chillies, mustard and curry leaves.

Uruli: Traditional cookware used in Kerala. An uruli is shallow and circular. It also serves an auspicious decorative function—it may be filled with water to float flowers.

Usnisa: The swelling or protuberance on Buddha's head. It is a symbolic representation of Buddha's wisdom and enlightenment.

Utsava murti: In a temple, it is the 'festival *murti*'. It is so called because it can be easily moved around for purposes of a festival—temple processions, ritual bathing and anointing ceremonies, special pujas, sacred marriage ceremonies, and so on.

Vada: A deep fried snack from South India. It is made from de-husked black lentils or de-husked black chickpeas.

Vadiyalu: Crispy and deep-fried, it is made from de-husked black lentils (black gram dal) and spiced with asafoetida, cumin and crushed green chilies.

Vahana or *vahanam*: A deity's mount. Typically an animal, bird, or a mythical creature that a particular deity or god is said to use as a vehicle. Nandi, the bull, is Shiva's vehicle.

Vata kozhambu: A tangy, spicy gravy eaten with rice. There are many variations of it. One of them is with manathakkali (dried nightshade berries).

Varaha Purana: One of the eighteen Mahapuranas (Hindu religious texts). It centers around Varaha, the third incarnation of Vishnu as a boar.

Varada mudra: The hand, palm facing out, is directed downwards. When the abhaya and varada mudras are combined in the same deity, the right hand in abhaya mudra makes the gesture of 'do not fear', and the left hand in varada mudra makes the gesture of wish fulfilment or granting of boons.

Vel: The divine spear of the deity Kartikeya or Murugan.

Venda: No.

Veena vidwan: A veena exponent.

Vibhuti: Sacred ash.

Vigraham: Idol.

Vimanam: The tower above the sanctum sanctorum.

Vishakanthemurti: Shiva, who drank the poison Halahala, and contained it in his throat.

Yagnasala: The enclosure in a temple where yagnas (Vedic rituals) and special pujas are performed.

Yajnopavita: The sacred thread worn by initiates after an elaborate religious ceremony called the *upanayanam* ceremony.

Yantra: It is a symbolic representation of aspects of divinity and creative forces of the universe. Its interlocking matrix of geometric figures, circles, triangles, and floral patterns have a deep symbolic/metaphysical significance.

Yogasutras: Patanjali's seminal and foundational text on yoga.